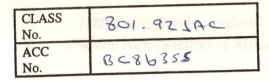

Please return this book on or before
the last date stamped below.

The Foundations of Modern Literary Theory Sequence

The Poverty of Structuralism: Literature and Structuralist Theory Longman 1991

The Dematerialisation of Karl Marx: Literature and Marxist Theory Longman 1994

Literature, Psychoanalysis and the New Sciences of Mind Pearson Education 2000 (formerly entitled *Making Freud Unscientific*)

Literature, Psychoanalysis and the New Sciences of Mind

LEONARD JACKSON

An imprint of **Pearson Education**

Harlow, England · London · New York · Reading, Massachusetts · San Francisco
Toronto · Don Mills, Ontario · Sydney · Tokyo · Singapore · Hong Kong · Seoul
Taipei · Cape Town · Madrid · Mexico City · Amsterdam · Munich · Paris · Milan

Pearson Education Limited
Edinburgh Gate
Harlow
Essex CM20 2JE
England

and Associated Companies throughout the world.

Visit us on the World Wide Web at:
http://www.pearsoneduc.com

First published 2000

© Pearson Education Limited 2000

ISBN 0-582-06652-2   PPR
ISBN 0-582-06653-0   CSD

British Library Cataloguing-in-Publication Data

A catalogue record for this book is available from the British Library

Library of Congress Cataloging-in-Publication Data

Jackson, Leonard, 1934–
Literature, psychoanalysis and the new sciences of mind / Leonard Jackson.
p. cm.
Includes bibliographical references and index.
ISBN 0-582-06653-0 — ISBN 0-582-06652-2 (pbk.)
1. Psychoanalysis and literature.   2. Freud, Sigmund, 1856–1939—Views on literature.   3.
Literature—Psychological aspects.   4. Art—Psychological aspects.   5. Psychology in
literature.   6. Psychoanalysis and art.   7. Cognitive science.   8. Subconsciousness.
PN56.P92 J28   2000
801'.92 21—dc21   99-043724

Set in Minion 10$\frac{1}{2}$/13pt by 35
Produced by Pearson Education Asia Pte Ltd.
Printed in Singapore

To
EJ   IMJ
and the memory of LJ

Contents

Acknowledgements

I am grateful to my students on OM25, OM325, EL381, EL385–6 and other versions of my courses in literary theory; and to Irving Dworetzsky for commenting on some sections of the book. As always, my main debt is to my wife and colleague, Eleanor Jackson. The defects of the book I put in all by myself, just as before.

Introduction:
where psychoanalysis stands now

Writing a book about *Literature, Psychoanalysis and the New Sciences of Mind* is not like mapping a large, settled intellectual territory. It is more like exploring the borders of several countries in time of war, where one may oneself at any time be shot. The wars are about literature, science, mind and sex. Can you have a science of mind? Some people argue passionately that the very idea is a philosophical absurdity. Could such a science throw any light on the way literature works – or did that notion die with structuralism, under the guns of Derrida and others in 1967? Is human sexuality to be explained by genes or by social construction of roles or by French metaphysics? And if the answer to that question seems too obvious, how about this: how do we explain the half-conscious metaphors in terms of which we experience sexuality, and represent it in literature?

Once upon a time there was a confident set of answers to those questions which went by the name of psychoanalysis. It offered a theory of mind, and a theory of sexuality. It offered a theory of dreams, and of symbolism, and it was the only theory with the slightest pretensions to being scientific that offered an explanation of the emotional depths at which literature affects us. But it is precisely the old territory of psychoanalysis that is now under attack from every side. Freud thought he had created a science. But almost no cognitive scientist – whether interested in brain structure, or computer simulation of thinking, or human or animal behaviour – finds Freud empirically satisfactory; and the Freudian variants – Jung, say, or Lacan – are very much worse; speculative religious nonsense, or empty rhetorical extravagance studded with pseudoscientific claims. Modern scientific theories of mind and sexuality generally have no place for psychoanalysis.

Freud is a live issue for the cultural and literary commentators, and they – we – are bitterly divided. Some – including some distinguished ex-Freudian critics – now agree with the scientists that Freud was wrong, and add that he

1

was not merely wrong, but wicked. Freud is blamed for denigrating women with theories like that of penis envy, and for excusing the sexual abuse of children by describing it as childhood fantasy. Others, including most modern literary theorists, have defended Freud in ways that would have appalled him. Far from complaining that his work isn't good science, they have *re-read* him as a non-scientist, actively *Making Freud Unscientific.*[1] In the last half-century, we have had Freud the humanist, the moralist, the hermeneuticist, the phenomenologist, the existentialist. We have now a feminist Freud who faithfully chronicles the internalisation of patriarchy. We have a post-structuralist one who is basically a set of texts, no less fictional than literary texts, and read alongside them to produce elaborate rhetorical studies of interimplication (rather than mere Freudian interpretations).

In this book I offer dispatches from several sides in this war. I give a brief introduction to the cognitive sciences and in the light of them look at the theories of Freud, of Jung, and, so far as one can make a rational reconstruction, of Lacan. I ask how, for example, Lacan's theory of language stands up against that of a modern linguist – Chomsky called him a conscious charlatan! And I argue that, even in the context of the new sciences of mind, which are often supposed to have rendered them obsolete, some of the ideas of Freud and Jung are an essential part of any coherent picture of the way the mind works. This is because they offer a theory of unconscious fantasy, which is as essential for explaining everyday decision-making as it is for explaining cultural forms like literature. I discuss traditional Freudian interpretations of literature – some of them my own – and contrast them with modern feminist and post-structuralist rereadings – none of them my own. I ask what general theories of literature underlie such interpretative practices.

Biological knowledge in the field of sexuality has been utterly transformed in the last ten years, and both the Freudian theory of sexuality and our standard theories of gender construction now seem indefensible. I summarise the radical version, by Baker and Bellis, of the standard modern biological theory of human sexuality, which I am sure many contemporary readers will find as utterly shocking as Freud's own theory of sexuality was in 1905, though the evolutionary and medical evidence for it seems very strong. In this theory, patterns of sexual behaviour are directly determined by the genes, for reproductive advantage. A naïve biologism, like Baker's own, moves directly from this to explaining individual behaviour as unconsciously calculated for reproductive advantage.

I argue, however, that even if the basic biological theory is correct, it is inherently incomplete. To explain human experience and behaviour we need an account of the cultural forms taken by biological drives. The study of literature – along with pornography, fashion and other discourses – is the royal road to a cultural unconscious. The value of an updated psychoanalytic theory is in linking the biological mechanisms that produce physical desire with the cultural history that produces both works of literature and ideological constructs like patriarchy.

The essential insight of dynamic psychology is that unconscious mental processes are real, active and creative. The whole time that we are alive, going about our everyday business and interacting with other people, we are constantly projecting unconscious fantasies upon the world – infantile fantasies, as Freud suggested, archetypal fantasies, as Jung suggested, and other socially moulded unconscious fantasies of sexuality and power. Our normal consciousness – including both our mental models of realities outside our own minds, and the internal objects of apprehension and desire in our wishes and our dreams – is constructed by combining such fantasies with everyday experience and culturally determined ideas. We see the world in the way that we do, we love and we hate, because we see the world through unconscious fantasy, we see the people we know through unconscious fantasy, we see ourselves through unconscious fantasy.

This is one of the most powerful explanatory theories of the twentieth century; I claim it is true, and has not been superseded by cognitive science. On the contrary, it fits easily alongside plausible cognitive models – mathematical models of language, computer models of brain functioning, studies of animal behaviour, genetic and ecological explanations of animal and human sexuality. It does not contradict, but provides an essential basis for, cultural and historical accounts of the development of complex ideas about sexuality and power. It also helps to explain how art and literature are produced, and why they can be compulsive addictions. It offers the only interpretations of literature and art that are based on biology and therefore potentially universal, though always incomplete.

Note and reference

1. *Making Freud Unscientific* is the title that was announced for the present book in the two earlier books of this sequence: *The Poverty of Structuralism* (1991) and *The Dematerialisation of Karl Marx* (1994).

Chapter I

Literature as psychotic fantasy

WHAT PSYCHOLOGICAL THEORY EXPLAINS LITERATURE

AND THE ARTS?

Literature as a test of psychological theory

All over the world, throughout the whole of history, people have been sing-
ing or reciting poems, acting in plays of various kinds, and telling stories.
Recently – that is, in the last five or six thousand years – they have been writing these down. We call them works of literature. All this time, other people
have been watching these works and listening to them, and sometimes reading them – not through compulsion, not through languid acceptance of a
social duty, not even as a formal religious or university study (though all
these things exist), but avidly, for the sake of personal desire, and sometimes with a total, if temporary, loss of self.

The cardinal question for literary theory is why this happens. This is a
question for a science of psychology. It isn't a philosophical question; it isn't
concerned with metaphysical categories, or the logic of value judgements. It
isn't a question for linguistics, since literature is only one of the arts; music,
dance, painting and sculpture can be equally involving and are equally old;
but none of them use words. It isn't a question for sociology or comparative
anthropology; these can perhaps explain the different forms literature takes
in different societies, but not its universality. If literature is a human universal, we need a universal anthropology based on a fully general theory
of psychology to explain its existence and functioning – and it becomes a
good test of such a general theory; perhaps, indeed, the ultimate test. But
associationist and behaviorist theories of psychology fail that test; and for
all its recent promise, cognitive science fails too. Cognitive science cannot
explain why any organism would want to spend hours entertaining false
cognitions about the world!

The theory I am adopting in this book is that human beings are innate
fantasists. Part of the time they are asleep – during REM sleep,[1] in fact – and

the whole time they are awake, they are producing fantasy material in the form of images or basic narratives, which is marked by not corresponding, as normal consciousness does, to the world about them: its structure and content are determined from within. In fantasy, residues from daily conscious experience are combined with other material that does not come from consciousness, and is emotionally compelling. Works of art in general, and works of literature in particular, are sophisticated fantasies driven by what Freud called primary process thinking – that is, thinking in images and elementary narratives rather than words and arguments – and reworked by what he called a process of secondary elaboration in accordance with whatever are the current artistic conventions. Works of literature are admired by critics, and to a lesser extent ordinary readers, for socially accepted reasons that can be consciously discussed, and that are different from one period to another. But it is the underlying fantasy that renders them compulsive; and this is because, whenever you entertain a fantasy in consciousness, you are repeating deeply unconscious fantasy material.

This theory has been familiar for some time as an adaptation of Freud's theory of dreams, and the obvious core of a Freudian theory of art. But recently Freud's whole theory of psychology has been widely rejected as unscientific nonsense, not only by the biologists, behaviorist psychologists, and cognitive scientists who have thought it nonsense for years, but by softer thinkers like sociologists and even literary critics. Can one rescue it, and reconcile it with cognitive science, say, to remove the arid emptiness and triviality of that discipline, and bring it into touch with deeper motivations? I think one can. I am going to argue, in fact, that cognitive psychology, placed in its proper biological framework, is perfectly compatible with several versions of dynamic psychology, and that dynamic psychology, which studies instinct, symbolism, fantasy and the transformations of desire, requires a solid framework of human cognitive psychology and even of animal behaviour studies.

The total theory of literature that I am adopting is in one sense obvious: one needs cognitive psychology and psycholinguistics to explain the mechanics of reading – how a set of words on a page is transformed into a narrative experienced in the head; one needs a biologically based dynamic psychology, including an account of the unconscious, to explain how that narrative moves, excites and satisfies. But there is more to it than that.

Such a model of the way we understand art has profound implications for the way we understand human beings in general. I am arguing that at the heart of any cognitive psychology that is adequate to deal with human beings rather than computers, or indeed, with animals rather than computers, there is a large Jung-or-Lorenz-shaped hole filled with archetypes or, equivalently, instincts, and the archetypal images and narratives through which we apprehend them; and at the heart of that, a large Freud-shaped hole filled with aggression and sex, along with complex unconscious psychic mechanisms for transforming these, first into fantasy, then into complex choices of action. I shall be arguing in fact for a dynamic psychology that has come to terms with ethology as well as sociology, and offering that as the foundation for the theory of fantasy we have to have at the heart of any serious literary theory.

Paranoia in the tutorial room: a thought experiment

I will begin with a thought experiment.

Let us suppose that a student comes into my office and claims he is a hobbit. He wishes to consult me about a serious problem he has – perhaps the most serious problem anyone has ever had. Some years before, he had acquired an old ring, apparently of little value save for one curious property: to put it on made one invisible. He has now discovered that the ring had originally belonged to a very powerful and exceedingly malevolent being, who now wishes to get it back. If the being gets it back, it will become even more powerful, and even more malevolent; it will take over the world, and it will certainly destroy the comfortable world of hobbits. Only one creature stands in the way of this – himself – since he, by very arduous means, has the power to destroy that ring. For that reason the powerful and malevolent being is hellbent on destroying him: so he – my student, the self-proclaimed hobbit – is the one person who could save the world, and he is encircled by spies and assassins.

I will recognise him as a paranoid schizophrenic, suffering marked delusions of reference and persecution. I will wonder how one begins a conversation that will end with advice to see a good psychiatrist and may lead to his being sectioned in a mental hospital. I will treat him, in fact, in exactly the same way as the student who tells me she is an illegitimate daughter of the Queen, or the one who told me that his landlord was persecuting him and trying to poison him with a quarter of a pound of strychnine in his soy sauce. (One of these examples is true.)

The young person who follows him into my office is bubbling with enthusiasm. The book he has just read seemed utterly real, utterly convincing, despite its fantastic nature. It took one out of oneself completely, and one believed every word. With all that, it was serious, too. It was an examination of the nature of good and evil, and of the responsibility of individuals in relation to apparently overwhelming power.

I shall respond with warmth to this; after all, here is a student who has actually enjoyed a book, even if the book is *The Lord of the Rings* rather than *Nostromo*. With impeccable political correctness, I shall raise a few questions about the book. Isn't there a degree of racism in the basic ideology? And perhaps a degree of immaturity – what about Edwin Muir's suggestion that all the characters are schoolboys with Aragorn as head boy?

It is, of course, exactly the same book. The difference is the quality of belief, and the nature of the identification involved. The first student is projecting a heroic fantasy onto the world and identifying with its principal character. He does this much of the time, his belief is a real one, and it may well affect his future actions. (For example, he might decide that *I* am an emissary of Sauron and stab me with his little dagger. This is a disturbing thought.) If he believes the book in this way, he has symptoms indistinguishable from those of paranoid schizophrenia. The second student also projects a heroic fantasy on the world, and the same fantasy at that; and also identifies with the principal character. But he does this while sitting down and scanning the pages of the book, as it 'takes him out of himself'. Disturb him and he'll blink his eyes and be back in the real world again. He is unlikely to stab a lecturer, but if sufficiently enthusiastic, they may talk each other to death. Talk to him, and he is anxious to link the fantasy to the real world in any number of analogical ways; but it never occurs to him that it actually happened. There is no loss of contact with reality – or perhaps it would be better to say only a temporary, controllable and defeasible one.

From the point of view of the psychiatrist, it is the difference between the two students that is all-important; he is in the business of cure. For the literary theorist it is the similarity between the two cases that is theoretically interesting. We are trying to understand how literature works. How and why do we produce it? How and why do we consume it? The striking thing here is that there seems to be no essential difference between the content of the most popular works of literary entertainment, and those of paranoid fantasies. The James Bond films or the thrillers of Patricia Cornwell would have done just as well for my example as *The Lord of the Rings*. I could also have chosen *Wuthering Heights*, or a gentler book than that. After a recent television adaptation, it is not impossible that there are people roaming the streets claiming to be Mr Darcy of *Pride and Prejudice*. I am not of course suggesting that the majority of paranoid delusional systems are taken from novels – they are not. I am noting, however, that they could be. In a sense, paranoid delusions *are* elementary novels. What is different is the secondary elaboration of the fantasy, the proliferation of realist detail, the depth and ambiguity of treatment, and so forth.

Let me venture an account of what the second student is doing. He is using the book to introject a rich and elaborated paranoid fantasy. He is then engaging in a series of mobile identifications with the narrator, and with many of the major characters, in that fantasy. In fantasy, he is performing heroic deeds, and suffering bravely too, and it's probably affecting his autonomic nervous system, though he's sitting still. If I had him wired up properly, I could demonstrate this. Then he comes out of the fantasy to tell me about it, using a special academic language we have developed for this purpose, that objectifies and impersonalises experience, but is pretty transparent for those who know it. As we talk, we create a common object, a common cultural reference, having value for both of us. (I wish it were *The Rainbow* though. Come to think of it, it was, for that slightly more mature woman student . . .) My second student is definitely not schizophrenic. Neither am I. But both of us show schizoid tendencies. We tend to withdraw from the real world from time to time and live in worlds of our own, or a common cultural world built out of those worlds.

My next student is a woman. She has been deeply affected by the book she has read, which is *Wuthering Heights*. She has read it passionately, in a kind of intense dream. We argue whether Heathcliff is a realistic character – after all, he disappears as an uneducated boy and comes back as an accomplished gentleman confidence trickster, with no explanation of how he made that change. She insists that Heathcliff is utterly real – more real to her than any real person she has met. She is not psychotic. She is not deceived. She knows he is a fiction. She may well end up writing an essay on the Byronic hero in the nineteenth century novel. She might end up arguing that Heathcliff's violence is a metaphor for the violence of sexual passion; it is projected onto him from his woman creator. But did she see, when she was reading the book, that it was her own passion she was projecting, to make this incomplete character seem intensely real? And does that mean that her own sexual feeling, in fantasy, was savage and masochistic? Would it be sexual harassment if I were to suggest as much?

Next I have two students in, a man and a woman, as if anybody cares; we are all egalitarians now, and I for one cannot tell the difference between a male student and a female one from an anonymous exam script. The text is *The Magus*. The girl, in this case, is cleverer; mildly post-structuralist, but clear with it; crisply she points out that this text is itself a study in the nature of novelistic illusion, brilliantly self-referential, but never finally disturbing our bourgeois complacencies in the way genuine French New Novel does. I admit she is right. Her companion, however, is the one who read the book passionately, and he is disturbed. Stammeringly, he tries to make sense of the sadistic role-plays in which Nicholas is trapped as victim;

seduced and tricked into showing himself to himself as sexual Nazi and suffering voyeur; and at last holding back desperately when invited to crack that whip again and again across the bare back of the girl who has seduced and humiliated him and is now so vulnerable, bound half-naked to a whipping frame with everybody looking on.

He is disturbed, it is clear, because it has become his fantasy; he is fighting against the sexual sadism it injects into his mind, and to which he, dismayingly, finds himself responding. The girl, meanwhile, is becoming most uncomfortable. John Fowles did not disturb her at all; but the revelation that she has a sexual maniac sitting next to her does. I wonder if she realises that she has one sitting opposite her as well? Fowles disturbs me a little, and used to, a lot. Yet none of us believes in Fowles's book; and all of us have read books with worse violence and sex. (Nobody actually gets hurt in *The Magus*, save in memories of the first world war, and the sexual encounters are consensual and not implausibly excessive in number. In Angela Carter, now, Little Red Riding Hood has sex with the wolf after he has eaten her grandmother. There's real violence for you.)

What on earth are we all doing, introducing these savage fantasies of sex and violence into our lives? Most literature is the same – from *The Iliad*, *Oedipus Rex*, *Lysistrata*, to Regan in *King Lear* getting off on the violence against Gloucester, as she helps put out his eyes. Sometimes the fantasies are more disguised than others; in *Pamela* there are hundreds of pages of restrained fantasy about a rape that never happens; in *Pride and Prejudice* both hero and heroine are humiliated and laid bare in a purely metaphorical way. Violence and sex are transmuted into conflict and romance; but do they lose their underlying quality? Is there not some level of fantasy in the reader's mind in which they are violence and sex still, and can sometimes provide the same autonomic reactions? And is that not the level at which we become addicted to literature, requiring our regular fix of readerly excitement to get through the day or the week?

A book – or the equivalent in other media, a film, a play, a painting, a piece of music, a dance – is a mind-altering drug, and hence a mood-altering drug, of infinitely greater precision than any chemical; it can reach the precise neural net that stores an archetypal image. I am a pusher, aiming to create or mould a lifelong addictive habit. I have the habit myself. I can read a couple of serious Victorian novels, or twenty detective stories, in a week and not think anything unusual has happened. And every one of those is a portable psychosis. It is obvious that these brief and controllable psychotic episodes we insist on having – several times a week, and in advanced cases of lyric poetry addiction, perhaps fifty times in a day – do something for us, though it is not in the least obvious whether it is good or bad.

In view of the content of violence and sex that these episodes often have, can they possibly be good? Some of the major religions have sometimes said 'No. You should read only the Good Book'. My students have in fact, read some of this; we included it in the first year course. Psalm 137 is unquestionably Good, though a layman might mistake it for a ferocious invitation to genocide. So are the accounts of how God allowed his only son to be tortured to death to purge the sins of mankind. Many Christians have supposed that it is necessary to mental health and salvation to spend an hour or so each day thinking about this delightful episode. It will escape nobody's attention that this is, psychologically speaking, simply another type of experience of literature. One can get a fix, not a thousand miles away from an artistic one, in a prayer meeting. If religions too provide an analogous fix, we are getting nearer to the universal claim: perhaps all human beings need their regular dose of psychotic fantasy?

Which science of psychology can explain fantasy?

The question that any literary theorist has to ask of a science of psychology is what produces the desire for literature, and the addiction to it. What is going on in the mind, in the brain, when we read a book? What reward do we get from entering into a fiction? If these questions are taken seriously they rebase our conception of human psychology. We have to conceive human beings as creatures that actively desire fantasy. We have to give a description of the human in which fantasy plays a central part. And we have to choose, among the numerous approaches to the sciences of mind, those in which these questions can be asked and answered. Can a behaviorist answer them? Or a new-style behavioral ecologist? Can a cognitive scientist? Can a psychoanalyst or analytical psychologist? Or a philosopher of mind?

We are not asking here for a theory of delusion or of false consciousness. Readers of literature are not deluded, though they are clearly entertaining false ideas and suspending disbelief in them. That is what we are trying to explain. It seems that consciousness is more than an awareness of the world, coupled with an awareness of our own awareness – which would be my first working definition. It is more even than an awareness of the self, as an entity which is aware of the world and acts in it – which would be my first working definition of self-consciousness. It must include the power to create imaginary worlds, and sketchy scenarios for possible worlds. A moment's reflection on one's own conscious experiences will confirm that a consciousness without this power – without the power to envisage the future and the counterfactual – would hardly be consciousness at all. And if we accept the existence of unconscious fantasy, then we have to recognise that the unconscious is more than the merely somatic, or biological-electrical functioning of the brain, and more than unconscious perception, or movements that have become habitual and need no attention paid to them.

If we ask why consciousness has to include fantasy, there is an obvious answer. Decision-making depends upon it. Human beings are capable of voluntary action, and rather more than that: they are capable of choosing between alternative courses of action. The capacity to decide what course of action you take depends on being able to envisage possible courses of action and their outcome. For human beings – and indeed for higher mammals – fantasy is not a luxury item, tacked on the end of human nature to give a little recreation. It is in itself an essential part of the consciousness of any organism that is capable of making decisions based on alternative futures.

If we ask why the unconscious should contain fantasy, the answer is not so immediately clear; but there is a speculative answer that is even more interesting. The deepest unconscious fantasy is the first stage of articulation of instinctive desires or drives. It explains why we want to do certain things rather than others. If we ask what these drives are, there is no certain answer to be found; but there is no reasonable doubt that they are sexual and aggressive in character, and involve not merely isolated actions, but sequences or patterns of action. The evidence of psychoanalysis and analytical psychology here goes along with the evidence from the general character of literature, and the evidence from animal behaviour studies.

What then is the function of relatively free-running fantasy, the fantasy we find in literature and the arts when decisions on action are not being made? One obvious possibility is that we are making a mental rehearsal of decisions that might have to be made in future. We might perhaps be building up a stock of fantasies to be used in some future decision, though not immediately. We might, without knowing it, and of course without knowing the reason, be attempting to translate some unconscious fantasy into a conscious one, thus bridging the gap between unconscious desire and possible actions. Or we might be attempting to modify our own moods – cheer ourselves up, or egg ourselves on – by running through some fantasy scenario in the head. If these are, as seems very likely, primitive psychological processes that may go on in all of us, it will go a long way to explain the functioning of the formalised versions of them that we call works of art.

Note

1. A part of sleep characterised by rapid eye movement; when woken, human subjects usually report dreams.

Chapter 2

The new cognitive psychology

BEHAVIOUR, THINKING AND FANTASY IN ANIMALS

AND HUMAN BEINGS

Summary

This chapter offers a brief and non-technical account of the cognitive sciences, which are transforming our conception of the human mind and its relationship to the body, and mean that we no longer have a simple choice to make between psychoanalytic theories and behaviorist ones.

It starts with the way even organisms without brains have information stored in their genes. It then looks – rather sceptically – at studies of the brain and at attempts to simulate on computers both the way the brain works and the structure of human knowledge. It goes on to consider the extraordinarily complex ways in which animals have to think, in order to produce the behaviour they do; and then to consider the place of instinct and of culture in human behaviour. There is a booklist at the end for those who wish to explore this rapidly expanding field in more depth.

I argue that the new sciences of mind entirely change our view of psychoanalysis, but don't make it obsolete. Spontaneously generated fantasy (with a possible physical basis in chaotic processes in the brain) is the basis of the mental life of most higher animals including human beings, and their capacity to make plans and decisions cannot be understood without it. Just as Freud thought, some form of dynamic psychology is needed to study the cognitive transformations of instinctually generated fantasy in ordinary living and in the arts.

Psychoanalysis and behaviorism

There was a time – and it was within my lifetime – when psychoanalysis could be defended as the best science of the mind we had. At that time, academic psychology was behaviorist.[1] It was also empirical, experimental and statistical: it had all the trimmings of serious and objective science, and in this respect made psychoanalysis look amateur. But its basic objective was absurd: to provide explanations of human behaviour in terms of external stimuli, learning schedules and so forth, that made little reference to the supposedly discredited notion of complex, species-specific action patterns (otherwise known as **instincts**) and no reference at all to 'mentalistic' notions like thoughts, beliefs, purposes or feelings. Such a restricted approach fails to distinguish human beings from experimental pigeons or rats; for it doesn't recognise that each species has its own characteristic set of instincts, controlled by its genes, and these determine what it can learn. And it fails to distinguish higher animals from cockroaches; for there is strong circumstantial evidence that many higher animals – like chimpanzees and even lions – can have complex mental representations of the world, and base their actions upon them, while lower animals cannot.

Within the behaviorist framework it was impossible in principle to describe the way human beings actually are: you could neither describe their instincts – whether simple, like sexuality, or complex, like language-learning – nor their ideas about the world, nor their feelings, beliefs and decisions. You were not allowed, with your scientific hat on, to say that a boy fantasised about being a fighter pilot or that a girl found herself pregnant and had to consider her options and decide whether to get married or have an abortion. You had to say that certain stimuli led to certain behaviours, and omit the unscientific bit about 'considering things' and 'making decisions'. But it is precisely this that constitutes human beings as persons! What we mean by a person is somebody who thinks, feels, perceives, imagines, understands others, makes decisions.

It seemed at times that it was actually part of the purpose of behaviorist psychology not to recognise people as persons. This objective became perfectly clear in the writings of B.F. Skinner, who explicitly claimed that his psychology enabled us to get beyond the outmoded vocabulary of humanism and mentalism: as he put it in the title of one challenging book: *Beyond Freedom and Dignity*.[2] To be fair, the anti-humanist literary theories of the post-Althusserians had similar grovelling aspirations, and denied human free will and dignity in the name of Marx rather than mechanism.

If behaviorist psychology made human beings into impossibly simple unconscious machines,[3] psychoanalysis respected the full complexity of conscious human thought and motivation. Only, beneath these complexities, it revealed further complexities of unconscious thought and motivation. The far more complex psychoanalytic account of mental life made sense of many experiences and symptoms that would otherwise have been wholly baffling. To that extent it commanded immediate imaginative assent; one said: 'That's how it must be!', just as behaviorism produced immediate imaginative rejection: one said 'It can't be as simple as that!'

But psychoanalysis did not merely leave us with an intuitively convincing account of complex mental life. It offered explanatory principles of its own – of the primary instincts of sexuality and aggression, of the way unconscious fantasies and daily experience are combined and transformed into the material of dreams or symptoms, of the stages of sexual development, of the structure of the psyche, and so forth – which appeared to provide fundamental explanations fully comparable with those of the hard sciences. And at no point did these explanations compete with the hard sciences, providing an actual conflict: one could be a neurologist and a psychoanalyst, as Freud himself was. There is no reasonable doubt that, even today, if the choice to be made were one between psychoanalysis and behaviorist psychology, a rational person would choose the former. But it isn't.

The bio-cognitive sciences

The last forty years have seen a revolution in biology, with the rise of a whole constellation of cognitive and behavioral sciences, which have changed our understanding both of sexuality and of the mind. There is **ethology**, which is the descriptive science of animal behaviour.[4] In lower animals we find fixed action patterns sparked off by specific stimuli – like the nest-building behaviour of wasps. In higher animals we find more generalised and variable action patterns – in hunting, mating, rearing and training cubs, establishing the basic dominance hierarchies which hold an animal society together, and so forth. For ethologists, human beings are a species of higher animal much like the others. They have a high learning capacity and can use language; these characteristics mark them off from other animals but don't cut them off in principle. The task of an ethological science of human behaviour would be to describe the basic instinctual behavioral vocabulary of human beings – which underlies, is logically prior to, and partially determines, the structure of human societies.

The purely descriptive account of animal behaviour and animal instincts given by ethology has been utterly transformed by **behavioral ecology** and **behavioral genetics**.[5] These provide an evolutionary explanation not only of animal but also of human instinctive behaviour in terms of what brings the organism ultimate reproductive success – that is, the largest number of ultimate descendants. Ultimate reproductive success is actually the fundamental principle of biological explanation. Every feature of every living organism that is determined by a combination of genes exists only because those genes have survived in reproductive competition. Even the features that are not determined in detail by the genes – for example, the learnt behaviour of a higher animal – are determined in outline by them. Indeed, it is behaviour that natural selection operates on, rather than bodies: organisms are selected for successful reproductive behaviour in a particular environment, and when they are successful, are said to be adapted to that environment. And the whole biological environment of life – the biosphere – is largely an effect of living organisms and evolves with them. The atmosphere only contains oxygen because living creatures provide it.

Our approach to the behaviour of higher organisms including *homo sapiens* is also being transformed by **cognitive psychology**. We no longer try to explain all behaviour in terms of sets of reflexes chained together, as a mindless reaction to some stimulus. Instead, we assume that the organism can acquire knowledge of the world, which explains what it tries to do. We then try to make a cognitive model of this knowledge. Take the case of language. It has always been known that in order to speak, you have to know some language, like English or German or Dyirbal. The behaviorists took on the absurd task of trying to explain *Verbal Behaviour*[6] without referring to our knowledge of language. Chomsky's **generative linguistics**[7] gave a rigorous mathematical form to the age-old discovery that when we speak a language, we put together items from a pre-existing vocabulary according to pre-existing principles of construction (otherwise known as rules of grammar). An associated **psycholinguistic** theory shows how we are preprogrammed to learn languages as children, and this provides us with a model of how we may be preprogrammed in other fields of knowledge and awareness; so that it now seems possible that we are born with an immense amount of knowledge before we ever learn anything. For the physical basis of all these cognitive capacities we look to **brain studies**, and to **computer simulations** of both knowledge structures and brain operations.

What these new sciences have in common is that they are even better based in empirical work than behaviorist psychology was. Much better based, in fact; they make the old studies of 'operant conditioning' look very thin. But they are far from developed yet. Brain surgeons are actually more like plumbers than electricians; they are nowhere near understanding the wiring of the brain, though they are quite good at removing blood clots when some boxer has been reduced to vegetable status. Cognitive psychologists can't provide a satisfactory model of any domain of knowledge, and certainly can't offer a computable one. All grammars leak, leaving linguistic data unaccounted for all over the place. And **sociobiology** – the science that derives social structures fairly directly from the operation of genes – is intrinsically as absurd a programme as behaviorism ever was, since it ignores the factors of culture, history and changing technology that actually distinguish human societies from termite heaps. Yet what these developing sciences have jointly is the potential capacity to model the full complexity of human mental functioning, and relate it to the fundamental principles of biology. It is this that offers the challenge to psychoanalysis.

Psychoanalysis is not, in fact, logically incompatible with behavioral genetics or any of the cognitive sciences. One of its fundamental principles – the explanatory primacy of the sexual instinct – can readily be explained from the fundamental principle of behavioral genetics – the explanatory primacy of ultimate reproductive success. (The sexual instinct is actually a name that we give to a set of unconscious behavioral patterns that evolved to ensure successful mating.[8]) But the scientific standards of psychoanalysis are very much lower than those of cognitive science. If psychoanalysis, over the past forty years, had developed in the way we might expect of a normal science, then there would be substantial agreement about its major claims, and an immense body of empirical evidence to back them up. We would be asking of the new cognitive sciences whether they were compatible with the established science of psychoanalysis, rather than the other way round. But in fact, for at least forty years now, academic psychologists have been asking in vain for satisfactory empirical evidence to support any doctrine of mainstream psychoanalysis, or to show that the practice of psychoanalysis cures anybody of anything.[9] Mainstream psychoanalysts have on the whole ignored this demand; Lacanians have wrapped themselves in resonant obscurity, attacked empiricism, and celebrated ritual formulations of their own dogma. The failure of psychoanalysis to respond to legitimate scientific criticism has become a public scandal.

Accordingly, the only people now who are prepared to give psychoanalysis priority over the new cognitive sciences are those who – for good or bad scientific or political reasons – are hostile to the idea that the study of mind could be a science at all. They like 'making Freud unscientific'. They wish, like Ricoeur, to see Freudian theory as a hermeneutic or cultural-interpretive procedure mistaking itself for a scientific one. Or like Foucault, they see it as a confessional procedure constructing sex rather than a scientific one studying it. There are plenty of people with those views in literary studies. But, for the rest of us, I suspect that the question of the scientificity of psychoanalysis has to be posed quite differently. It is no longer possible to defend psychoanalysis as a total science of the mind. The question is, are there parts of it that one can rescue, by fitting them into appropriate places in the spectrum of the biological and cognitive sciences?

As this book shows, I believe that there are. I believe that the cognitive sciences, taken as a whole, have very large Freud-shaped gaps in them.

There are, that is to say, things the cognitive sciences ought to explain, that they cannot explain without being supplemented by concepts taken from Freud: specifically, concepts involving the transformation of underlying sexual fantasies into the complex products of civilisation. They also – and this will astonish those who have thought of Jung as a low-grade religious thinker – have rather large Jung-shaped gaps; the Jungian concept of archetype is indispensable, and can be made essentially scientific rather than religious in nature. In this book I will try to summarise behavioral genetics and the cognitive sciences in a way that shows how they might fit together with the dynamic psychologies. In order to combine them, one may well have to splinter Freudian theory, accepting some parts and rejecting others; and to take material from some non-Freudian theories, including those of Jung but probably not including those of Lacan, which seem to me suggestive but scientifically irredeemable.

Cognitive science and DNA

The cognitive sciences are based on a single insight: that organisms aren't just pushed around by external stimuli; they carry an internal representation of the environment in which they act, and they respond to stimuli selectively on the basis of this. An internal representation does not necessarily mean a mental representation. You do not need to have a brain to have an internal representation of the world, or a functional behavioral pattern. Philip Johnson-Laird begins his excellent introduction to cognitive science, *Computation and the Mind*, with a creature that has no brain at all. This is the bacterium, *Escherichia Coli*, which lives in the human gut. *E. Coli* seems as capable of purposive behaviour as its host: like *homo sapiens*, it hunts for food! Though it has no brain it does have chemical receptors: what we might think of as a sense of taste; and (as with an old-fashioned literary connoisseur) its sense of taste directly controls its flagellae. In the presence of food, these hair-like organs rotate anti-clockwise, and propel it forward; in the absence of food, they rotate irregularly and often clockwise, and then collapse; the organism then moves all over the place. It therefore spends its time either directly (if rather raggedly) pursuing food particles, or moving about at random till it finds a trace of them. You don't need a brain to hunt if you are a bacterium.

One is tempted to say (as Johnson-Laird actually does say) that you don't need an internal representation of the environment. But this would not be quite true. The bacterium is adapted to its environment. Thus, in a sense – the sense in which the same template represents both a key and the lock which that key fits – its genes, which encode the information that specifies that particular species, are also a representation of the environment to which that species is adapted. To make an organism that will hunt for food in the human gut, the genes have to specify a design that will work in that gut; and any such design presupposes a specification for the relevant aspects of the human gut itself. In that rather special sense, the organism is born 'knowing' that there are food particles around, and how to find them. In the sense that a functioning brain is necessary for knowing, the organism does not know anything at all. Its information about the environment is stored in its genes, not in its non-existent brain.

As we move up the scale of complexity in life, so we find that organisms store more information: this is the only objective measure of how 'high' an organism is in the scale of being. Bacteria have a million or more binary units of information (bits), all stored, like any other genetic information, in DNA nucleotide pairs. Amphibians like frogs check in at a couple of billion bits. Reptiles make three billion. Human beings have 10 billion. Remembering the fundamental ecological principle, that the form of the body is an adaptation to the environment within which the organism has evolved, we may say that simply by having human bodies, we handle 10,000 times the environmental complexity that a bacterium does. Our bodies 'know' – without ever thinking or learning – 10,000 times as much as the bacterium.[10]

But this greatly understates human complexity. Many lower animals have a nervous system; higher animals have a brain. A brain is basically an information processing device for controlling the operation of a complex body. It is, like any other organ of the body, specified by the DNA; a certain amount of information is built into it. But it is the nature of the organ that it can acquire and store information about its own bodily states and about the world outside. In the case of an amphibian, that is not very much information; the brain can store about 200,000 bits, which is only a hundredth part of the information stored in its genes. A reptile has a much more efficient brain; it can store three times the information that is present in its genes, or more. A reptile is thus capable of complex learning behaviour. Some mammals have brains that can store about thirty times as much information as is found in their genes, or more; their adaptation to the world is largely an acquired one, though it is built on a genetic base. Human brains go far beyond this.

The function of brains

The way that brains represent information is much less well understood than the way that DNA does; and the best thing a commentator can do nowadays – when people are going mad about the cognitive sciences – is to sound a note of caution. We don't know how brains work, and we can't yet make reliable inferences from brain structure to behaviour. Most people accept some kind of computer analogy for the brain. But there are two questions about this, one philosophical, one practical. The philosophical question is: suppose we were to complete the strong artificial intelligence project, and simulate on a computer absolutely everything that goes on in a brain; would the computer actually think, and feel, and experience things as an animal does? No one actually has an answer to this question, though it is passionately debated. I suspect that this philosophical question will never be settled by argument; it will be like the old philosophical question about the nature of life, which everybody was arguing about in the time of Bergson and Bernard Shaw, but which became obsolete with the discovery of DNA mechanisms and is now forgotten. It may be – and it may not – that the philosophical question about the nature of mind will be forgotten when we understand in detail the workings of the brain.

We don't understand them yet. We understand exactly how a real computer operates. A computer designer can specify the exact circuitry; a programmer can explain exactly what programs are running on it, and what they do; and there are computer technicians who can explain what is happening in physical, electrical terms, when a program runs. Our understanding of DNA, though incomplete, is of the same order as this. We are mapping the human genome and relating it to somatotype, diseases etc; when we have finished, we will probably know what genes, in what combinations, produce what features of human form and instinctive behaviour. But we don't have the beginnings of such a specific understanding of the brain and its workings. We can't trace the circuitry; we don't know what the programs are, or even what kind of programs they are. One can't appreciate the little we do know – about blood-flows, neuro-transmitters, electrical discharge rhythms and so forth – until one realises what a tiny proportion that is of what is to be known; and even, how far the little we do know is mythological and speculative – like some of the strange interpretations of its bilateral structure.

The central problem for the computer model is to simulate something like human decision-making. IBM's chess-playing program – which has just beaten the human world champion – works by calculating the consequences of every possible move, as far forward as it can, and taking the best. We know real human players don't work quite like that; they haven't the speed or the memory. But they certainly envisage some alternative futures, and choose the moves that seem most promising. It may be that the way a creature with an advanced brain differs from *E. Coli* is that rough models of the consequences of alternative actions are set up in its brain, and the random search that *E. Coli* has to conduct in the real physical world is here conducted in a virtual, or imaginary world, with less risk and effort for the whole organism. It will be seen that what we are suggesting here is that the very basis for the higher mental functions is the ability to construct alternative stories about the future.

It is probably essential to the functioning of an animal brain that it should not function deterministically, like an ordinary digital computer. These will respond in a predictable way to any input they receive. A determinist brain would go very well with a behaviorist psychology; and both fit well with the eighteenth and nineteenth century view that for a scientist, the world as a whole is a determinist one; but it is hard to see how one could recognise any logical possibility of human free will in such a world. In the twentieth century we have learnt that there is uncertainty built into the very structure of the world, at the quantum level. The world is ultimately non-deterministic, and so, probably, is the brain. That doesn't solve the whole problem of the relation between mind and brain; but it removes the flat logical contradiction of a person with free will whose body is a deterministic machine.

A brain is one of the most complicated and interconnected things in the universe, comparable to the atmosphere of the entire planet, which as weather forecasters know, can't be simulated in detail by any computer. As chaos theory in mathematics warns us, when a system is as complicated as that, very small differences in input can produce colossal differences of output; as the catchphrase has it, the flap of a butterfly's wings can produce a typhoon six months later and six thousand miles away. Some of the inputs to the brain can operate at levels where quantum uncertainties appear. The brain as a whole may well be a machine which amplifies quantum uncertainties to the point where they affect gross behaviour: a non-deterministic automaton. This may be the physical basis of our ability to generate fantasies – that is, accounts of the world that are not simply mechanical responses to stimuli.

The thinking of animals and the biological function of fantasy

So what functional difference does it make to have a big brain with a large cerebral cortex? Compare the way the lioness hunts to the way *E. Coli* does it. Lions form social groups called prides, with one or more mature males and a rather larger number of mature females and cubs. The lionesses hunt cooperatively, against formidable, mobile and wary herd animals, often by complex manoeuvres designed to cut out weaker animals from the herd. If we think what kind of computer program we would try to put into a robot to achieve a performance like this, we can get some idea of the minimum of mental operations lionesses must engage in. They are very complex.

Every individual lioness must have a detailed internal model of its environment, which is capable of being remembered throughout the active life of the lioness, but is also capable of being instantaneously updated as new information comes in. That model covers not just the inanimate or vegetable environment, but the mobile prey animals and also the other lionesses. It cannot be just a model of the physical shape and velocity of the prey; it needs to be a complex model of the prey's intentions and possible strategies, and must be sensitive to changes in these – it needs, for example, to be able to tell when a particular prey animal is getting weak or exhausted. Furthermore, since hunting is cooperative, the lioness must have corresponding models of the interiority of all the other lionesses as well. You can't cooperate with another living creature unless you have an updateable model of its mind inside your mind – and that is true whether you are a lioness or a person.

It doesn't stop there. In order to perform the actions of a hunt, the lion-robot must be capable of entertaining many complex counterfactual scenarios, and working out its responses to them. In human and linguistic terms this might be: 'If that deer breaks to the left I can leave it to be taken by Emma, who is concealed behind the ridge; if it breaks to the right, I must move to cut it off.' The lion-robot operates without the benefit of human language; but this is what it has to 'think'; and some internal language of representation, or the neural-network equivalent, has to be supplied that enables it to 'tell itself' these little stories, and act upon them. The real lioness must have a mind that is no less complex than this robot-model. The human being must have a mind that is immensely more complex, since as we shall see he has the use of a human language to construct concepts of an indefinitely high order of complexity, and has access to a far more extended culture.

What do we learn from this little thought experiment? What we learn, I suggest, is something crucial to the basic structure of action and decision-making in all higher animals, including human beings. A higher animal forms an updateable internal model of the world it lives in, including other creatures and itself, and imagines alternative courses of action within that model. It then chooses between these imagined courses of action. And all this happens in real time, while action is proceeding.

The animal behaviour we have been talking about is often called instinctive – that is, determined by genetic rather than cultural transmission – and there is no doubt this is broadly correct; although there is cultural transmission within the pride, as cubs are shown how to hunt. But what exactly is the instinct that is inherited? It isn't limited to what the ethologists call a specific action pattern, as it might be for *E. Coli* or even a wasp. It is, or at least includes, a generalised capacity for cooperative hunting, which rests on the ability to envisage many patterns of action, and choose between them. It looks as if instinct, in a higher animal, directly produces, not behaviour, but the pattern of thought that leads to behaviour. Let us press this argument to its conclusion.

What we have just established, with a pretty high degree of confidence, is that there is a central role in higher animals, no doubt including man, for genetically controlled abilities to generate counterfactual self-referring narratives, otherwise known as fantasies; and to choose among these fantasies which ones, if any, shall be realised in action. Such fantasies are not, on this analysis, the marginal luxury of a mind running out of control; they are the basis of the central function for which the mind has evolved, which is, of course, to make decisions that are crucial to survival in complex situations.

On this analysis the brain evolves as the control system and regulator of the body, and also to specify gross behaviour patterns. The mental functions of the brain evolve in order to make it possible to run through counterfactual narratives about behaviour, predict their consequences, and choose which particular course of action to take. For this to be possible, the brains of higher animals must have a built-in capacity to generate stories. We thus discover the roots of imaginative activity – the formation and elaboration of fantasies – in the ordinary functioning of the mammalian brain. It exists in animals without language, and it is therefore reasonable to postulate that it exists in human beings at a level below language: perhaps the level that Freud called primary process thinking, or perhaps that which Lacan called the imaginary, or perhaps that which Jung called the archetypal.

Instincts, language and culture in human beings

There has been an extraordinary consensus in the last fifty years, in the pretentious and unreliable fields of sociology and cultural theory, that everything of importance about human beings is cultural; *homo sapiens*, unlike other animals, has few or no instincts. This view is nonsense, and has now been abandoned by most serious thinkers. Human beings have the richest and most complex instincts in the animal kingdom. No other animal, for example, has the immensely complex instinctual equipment that would enable it rapidly to acquire and use a language, as human children do; or to handle, with precision and skill, a wide range of physical tools. It is because human beings have rich and complex instincts that they are capable of rich and complex learning. What is true is that we have extraordinary capacities to acquire and use further information, realising our basic instinctual fantasies in complex cultural forms.

The brains of human beings can store a thousand times the information that is in our DNA. And this still enormously underestimates the amount of information – still keeping to the sober, computer-science concept of information – that human beings and, even more, social groups of human beings, can handle. Human beings, like many higher animals, have cultures; uniquely, human cultures employ language to construct complex concepts with which to articulate themselves. Language has many functions; but overwhelmingly the most important one is that of encoding complex information in a form which the human brain can handle. Consider a concept like 'the British economy'. Many hours of explanation would be necessary to explain the meaning of this phrase in terms which address everyday experience; but language enables us to manipulate it as a single unit in discourse. Language acts, therefore, as an information-compressor or, what is the same thing, as an amplifier of the information-processing capacities of the brain. What order of amplification it gives is difficult or impossible to estimate, but one would be surprised if it were not several orders of magnitude – perhaps tens of millions of times – and it is this which makes possible the great complexity of human cultures.

This is what casts doubt on the simple common-sense assumption that the mind is a biological entity somewhere in the head. Although the capacity to acquire language and to learn a complex human culture is hard-wired into the human brain, actual languages, and actual cultures are not. These are learnt from a pre-existing society. But these – which, if the brain is seen as a computer, would be its programs – are the very basis of mind. The culture of a society is a kind of collective mind, or perhaps the collective matrix of any individual mind; and it is also a perpetual partner in dialogue for any individual mind. (This is the only sense that can be given to the detestably vague metaphysical concept of 'the Other'.)

We have not finished yet. The instinctual capacity of human beings to use tools interacts with their intellectual capacities to make possible the external storage of information. Developments within human cultures in historical times, beginning with the invention of writing, and ending currently with the development of computers, have increased the amount of information stored and available to human beings by many orders of magnitude again. Computers cannot yet, and may never, replicate human brains. But they amplify the information-processing capacity of human brains at least as much as language did – though, obviously, acting on top of language, not replacing it.

The location of fantasy in human thought

If the argument so far is correct, the direct operation of instinct in higher animals is to produce not action but phantasy. The hunting instinct in lionesses or men produces not a set of reflex actions ending in the grabbing of the prey but a desire for prey coupled with a generalised idea of the actions that might secure it. The sexual instinct in lions or men produces a desire for a lioness or a woman coupled with a generalised idea of the actions that might secure her. These phantasies (so spelt) exist at what a Jungian might call the archetypal level of mind. It is a part of the intellectual ability of a higher animal that it can combine such an archetypal phantasy with information about actual prey animals, or actual females, in the world around, to produce alternative provisional plans of action – fantasies, in the other spelling of the word – which are then, in some cases only, used as a guide for action. Higher animals think about more prey animals than they actually try to take, and the males think about more females than they actually impregnate; and it is clear that for a higher animal some satisfaction is gained merely by fantasising the achievement of an instinctual goal.

All this happens at a non-verbal level of the mind that roughly corresponds to Freud's primary process or perhaps to Lacan's 'imaginary'. For human beings there is however a further level of mind at which culture, and the complex concepts constructed in language, come into play: it corresponds to Freud's secondary process and perhaps to Lacan's 'symbolic'. It is the mark of human beings that they can integrate complex cultural ideas into fantasies or plans for action, and communicate these by means of language; this ability is vital to human survival, which depends on complex social actions. It is this general ability to fantasise that underlies the capacity to produce those complex and sophisticated fantasies that we call works of literature.

Notes and references

Suggestions for further reading are on page 211.

1. In the 1950s. For a more balanced view it is worth looking at one of the older histories of psychology – e.g. **Flugel**, 1933.
2. **Skinner**, 1972; see also 1938, 1953, 1957, 1959.
3. Strict psychological behaviorism does this. There are varieties of philosophical behaviorism that don't – at the cost of counting a whole range of intelligent activities as behaviour, and thus explaining nothing. Cf. **G. Ryle**, 1949, *The Concept of Mind*; and for social behaviorism, **George Herbert Mead**, 1956.
4. **Lorenz**, 1952, 1963, 1973; **Tinbergen**, 1951, 1953a, 1968.
5. **Dawkins**, 1976, 1982; **Diamond**, 1991; **Ridley**, 1993.

6. **Skinner**, 1957.
7. **Chomsky**, 1956, 1957. Chomsky's main mathematical papers are collected in **Luce, Bush and Galanter**, 1963, 1965.
8. See Chapter 8.
9. Not quite in vain: see **Fisher and Greenberg**, 1996 for evaluation of about 2,500 references. See Chapter 3 for discussion.
10. All figures rough estimates from **Sagan**, 1977.

Chapter 3

The sceptical Freudian

PSYCHOANALYTIC THEORY AND ITS DISCONTENTS

Summary

This chapter gives an account of the main claims of Freud and some immediate followers, along with some of the familiar scientific criticisms and some putative answers to these. Freud's theory was developed over a very long working career – roughly 1884–1939 – and it changed greatly. I have summarised and simplified in an attempt to show Freud's thought as an interconnected whole; I have represented his development by mentioning one or two major changes only. I have also added comments in which I have tried to estimate the scientific credibility, in modern terms, of each claim in turn.

The argument about Freud is here treated as a scientific one, about the truth and the force of his explanatory theories, rather than a hermeneutic one about the interpretation of his texts, or a literary critical one about the mobilisation of his metaphors, or a cultural one about his significance for the twentieth century. Freud believed himself to be an objective scientist, though both his critics and many of his later followers strongly disagree, and he deserves to be evaluated as such.

In academic psychology nowadays an almost overwhelming consensus is emerging that Freudian theory is unscientific nonsense; but in literary and cultural studies scientific criticism is often seen as irrelevant, as if it were an obvious mistake to see him as a scientist of any kind, rather than, say, an imaginative writer.[1] I argue against both these positions. Freud's interpretative approach rests firmly on his theory: it is inconsistent to keep one and reject the other.

The system of Sigmund Freud

The philosophical problem of unconscious mind

Freud's theory starts with a crazy paradox, though it has grown so familiar now that we don't see its craziness any more. The paradox is the concept of 'unconscious mind'. Consider what we mean by 'mind'. When we use the word normally, we are not thinking of an object that we could examine, like the body, but of kinds of activity – thinking, feeling, perceiving the world, imagining future possibilities, deciding what to do. And all of these are activities we are directly aware of performing – that is, they are conscious. Mind **is**, on the face of it, consciousness, awareness, subjectivity; and it includes the ability to reflect on the world and to choose and decide. It seems nonsensical to speak of unconscious consciousness, unaware aware-ness, or a subjectivity that is outside the subject and stops it doing what it wants.

Literary people probably find it harder to see the force of this argument than scientists, because they love paradoxes like these, which come over as powerful metaphors, suggest great profundity, and remind them of modernist art. For forty years now, literary theorists have preferred formu-lations of psychoanalytic theory like those of Jacques Lacan, which are high on paradox and rhetoric – 'desire is the desire of the other', 'a subject is a way of representing a signifier to another signifier' and so forth. Phrases like 'the decentring of the subject' have been used in literary theory as mantras, to be chanted for effect whether or not they make scientific or philosophical sense. But if we are to discuss the scientific claims of a psychological theory, we have to remind ourselves that any theory from which we can derive a paradox is thereby proved false.

The argument against the unconscious

On the face of it, a thought only exists if we think it, and a feeling if we feel it, and to think or feel something is to be aware of thinking or feeling it, just as to decide something is to think of alternative possibilities and choose between them. An unconscious thought is not a thought. An unconscious perception is not a perception. An unconscious feeling is not a feeling. An unconscious decision is not a decision: it is simply doing something without making **any** decision to do it; or it is something that happens to us rather than something we do. Unconscious mental processes are not **mental** processes. What sense can be made of the notion of an impalpable container – the unconscious – in which are ghostly objects – thoughts, feelings, etc. – that we 'have' without being aware of? If it is the very essence of thoughts and feelings that we are aware of them, then if we are not aware of them, we surely don't 'have' them!

If we want an opposite to conscious mind, it is not unconscious mind but body: physical brain processes, for example. Isn't it the natural thing to say that 'thoughts' exist when physical brain processes are accompanied by conscious awareness: and they don't exist when physical brain processes occur without conscious awareness? Insert an electrode at a certain point in the cortex of the brain, and a vivid image will be elicited: a 'thought' exists. Insert it elsewhere, and there will be no such image; though there might be an involuntary twitch. There is no case for saying that an involuntary twitch is an unconscious thought, or even a symptom of one: it is just a twitch, as innocent of thought as the knee-jerk reflex. The cerebellum works very hard at keeping us upright when we walk, but no mental process accompanies this. We are conscious of walking, but have no idea of the complex control process that makes it possible. But that does not mean that it is an unconscious mental process. It is a physical control process; there are no grounds for calling it a mental process of any kind.

If this argument were correct, we would have to reject not only Freudian theory, but the most obvious interpretations of modern cognitive psychology, and most forms of psychological science, on purely *a priori* grounds.[2] If we are to preserve them we have to ask what sense we can make of the claim that a process can exist that is at once mental and non-conscious.

The answer from cognitive science

A good first step toward an answer is to consider the basis of our knowledge of other people's thoughts. We are never directly conscious of these; but we are perfectly confident that they do think and feel. What those thoughts and feelings are, we infer from what they say and do. We can apply this same principle to ourselves. Suppose we find that there are things which we say and do which appear to be the outcome of trains of reasoning, or intentions, of which we are quite unaware. Suppose for example that I go to sleep contemplating a difficult mathematical problem, and wake up having solved it. In that situation it is reasonable to argue that the steps of that solution have been gone through without my being aware of performing them; and it would be absurd to argue that they lose the entire character of mental processes merely because I was not aware of performing them. What could be more mental than mathematical problem-solving? But once the principle is accepted that we can sensibly attribute mental operations to ourselves or others, in order to explain observed behaviour, without necessarily assuming that we or others are aware of those operations, a whole world of unconscious mental life becomes available for examination.

The basic claim, then, which is as much cognitive as Freudian, is that in addition to the ordinary mental processes of which we are aware, there are processes going on within us, which we have overwhelming reasons to describe as mental, and of which we are unaware. These processes range from apparently trivial – but actually very complicated – processes of perception, movement control, language-speaking and language-learning, to apparently profound – but probably rather simpler – matters of emotional attitude.

Human beings can do something that no robot ever devised can manage: we can walk along a crowded pavement, without bumping into any of the people there. To do that, we must in some sense have seen the people on the pavement, made very complex judgements about them – judged, for a start, that they were people, not lamp-posts, and therefore were likely to walk in directions of their own choosing – noticed their positions and the way they were going, and executed all sorts of complicated pavement manoeuvres to avoid them. The astonishing thing is that we can do this without noticing we are doing it, or remembering what we have done. This means that we have **not** consciously seen the other people; but we have unconsciously perceived them, and thought about them. We continue to rely on these unconscious processes of perception, cognitive analysis and movement control for sophisticated and dangerous purposes like driving a car in heavy traffic.

Human beings can be equally oblivious of their own emotional attitudes. We can be furiously angry without noticing the fact, and indeed, while being confident that we are calm and controlled, though any observer could tell us to the contrary. We can hold a grudge, or be passionately in love, for a whole lifetime without ever noticing the fact. We can sleepwalk into adultery, contriving the situation without ever acknowledging our intentions. Writers and philosophers have always known this; to judge by the latest work of Baker and Bellis, the biologists have just discovered it, too.[3]

There are, then, mental processes we are aware of, and mental processes we are not aware of; and we call these conscious and unconscious mental processes, though this is a slightly misleading formulation: it would be better to say, mental processes we are conscious of performing, and mental processes we are not conscious of performing. For this reason we cannot identify consciousness with mind, as my first remarks suggested, and as those influenced by Cartesian philosophy and phenomenology have often tried to do.[4] One might even go in the other direction, and say that conscious thoughts are a second order phenomenon – we all the time have a certain level of awareness of the world and of ourselves; but part of the time we are aware of that awareness, and that is consciousness.

This is a broader position than Freud's, but Freud was very familiar with it; it is fairly close to the view of his contemporary Theodor Lipps, whom he read in 1898 (there is a letter to Fliess about him). Lipps said he believed not merely that unconscious mental processes exist side-by-side with the conscious ones, but that unconscious processes lie at the bottom of all conscious ones and accompany them. 'The conscious, when fortune favours, arises from the unconscious and then sinks back again.'[5]

Lipps seems obviously correct here, but there is a startling implication of this view. There is no logical absurdity in the notion of a person leading a fairly complex mental life without ever becoming conscious of it! It looks as if this can actually happen in certain types of brain injury, and in sleep-walking and certain hypnotic states. It raises the interesting question: what is the function of consciousness? Why do we ever need to be aware of our mental processes? Why not just perform them?

The Freudian unconscious and the concept of repression

Freud had a much more specific notion of the unconscious than we have considered so far. He thought of the unconscious as the domain of the repressed. Complex mental phenomena like images, ideas, motives, feelings, beliefs, memories etc. are often unconscious only in the sense that they are not present in the mind at some particular moment; but we can usually recall them to consciousness any time we want. Sometimes it is necessary to call them into consciousness by some special technique – hypnotism, for example – or merely by asking someone to keep on saying everything that pops into his head – the 'free association' technique. Material like this Freud called 'pre-conscious'. The interesting point is that it is sometimes not possible to recall items to consciousness: there is a 'resistance' to the search. In this case, it is postulated, there is an active force in the mind preventing recall; the memories, motives, etc. are then said to be repressed. The specifically Freudian unconscious is the domain of the repressed, and the first line of evidence for it is that there are gaps in conscious memory which become evident in the analytic session, and which can only be filled if we assume the existence of repressed material.

The notion of repression, and of the Freudian unconscious, grew up in the context of a set of studies on hysteria.[6] Hysteria was an immensely complicated syndrome including many different pathologies – fainting fits, strange fantasies, paralyses with no organic foundation, and so forth – and was one of the most widely diagnosed mental illnesses of the 1890s.

Nowadays it has almost disappeared; the symptoms that would once have given rise to a diagnosis of hysteria would either be attributed to some brain damage too subtle for the science of 1890 to recognise, or attributed to a different mental illness like schizophrenia. Freud and Breuer, however, thought of it as a unitary disease with a wide range of symptoms and a uniform cause. It was always caused by some stressful incident – anything from being involved in a railway accident to the death of a parent – which had been insufficiently reacted against; the cure was a conscious variant of the Aristotelian concept of 'catharsis' – the way in which a great tragedy was supposed to purge and purify the emotions. It was to work on the patient's resistances, get him to bring the incident to mind and react to it emotionally now. Ideas of repression and the unconscious were of course broadened greatly later on.

Comment: The most up-to-date, perhaps the most ingenious, and certainly the most trivial argument against the reality of repression and of the Freudian unconscious is a post-structuralist one of a broadly literary kind. This is that when we postulate repressed materials in an unconscious mind we do so in order to fill gaps in the patient's narrative about himself; we are not satisfied with what the patient says because it lacks narrative closure. The unconscious is therefore an artefact of our demand for narrative closure. There is a sense in which this is trivially true: we wouldn't postulate anything about a patient's unconscious mind if we weren't trying to make sense of the conscious one. But it doesn't follow that the patient wouldn't have an unconscious mind if we didn't investigate it!

From a scientific point of view, there is nothing particularly implausible about the existence of a Freudian unconscious – an unconscious that contains repressed material – and a good deal of empirical evidence for it. In fact we can actually create such an unconscious under controlled experimental conditions. A subject can be hypnotised – that is, placed in a light trance by suggestion – and then intentions, motives and beliefs can be suggested, within fairly wide limits set by the strength of the existing belief system of the subject under hypnosis. The subject can be instructed not to be aware of what has happened, or what he now believes. On waking, he will act on his new beliefs and motives, but honestly deny their existence.

In a typical experiment, a hypnotised subject, sitting in a group of observers, might be instructed to open a window as soon as she wakes up, but to forget that the instruction has been given. On waking, the subject will become progressively more uneasy, and finally go to open the window: on being asked why, she will fabricate a reason – saying 'It's stuffy in here' even if in fact it is not. In this trivial case, an unconscious motive has been injected into the subject's mind. We here have a controllable experimental procedure, no less, which demonstrates the production and the existence of unconscious motivation. But since, as I pointed out above, a wide range of unconscious learning is possible, it seems equally possible that unconscious and repressed thoughts might be acquired by unconscious learning without the intervention of a hypnotist. Freud's general claim is therefore a perfectly reasonable one.

Freud himself used hypnosis for a time, in the period round about 1889. In the case of Emmy von N, described in *Studies in Hysteria*, he gives extensive notes of such a treatment. He used the technique, consciously following Breuer's example, both for investigation – to discover what forgotten traumatic episodes were responsible for Emmy's hysterical pains and so forth – and for treatment – to banish symptoms like pain, or to erase memories which he thought were responsible for the symptoms – and even to impress his patient with the reality of hypnosis by giving her post-hypnotic commands which she later obeyed without remembering them. (She was a non-drinker, so he told her to ask him for a glass of wine at lunch that day; then refuse it. He told her the very words she should use, and wrote them on a folded paper which he gave to her. A few hours later, she did exactly as he had commanded; then looked with astonished surprise at the piece of paper on which her words were written. This may be a stage trick, but it could easily be the basis of a valid experiment.) If we ask ourselves why Freud and others were so ready to accept the existence of an unconscious mind containing repressed memories and desires, the answer is that they were all familiar with the phenomena of hypnosis, so it didn't seem unreasonable.[7]

Once the reality of hypnosis and the possibility of spontaneous repression are accepted, it is easy to see that there may well be, in a normal person, whole systems of thoughts (complexes), or perhaps whole subpersonalities, that are unconscious because they are repressed. The symptoms of many mental disorders, both in Freud's time and our own day, can readily be explained on this basis. There is even a disease – multiple personality disorder, once rare, now commonplace – in which apparently complete personalities can alternate in the same physical body, with varying degrees of awareness of each other; sometimes one personality has complete amnesia for the doings of the others. Some psychiatrists think that this is a fake illness that is actually produced by hypnosis; but there are well-attested spontaneous cases, usually the result of great stress in childhood; and a famous one was described by Morton Prince in 1905.[8]

The evidence from hypnotism is very well established. It was familiar to Freud himself, and to his distinguished teacher Charcot, and to workers for a century before that.[9] Some modern researchers, however, are still so disturbed by the notion of the unconscious mind, that they are prepared to deny the reality of hypnotism – even when they themselves regularly produce the whole range of hypnotic phenomena reported in the literature, from false beliefs to hysterical paralyses, by suggestion in their own classes. What they do is to produce the phenomena but also strongly suggest to their subjects – who are often their students and therefore peculiarly susceptible to pressure – that their cooperation with the hypnotist is voluntary, and could be suspended at any time. The subjects, and the observers, believe this, and confirm it. The researchers conclude that hypnotism does not involve the production of trance, or the subjection of the subject's will to the hypnotist, or amnesia for the commands given. It involves more or less conscious cooperation. They extend the same aggressive scepticism to multiple personality disorder, and indeed to any phenomenological account of a mental disorder that supports the reality of the unconscious.[10]

The subjects of the traditional hypnotist, on the other hand, are told that they will be put into trance, and that they won't remember the instruction they have been given. So they obediently go into trance, and they don't remember it afterwards. They thus provide evidence for the traditional account of hypnotism. There is thus a common mechanism of suggestion in both cases; but there is artificially produced unconscious motivation only in one. Psychologists of the sceptical camp claim that this refutes the notion of hypnotism, and of unconscious motivation. But in fact it does not. Neither procedure discredits the other! On the contrary: it seems that it is possible sometimes to have hypnotic effects associated with traditional trance-like phenomena, and sometimes 'hypnotic' effects not so associated. It seems that one may sometimes have amnesia for commands given, and sometimes have no amnesia for commands given.

These facts actually reinforce the possibility on which psychoanalysis is based, that one may have a patient whose condition is affected by material of which he is not conscious, and one may be able to give a treatment that makes that material conscious.

The concept of repression has however been criticised on more materialist grounds. Modern paediatricians usually reject the Freudian view that infantile amnesia – our habit of forgetting the most significant and traumatic things that happened to us when we were young children – is a result of some mechanism like repression. They claim that the brain is in such a state of turmoil in infancy, so rapidly losing cells, that it is very unlikely that stable memory traces are ever laid down. If they are laid down, they are probably lost through the extensive brain reorganisation that is still taking place up to three or so. The question arises whether our so-called 'infantile memories' are not actually reconstructions, produced later and projected back?

In fact, for modern psychologists, most memories are reconstructions, based on stored cues. This changes the question into: 'How adequate are the cues remaining for reconstruction of memories from infancy?'; and it may be that they are not very adequate, so that when we try to remember, we tend to confabulate, or at best, reconstruct our infancy from what members of the family have told us. Indeed, we may have to be cautious about later stages of childhood and adolescence. Is the psychotherapist who purports to lift a veil of repression and show childhood traumas, real or fantasied – child abuse by a loved father, satanist abuse, or in some cases kidnapping by aliens in spaceships – actually projecting a false memory of something that never happened either in reality or fantasy? Where one therapist might see repression lifted, another might see false memory syndrome.

We have to beware of excessive scepticism. Suppose we decide to follow those aggressively sceptical psychologists who reject repression and hysterical dissociation, multiple personality disorder, hypnotism, and indeed virtually anything that conflicts with the notion of the unified conscious social self or that attempts to recognise irreconcilable conflicts inside the self. Such an approach throws us back on a kind of social behaviorism, perhaps supplemented by some cognitive psychology: a very limited view of human nature. One wonders if this is not a fear of the irrational, leading to a denial of the existence of irrational forces and processes inside the mind. What do psychologists who take this view say about fantasy? About unconscious fantasy? About art and literature? About the Romantic movement, or Surrealism? It is probably in these areas that the most convincing evidence for the existence of mechanisms of repression or dissociation may lie.

Consciousness, the unconscious and freedom of the will

For Freud as therapist, the fundamental point of psychoanalysis is to bring material from the unconscious, which is causing neurotic or compulsive behaviour, into consciousness, so that the patient can freely and rationally make decisions of his or her own. The purpose of therapy is therefore to increase human freedom. But Freud has a mechanistic and determinist model of mind as a whole, though not of consciousness by itself. Consciousness, for Freud, is not self-determining. And the unconscious part of the mind does not wholly determine the conscious part. They interact. Our mental life is determined by the interplay of unconscious and conscious elements. The mind as a whole is a deterministic system.[11]

Comment: There seems to be a fundamental contradiction here, between Freud's view of the nature of psychotherapy, and his deterministic model of the mind as a whole. The very concept of free human action seems to require that decisions are not predictable or causally determined, and that any decision to act one way or another helps change the possibilities for the whole future of the world. This is the common-sense view of human action that at some level we all share, and it gives meaning and dignity to our lives: it means that we make a difference to the world.

If the system of the world as a whole, or even the system of the mind as a whole, is determinist, consciousness can never be more than a mere spectator, becoming aware of each preordained 'decision' as it arises on the basis of purely causal mechanisms. How then can the patient be said to 'make his own decisions'? He is just as determined after therapy as before. The notion that the subject has any freedom at all seems to belong to a Kantian conception of mind, which places it outside the causal order of nature, rather than to Freud's mechanistic determinism. There is a *prima facie* conflict between determinism and freedom of the will.

This is a problem that would not be cleared up if we were to drop psychoanalysis and adopt a cognitive model of the human mind. It would still be impossible to reconcile the notion that every action is determined by causes that can be studied scientifically, with the notion that every person has free will, and decides for himself what action to take. Only a mind, or a device like a non-determinist computer, that can represent genuinely possible alternative futures, can make decisions. It is not only psychoanalysis that needs to postulate a mind of this character. The point is crucial to all approaches to the mind.

A long series of philosophers have attempted to demonstrate that this conflict does not really exist: that it depends on some type of logical confusion. Peter Gay quotes Donald Davidson's version of this series: 'Hobbes, Locke, Hume, Moore, Schlick, Ayer, Stevenson, and a host of others have done what can be done, or ought ever to have been needed, to remove the confusions that can make determinism seem to frustrate freedom.'[12] One can readily add to this list: the vituperations of Christopher Caudwell, for example, could stand for the Marxist tradition,[13] in which ordinary freedom of the will is a bourgeois delusion, and true freedom is the consciousness of necessity. Ted Honderich, 1988, even offers *A Theory of Determinism* which requires us to affirm determinism joyously!

What I chiefly notice is that philosophers get very bad-tempered when they are trying to explain why free will does not conflict with a deterministic model of the mind or brain: as if this is a problem that has no right to exist, yet keeps on coming back like a buzzing fly. But the very fact that the problem has such antiquity, and has been treated unsuccessfully by so many major thinkers, shows that it is a serious one. My own feeling is that human free will is a fact; that it does conflict with the nineteenth century determinist model of science, and that that is a good reason for thinking that the determinist model of science; is wrong, even if we did not have independent evidence from quantum theory that it is wrong.

In some ways this is reassuring. If Freud is wrong about determinism he might be right about the liberating effects of his therapy.

The content of the unconscious

Freud's greatest achievement was to see that you could apply the principles of conversion hysteria – in which, according to Freud, mental contents of the unconscious are converted into physical symptoms – to a wide range of everyday phenomena – in particular, jokes, slips of the tongue and other mistakes, and dreams. He worked out a single, uniform psychological process in which underlying unconscious wishes were combined with everyday experience to form manifest phenomena. This process, in its application to dreams, is called 'the dream-work', and is briefly described below. Because there is a known process of production of these phenomena from unconscious material, it is possible to interpret them by tracing the process of formation in reverse. One examines symptom, mistake or dream, making hypotheses about what has led to them, following up immediate associations, and interpreting any resistances that might appear. Freud thus has available not merely a therapeutic method, but a powerful research tool comparable with X-rays in medicine, which can work back from many kinds of conscious phenomena to discover what is in the unconscious mind.

Freud offered three main types of indirect evidence for the content of the unconscious.

(1) *Neurotic symptoms and conversion hysteria*   According to Freud, neurotic symptoms are fulfilments of, or devices for fulfilling, repressed wishes. The woman who had reached a stage at which she could no longer bear to go on nursing her father, developed a hysterical paralysis (a paralysis with no basis in organic injury) which stopped her from nursing him. She was not faking the paralysis; it was not consciously intentional. But it was unconsciously intentional.

As with dreams and parapraxes, the interpretation of neurotic symptoms is something that must be made one case at a time. The same symptom will mean diferent things in different cases. However, it is perfectly possible, even while attending to the individuality of each particular case, to discover a deep layer of commonalty in all the cases. Freud came to think that underlying all hysterical symptoms were deep sexual disturbances.

(2) *Mistakes (Parapraxes)*　These include slips of the tongue and pen, forgetting, clumsy behaviour, etc. It is commonplace that slips of the tongue and other mistakes may reveal some underlying purpose, at odds with our overt and admitted purpose, or reveal an opinion that we wish to keep concealed. 'Hello Mr Wart!' one says – he is actually called Waugh, but has an obtrusive deformity. Freud's point is that sometimes we are unconscious of the interfering motive, or perception, until we interpret the mistake that we have made. Freud himself went to enormous lengths in interpreting parapraxes, even to the extent of interpreting verbal errors as trilingual puns, as if all errors were necessarily meaningful, and meaningless mechanical errors did not occur at all. Again, at a deep level, he always discovered sexual problems.[14]

(3) *Dreams*　Freud argued that night-dreams, like day-dreams, are wish-fulfilments. Night-dreams, however, are usually disguised fulfilments of repressed wishes. The disguise comes about in the following way. Dreams are the product of primary-process thinking: thinking that is motivated by infantile sexual desires which combine with residues of daily experience to produce fantasised goals. This contrasts with the secondary-process thinking that inhibits and postpones primary-process thinking and redirects thoughts toward changing reality. Dreams are vivid and pictorial, and cannot contain much in the way of abstract thought. The repressed wishes which are the latent thoughts underlying the dream are translated into the manifest dream by a process which Freud called the dream-work. The dream-work involves a condensation of the underlying thoughts; a displacement of emphasis so that what is important in the underlying thought becomes unimportant in the manifest dream, and vice versa; and some degree of translation of the underlying thoughts into concrete, vivid imagery – so that, for example, the logical relationship of cause and effect will be translated into the serial relationship of one event simply following another; and thoughts will be translated into pictures and dramatic scenes – sometimes on a basis peculiar to the individual, and sometimes by fairly universal symbols.[15]

The interpretation of dreams was described by Freud as 'the royal road to the unconscious'. It involves reversing the action of the dream-work and proceeding from the manifest dream back to the latent dream-thoughts.

Since these are so much fuller than the dream itself, interpretation requires the analyst to build in material he acquires within the analysis: it is not a matter of mechanical translation according to a dream book. (This is also true of parapraxes and symptoms.)

Comment: It is a stunning theoretical coup to explain mistakes, jokes, hysterias and dreams – and as we shall see, myths and works of art as well – by the same unconscious processes, thus offering what looks very like a general theory of human creativity. The jury is still out on this proposal;[16] but I have to say that I don't believe there is a better one on offer. It was Socrates who first pointed out that authors couldn't offer a full account of the meaning of their own work. His solution was that part of the work depended on divine inspiration. The theory of unconscious processes is a modern alternative to that two-and-a-half-thousand year old theory.

Some would say the concepts of the unconscious mind and of repression merely enable Freud to **interpret** as purposive or meaningful behaviour many things, like these mistakes, dreams and neurotic symptoms, which are not consciously purposive. There are many criticisms of this procedure. Some scientists reject purposive explanations in science even when one is discussing human actions: this seems crazy to me. Others point out that the realm of purely mechanical and meaningless error is actually quite large, and accounts for most parapraxes. As any mediocre typist knows, the major reason one sometimes mistypes a comma as the letter 'm' is that they lie side by side on the keyboard; it has little to do with the fact that 'm' is the first letter of 'masturbation'. (There is an excellent study of **The Freudian Slip** by Timpanaro, a Marxist philologist who knows what it's like to handle texts.)

My worry would be that the principles of the dream-work, for example, are too general and too vague. They can explain any transformation what-ever, and map virtually any underlying set of dream-thoughts you like to postulate, onto any manifest dream. The only control here seems to be the psychoanalyst's knowledge of his patient, acquired during the analysis. But theories that can explain anything are not scientific. They are merely terminological frameworks into which you can push anything.

The concept of primary-process thinking corresponds roughly to that of phantasy or inner reality in later theories and perhaps to 'the imaginary' in Lacan. Secondary-process thinking might correspond to Lacan's 'the symbolic'. This distinction is close to, but not identical with, that between non-verbal and verbal thought, and with that between unconscious and preconscious thought. It makes for a baroque theory, but we probably have to recognise all these distinctions – primary and secondary process, inner and outer reality, verbal and non-verbal thought, the imaginary and the symbolic, the id and the ego – as important and as different from each other.

The development of sexuality

It was a commonplace of medicine in the 1890s that sexual problems played an important part in the aetiology of hysteria. Freud went further: he began to claim that they played the major, if not the sole part, and even to try and classify the neuroses according to which particular sexual practice they originated from. One of the more comical aspects of the letters to his friend Wilhelm Fliess is the way that they reveal Freud as a nineteenth century doctor, typical in his prejudices, arguing that 'neurasthenia' is caused by masturbation. Eventually, he came to claim that the initiating trauma that led to hysteria was invariably sexual seduction, in infancy, by adults (almost always the father). Such 'seductions' had usually been repressed by the victim and required brisk work by the analyst to recover them. Modern practitioners of recovered memory have in effect revived this view of Freud's, with all its terrible potential for disrupting families on the basis of evidence one wouldn't hang a dog on.[17]

Later on, in a move fateful for the future of psychoanalysis, Freud changed his mind, and argued that these seductions were in fact childish sexual fantasies; after that, for forty years or so, therapists would routinely dismiss patients' reports of childhood abuse as fantasy. But the notion that children were capable of sexual fantasies helped Freud to the enormously important theory of childhood sexuality; so, for good or evil, we owe virtually the whole of psychoanalysis to it.

According to Freud, taken along with some of his followers, like Abraham,[18] the foundations of adult sexual perversions (voyeurism, exhibitionism, oral–genital contacts, anal–genital contacts, sexual fetishism etc.), of adult neuroses (which are the negative of perversions – they are perversions repressed and defended against) and of normal adult character (oral-dependent, anal-obsessive, etc.), are to be found in the development of sexuality, or libido, in infancy, through a series of fairly well-marked stages, at any of which the child may get partially fixated (or stuck). Fixation shows up in the adult patient by the persistence of the early sexual aim in unconscious fantasies – which are uncovered, of course, by interpretation in the course of the treatment, and so are subject to all the methodological doubts noted in this chapter.

Here are the stages, as set out in the early book, *Three Essays on the Theory of Sexuality* (1905) supplemented by articles of 1923–4.[19]

Babies show a diffuse sexuality not yet united into a single directed instinct, but containing the roots of all the perversions; they are **polymorphously perverse**, and this disposition may persist in children and in the 'average uncultivated woman' who 'if she is led on by a clever seducer . . . will find every sort of perversion to her taste' (*Three Essays*).

The first major sexual centre is the mouth; the activity is nipple or thumb-sucking; the aim of gratification is sucking, incorporating, biting; the baby's interaction with the external world is through breast or bottle-feeding schedules; the associated adult 'oral personality' is emotional, dependent, talkative, and given to sweet-eating, smoking and pencil-chewing. Oral fixation seems to be associated with hysterias.

The second major sexual centre is the anus; the activity defecation; the aim of gratification is retention or aggressive expulsion; the interaction with the external world is toilet training; the anal character, one of stubbornness, independence, and possessiveness 'derived from the retentive pleasure of the child who in face of parental entreaties responds in effect "what I have I keep"' (ibid.). Faeces come to be associated with possessions and money; money is muck; but by **reaction-formation** anal characters are obsessive, methodical and tidy. Anal fixation is associated with obsessional neuroses.

The third major sexual centre is the phallus – that is, penis or clitoris. The sexual activity is, for both sexes, masturbatory; interaction with the external world is chiefly that with the parents, both affectionate and disciplinary. The taboo on masturbation, and possibilities of sexual seduction – both in reality and fantasy – belong here.

In this period (from three to five, say) the Oedipus complex is formed: the boy falls in love with his mother and wishes to kill his father. But his father is large, and feared; the boy forms, in fantasy, the fear that he is going to be castrated (like his mother, or sisters!) He therefore represses or even destroys his Oedipal feelings, and starts to identify with his father, thus resolving his Oedipus complex (more properly shattering it to pieces and leaving little trace) and beginning to model himself as a man. He then enters a sexual latency period, until puberty. If his Oedipus complex was satisfactorily resolved, he will be able to make a satisfactory external choice of sex object; if not, this complex may form the nuclear core of a neurosis later on. (The commonest of these is being impotent with respectable women like one's mother, since they are taboo, but potent with whores, who are not.[20] Another is sexual fetishism, where a part-object, like a pair of shoes, becomes a substitute for the mother's missing penis, in an unconscious disavowal of her castration.[21])

Little girls think they **have** been castrated; and this is only one of the differences between them and boys, in a vastly more complicated developmental scenario. Freud at first thought that the woman's case was that of the man, but with the sexes transposed. Women love the father and want to kill the mother. Jung called this the Electra complex. But the girl actually starts, like the boy, in a dyadic relationship with her mother, in which the father intervenes as a third party. And in the phallic stage the little girl is still a little man whose sexuality is centred on her clitoris. She has to change her object of love from mother to father; and her centre of sensitivity from clitoris to vagina: the first is a difficult psychological feat to achieve, and the second an anatomically impossible one: the vagina doesn't have the right nerve endings.

It is castration that helps her on her way: in boys, as we have seen, the threat of castration puts an end to the Oedipus complex; in girls, it creates one. Believing that they have been castrated, they envy the father, or boys, for having a penis, and identify with the mother in order to get the father's. Frustrated in this, they settle, after their latency period, for some other young man's penis; and finally for the ultimate substitute for a penis, which is a baby. (That proud mother returning to the workplace after maternity leave, to strut around displaying her baby for all to admire – it is really her penis! She is equal to the men at last! In fact she has a bigger one, and it makes noises.)

These views have become a byword for sexism and bad biology. But the case is not so simple. Very early in his career, Freud had taken from Fliess the view that human beings are essentially bisexual; and he retained this view. What this means – as Freud explained in one of his later metatheoretical papers, *The Ego and the Id* – is that the full version of the Oedipus complex includes both the masculine and feminine versions; and both sexes have it. The boy will normally abandon his object-love for the mother and identify with the father; but he may identify with the mother. Contrariwise, the girl may identify with the father. Where the final identifications will lie depends very much on constitutional factors. This is not a particularly clear view; it could point the way either to a position in which constitutional factors determine everything, or one in which final sexuality is determined by a complex set of abandoned objects and identifications, and has little to do with biological sexuality.

Freud continued to waver on this issue to the end of his life, taking an ever more nuanced view of female sexuality and its origins; and some feminists, like Juliet Mitchell, Jacqueline Rose and a whole tribe of Lacanians, have found Freud's account, precisely because it makes of femininity a wavering, uncertain, constructed thing, far more useful than the approaches of writers like Ernest Jones or Karen Horney, which appear to pay much more respect to the natural sexuality of women.

Comment:	Again we have a theory of stunning comprehensiveness; it brings together all the sexual perversions recognised by nineteenth century sexology, plus the neuroses, adult character-types and normal infant sexual development.

Nobody nowadays would deny the existence of infantile sexuality, and this developmental narrative still meets some of its original purposes: it explains the nature of the sexual perversions (and the content of much pornography) and relates them to normal sexuality. But many of the details above seem fantastic, and have been difficult to confirm empirically; nor do all analysts agree. Non-Freudian psychologists often doubt whether there are such character-types as 'oral' or 'anal'; they wonder whether the characteristics listed under each type actually belong together at all.[22] Some of Freud's judgements now seem projections of the *mores* of his own society: particularly his judgements of women. The concept of penis-envy, with the baby seen as a substitute penis, has attracted particular derision from feminists: there are plenty of real privileges that men have, which may reasonably lead to women's envying them; one should not postulate that female grievances are merely cover-ups of resentment at not having a penis.

Not all of these criticisms are sound. It is not actually as damaging as it sounds to say that the details of infantile sexuality are fantastic: most of them actually relate to fantasy material. Very few little boys actually murder their fathers: the claim is only that they unconsciously want to. Moreover, in the Freudian unconscious, many of these fantasies are not even verbalised: the verbal forms analysts give them therefore stand to them in the relation of vivid metaphors. Having the penis is a metaphor for power and aggression; castration a metaphor for powerlessness. This is something that we fully recognise at the conscious level: a man can use the word 'ballbreaker' for a dominant woman, and Germaine Greer could use the title '*The Female Eunuch*' for a pioneering feminist study, and neither would expect to be taken literally.

The question then becomes: why should these sexual metaphors be privileged over other, non-sexual ones in our account of child development? The answer would have to be that they are the metaphors that fit the clinical material: they enable the analyst to make sense of the dreams, symptoms, and associations he is presented with. And this evidence leads to a substantive universal claim of great importance: that our fundamental, instinctual understanding of human relationships of power and subordination, on which all later cultural vocabularies are built, is constructed on the basis of primitive unverbalised responses to sexually sensitive organs, and almost equally primitive preverbal object relationships in the mother–child dyad and the triadic relationship that includes the father. (I believe some such claim is almost certainly true.)

Some psychoanalysts drop the literal, physical details in Freud's account altogether, and treat it as almost wholly metaphorical. For the Lacanians, the penis – which is a physical organ – is replaced by the phallus – which is 'a signifier'; and the position of the sexes is equalised, for we are told that no-one can have the phallus. The Oedipus complex is replaced by the name (*nom*) or the 'no!' (*non*) of the father, which provides entry into the realm of the symbolic (language and culture). Lacan speaks of 'the paternal metaphor'. But it is not clear that an account as metaphorical as this would be recognised by Freud as psychoanalytic at all. He would have seen it as unscientific in tone and as evading the central dogma of sexuality.

More worrying than any of the formal theoretical arguments about the logical status of our claims about early sexual development is the practical question of its relation to the cure of neuroses. Freud sees the Oedipus complex as the nucleus of these. There is little doubt that some neuroses have partial roots in childhood conflicts. But Eysenck and others have argued that psychoanalysts, who always try to resolve such conflicts, are no better than other psychiatrists, who do not, in actually curing neuroses – are no better, in fact, than the passage of time, which produces as many cures as analysts do, or more. In view of the inordinate time taken by psychoanalysis, this is a very serious criticism indeed, though Fisher and Greenberg give a partial answer. Practically, it destroys the case for psychoanalysis as a therapy; theoretically, it weakens the case for the very existence of the stages of sexual development and for the Freudian account of neurosis-formation.[23]

Some analysts, I am afraid, and very many literary-critical users of Freudian theory, including a good many Lacanians of my acquaintance, cut this knot by effectively rejecting the notion of a cure, or at least taking no effective interest in the question. This approach would align psychoanalysis with the anti-psychiatry movement. Cure is admittedly a very difficult thing to define. Freud said it was the reduction of neurotic suffering to ordinary unhappiness. The early Lacan said that the patient begins by talking about himself but not to the analyst; or to the analyst but not about himself; when he starts to talk to the analyst about himself, the analysis is over. This seems to be a typically Lacanian contribution: the profound wisecrack. It does nothing for the scientificity of the theory.

On the feminist point, there was a long and elaborate debate from 1920 on, to which many women analysts contributed. Some quite convincing attempts were made to provide women with a development that paid more respect to their own anatomy and biological functions. My own slightly irresponsible intuition would be that at the literal level womb-envy among men is more probable than penis-envy among women; men produce and dominate culture because they can't have babies. Karen Horney and Melanie Klein both suggest something along these lines; for girls Klein has a phase of penis envy sandwiched between two phases of desire for a baby, which must cast doubt on the notion that the baby is a mere penis-substitute.[24]

The terms of this debate have been entirely changed by second wave feminists. They have argued that 'psychoanalysis is not a recommendation for a patriarchal society, but an analysis of one'.[25] The task of psychoanalysis is 'to decipher how we acquire our heritage of the ideas and laws of society within the unconscious mind'. The heroes and villains for feminists now change places. Freud's value is that he shows how patriarchy comes to be installed in the mind, and therefore how it might be not installed; and how wavering and uncertain is the creation of masculine or feminine identity: he is an ally. Those like Jones and Horney, who favoured an account of female sexuality closer to a woman's actual biological nature, are enemies: they are supporting biological essentialism, which, as always, is an obstacle to revolutionary change.

The same perversely ingenious mode of reasoning was then applied to Jacques Lacan. Lacan replaces Freud's rather literalistic Oedipus complex with something like 'the institution of a paternal metaphor' – his work, that is, can be read as giving an account of how patriarchy gets into the unconscious. Reading Lacan in this way has given rise to some of the most brilliant arguments in all feminism.[26] Feminist literary theorists seem mostly to be Lacanian, and stress the name-of-the-father. Most feminist analysts outside literary theory, however, seem to be far more interested in the role of the mother. (Cf. Dorothy Dinnerstein, *The Mermaid and the Minotaur: Sexual Arrangements and Human Malaise* (1976); Nancy Chodorow, *The Reproduction of Mothering* (1978); Chodorow began as a sociologist.)

What everybody agreed upon, for many years, was that biology could not be allowed to have anything to do with the matter. Unfortunately, in recent years evidence has piled up that there are systematic sex-linked behavioural differences between men and women, produced in the ordinary course of evolution, carried in the genes, and effected in the individual by hormonal processes affecting brain development that have nothing to do with ideas about the penis or castration, but a good deal to do with the physiological, hormonal effects of testicles at the embryo stage. See Chapter 8 for a current biological view of sexuality. Of course, on any account, biology does not settle the matter; there is still a question of how masculine and feminine roles are learnt. But this is a matter for sociology. A satisfactory theory of sexuality thus may fall right outside psychoanalysis; it depends on whether there is a logical space, between the now undeniable biological basis for sexuality and the ordinary social learning of sex-linked roles in the culture, for a specifically psychoanalytic process linked with the stages above. See Chapter 8 for an argument that we must still recognise dynamic processes of identification and projection.

Instincts or drives; the pleasure and reality principles

Freud offers, as his ultimate explanation for all human behaviour, the operation of a limited number of instincts, or rather drives, which are modified or transformed by experience. How many different basic instincts Freud recognises is not clear; but the most important, in the early work, seem to be those of (i) self-preservation and (ii) sexuality (species preservation). In the later work, the concept of sexuality becomes even broader than it was to start with and includes some elements of self-preservation; Freud called it *Eros*. The second instinct is then the death instinct – a version of aggression against the self, and part of a biological programme that leads us toward death. Later Freudians called it *Thanatos*.

In the first version of the theory the basic drives are both positive ones; aggression would in this version be a mere derivative formed when a basic drive was frustrated. This version of Freudian theory is therefore very optimistic and perhaps rather shallow. It implies that we can ensure social progress by reducing sexual frustration. It deserves the immortal rebuke of *Brave New World* (Aldous Huxley, 1932). In this classic nightmare dystopia, social peace is assured by avoiding sexual frustration; sex is never forbidden, and hence becomes humanly meaningless. In the 1960s some groups started to put this into practice.

In the second version of the theory – that of Eros and Thanatos – one of the major instincts is itself destructive; and even infantile aggression plays a crucial role in the development of personality. The second model led Freud to the gloomy views of *Civilisation and its Discontents*, in which he argued that the advance of civilisation inevitably increased frustration and therefore neurotic misery.

The constant element in all versions of the theory is the centrality of the sexual instinct. Freud broke with two of his major followers – Adler and Jung – when they disagreed with him on this issue. Adler argued for the centrality of aggression as a primary instinct. Jung attempted to widen the concept of 'libido', which for Freud was purely sexual, and treat it as a 'designation of general tension'.[27] On Freud's view both men were weakening the explanatory power of the theory in order to make it acceptable to a prudish public. I believe he would have treated Lacan's version of desire as a linguistic effect (discussed later on) with the same contempt.

Wilhelm Reich was later rejected for the opposite reason. While fully accepting the sexual side of the theory, he had attempted to integrate it with Marxism, which, as Freud said, 'culminated in the nonsensical statement that what we have called the death instinct is a product of the capitalistic system'.

Freudian instincts are actually rather unspecific, compared with the complex 'fixed action patterns' recognised in studies of animal behaviour. In fact a correct translation of the German word would be 'drive' rather than 'instinct'. This leaves Freud with the difficult task of explaining how generalised instincts are shaped into the detailed pattern of ordinary behaviour. He argues that the instincts are shaped by the operation of three principles. The first two of these are discussed in 1911; the third is extensively discussed in 1920.[28] They are the pleasure principle, the reality principle, and repetition compulsion.

The unconscious mind is originally regulated by the pleasure principle. Left to itself it would simply hallucinate satisfactions; but experience rapidly shows that this leads to unpleasure; so that consciousness substitutes a 'reality principle', and this leads to the development of attention, and thinking. However, a part of our thought remains walled off from the reality principle: this is fantasy. Because of the existence of auto-erotism as a way of satisfying sexual needs, and because there is a latency period, fantasy remains connected more closely and longer with the sexual instincts than with others.

Freud devoted considerable effort to showing the importance of the pleasure principle, deriving almost all products of the unconscious from wishes, even when this was quite counterintuitive (as in the case of anxiety dreams). But by 1920, he had admitted the existence of a further principle of mental functioning: the compulsion to repeat. This accounts not merely for the repeated appearance in dreams of traumatic material, but also repetitive children's play.

Comment: Freud's main claim, and his most controversial one, was that the driving force of almost all human action and culture was the sexual instinct. Every attempt to make Freudian theory, or some successor ideology, more respectable, more humanist, or more politically correct, from Adler and Jung to Lacan and Foucault, has modified or moved away from this central dogma. Yet in biological terms Freud is obviously correct. The fundamental principle of biological explanation, from Darwin to Dawkins, is that everything that is genetically determined, including all genetically determined behaviour patterns (instincts), survives only by contributing to ultimate reproductive success. The modern biological theory of human sexuality, which is outlined in Chapter 8, shows how this biological imperative works to produce both social institutions like marriage, and unconscious desires by individuals to violate those institutions by committing adultery. Most biologists reject Freud; but they are with him on this point.

However, the picture of the sexual instinct as an undifferentiated drive is actually too simple. The mechanisms Freud postulates for moulding simple drives – the pleasure principle and the reality principle – are nothing like powerful enough, or precisely enough formulated, to construct the labyrinths of a Freudian childhood, or explain just how the powerful but generalised impulsions of Eros and Thanatos can lead to the details of our daily discontents. The pleasure principle seems to consist merely in the need to reduce excitation. But organisms in general need excitation: if they don't have enough, they will spontaneously seek it out; and pleasure often comes from an increase of excitation. The reality principle is given no explanation at all, save what is implicit in the name. The third principle – repetition compulsion – was admittedly forced upon Freud late in his theory building. But once it is there, it seriously undermines the pleasure principle, offering an alternative explanation for many phenomena like anxiety dreams that Freud wants to derive from wishes.

Modern ethology – the study of animal behaviour – shows that all species have characteristic unlearnt or only partially learnt complex behaviour patterns, which appear at definite times in the life cycle. Why not man? (Even the anti-biological Jacques Lacan made considerable use of ethological results in supporting his concept of a mirror stage of development, when a young child starts to recognise his own identity in a reflection.) Once one has accepted that instincts may be complex and well-defined generalised action patterns, the pleasure principle and repetition compulsion both look very different. We can now think that human beings, like other higher animals, have sets of defined action patterns which they have a compulsion to repeat; completing any one of these gives pleasure. The phrase 'action pattern' is, however, slightly misleading here. What an instinctual impulse in a higher animal leads to, in most cases, is not an action but a fantasy of action. It is completing the fantasy which gives pleasure. As Freud says, we move from fantasy into real action under the pressure of reality, as we discover that there is a world impinging on our experience that fantasy alone, not accompanied by action, will not change.

Stating what the elementary basic instincts are is difficult. I would want to recognise some quite specific ones – e.g., a genetically determined drive to learn languages, and to talk, independent of general curiosity, developing in early childhood, and supported by inherited physical structures of the vocal organs and the brain, and by inherited mental capacities that presumably depend on the structure of the brain. I have no doubt that there are many other specific instincts as well, but offer no views on what they are. In particular – to take a question that is still very live – I don't know whether Adler or the early Freud was right about the independence of aggression as an instinct; but the question seems to me a real one. Equally, I would not rule out the existence of a whole set of inherited archetypal ideas, as Jung later proposed – such as **wise old man, devouring mother, eternal child**. But whatever their specific character, ultimately all the instinctive characteristics have to serve the purpose of ultimate reproductive success, and are therefore part of Eros.

Some later psychoanalysts, like Melanie Klein, have made considerable use of the death instinct, but many have found it rather mystical. We are all going to die, but why should we need an instinct to do so? It is worth noting that the existence of a biological death instinct has been stunningly confirmed by modern cell biologists, who have discovered the phenomenon of programmed cell death. While the general biological phenomenon of death is not nearly so well understood as that of reproduction, it is clear that it is just as much a part of our biological inheritance: we are designed to die. What is not clear is that this biological programme has anything to do with a psychological instinct of aggression against the self or others. Aggression directed against others has a considerable biological value of its own; we would expect a species that had it to survive when a non-aggressive one did not.

Lacan is one of the later commentators who takes the death instinct seriously; but this goes with his generally teleological and non-causal view. The death instinct seems to become something much more like Heidegger's concept in which authentic being is Being-for-death. This seems to be a version of a religious view that we are only living seriously in the world if we keep death constantly in mind. It is a view that is not merely Christian, but pre-Christian; it goes back to the Neolithic, as the funerary monuments demonstrate. Otherwise one might think that Reich was right: the death instinct is a way of mystifying some of the contradictions of capitalism. It is at least worth reading *Civilisation and its Discontents* from that point of view.

The structure of the mind

From the beginning, Freud believed that mental life went on, whether we were conscious of it or not. Consciousness is merely our temporary awareness of some of our thoughts; and its contents can change from moment to moment. Not all the contents of the mind can enter consciousness; some are walled off by a barrier of repression. In his early, **topographical** model of the mind, Freud called that part of which we can become conscious the **preconscious**; that part of which we cannot directly become conscious, the **unconscious**. Unconscious material – like the latent content of dreams – can transfer across the repression barrier and attach, in a distorted form, to contents of the preconscious – as in the manifest content of dreams. **Transference** occurs regularly during psychoanalysis when infantile sexual feelings transfer across the repression barrier and project onto the figure of the analyst. The patient falls in love with the analyst. The analysis is unlikely to work otherwise.

Freud's later, **structural** model is more complicated. There is a wholly unconscious part of the mind – the **id** – containing not only infantile libidinal feelings (sexual ones) but infantile aggressive or destructive ones – both of these are held in check by a barrier of repression. Outside is the world of reality. It is the business of the **ego** to mediate between the desires emanating from the id and the demands of reality. Part of the ego is unconscious; it consists of defence mechanisms which transform the desires of the id into forms acceptable to the ego. The rest of the ego is preconscious; it is this which reconciles the (transformed) desires of the id with the demands of reality. A third major component – corresponding roughly to conscience – is the **superego**. This consists of social, and in particular parental, standards introjected into the mind. The superego is partly unconscious: it issues blind commands, just as the id issues blind desires, and produces feelings of guilt when its commands are disobeyed.

Freud has an extraordinary narrative to account for the way these structures come into being. The id has certain objects – that is, objects of sexual desire – starting with the mother's breast, which are then lost; these are introjected into the mind and identified with. The ego is the precipitate of these lost objects. The superego is the heir to the Oedipus complex; it is constructed by introjecting the parents as an ego-ideal. The process of introjection, in which an image of the object is set up within the ego, is a more sophisticated version of the original infantile fantasy of incorporation – eating the object.

The model of the mind as containing internal objects was of great importance for later developments in Freudian theory – for example, in work of the school of Melanie Klein. As time went on, some psychoanalysts went way beyond Freud in the number, variety, and function of the internal objects they recognised, and some began to argue that the instincts themselves are object-seeking rather than gratification-seeking. If this is taken seriously, it undoes Freud's own insistence on a generalised sexual instinct, which finds its object only after many vicissitudes, during which it is aimed at the mouth, the anus, the phallus . . . On the contrary, the organism will have specific built-in instincts, each with its own specified and quite complex object. This has some similarity with ethological accounts of instinct in animal behaviour, and some with Jung's theory of archetypes and archetypal images.

Comment: Both the topographical and the structural models are often criticised as metaphorical or even mythological in character. I am not sure how damaging this criticism is; many sound theories started as metaphors. There is also some resemblance to the ancient Platonic picture of the three-fold structure of the mind. I find this encouraging; perhaps both Plato and Freud are broadly right.

There is also a much more philistine comparison that materialists might take comfort from. Ordinary computers can have several programs running on them at the same time; it is called **multi-tasking**. The programs can be made to interchange data and react with each other in quite complex ways. There would be no difficulty in setting up either of the Freudian dynamic models of the mind as a computer game; played between say an ego-program, an id-program and a superego-program; and if Freudian theory is genuinely scientific, in the ordinary sense, such a game might actually be predictive. Jung's version of the theory could also be computer-modelled: he has many semi-autonomous **complexes** of ideas in the mind, each one built round an **archetype**, and these interact.

There is even a place for the ordinary physical concept of energy in this picture. Computation requires energy; the human brain consumes more oxygen (required for energy production) than any other organ of the body; and different parts consume oxygen as different mental activities occur. There really are energy flows in the brain, though they don't have quite the function Freud's metaphors suggest.

Two post-Freudians: Melanie Klein and Anna Freud

Despite what is sometimes said, in the real world of psychoanalysis the development of Freudian theory did not stop with Freud. There have in fact been numerous theoretical innovations, and not all of them were made by Freudian heretics, cast out of the movement as a result. One particularly interesting set was offered by Melanie Klein, who extended the developmental phases forward in time to include a **paranoid** position and a **depressive** position in the first year of life. Klein held that object relations start very early, with the first sexual object not a whole person but a part-object, the maternal breast; the instincts of libido and aggressiveness are present from the beginning and produce intense emotions of greed and anxiety with fantasies of devouring and tearing: in fantasy, the single breast is split into a good supportive breast and bad persecutory one. It is these first objects which, when introjected, form the core of the superego. The postulation of a phase like this gives a possible etiology of the psychoses; Kleinians might therefore have a line on schizophrenia, which defeated Freud.[29]

The depressive position is reached in about the fourth month of life, when the mother is apprehended as a whole object: libidinal and aggressive instincts now have to focus on the same object instead of different ones and anxiety arises as a fear of destroying the loved object. It is overcome when the loved object is introjected in a stable way as a guarantee of security. For Klein, the early stages of the Oedipus complex begin with the depressive position. Klein, and most later workers, are much less temporally schematic than Freud was; that is why Klein speaks of positions rather than phases.

Klein's account has been criticised for attributing complex fantasies and object relationships to children too young and ill-organised to have them; but this may be a false impression due to the necessity of describing the fantasies in terms intelligible to an adult. There is nothing biologically implausible in the notion of a young human born with a preformed capacity for forming an object relation with the breast; some chicks have preformed responses to coloured patches on the beaks of the parent bird, and automatically peck at them (which causes the parent to regurgitate food). And there is nothing implausible in the idea that a very young child should have fantastic and infantile notions about that object relationship.

One might, perhaps, speculatively, put the Kleinian account of infancy together with the views of an early Freudian, Otto Rank, on the importance of the first traumatic experience, that of birth (when, of course, the brain is even less well-organised). The history of the infant then becomes a long succession of experiences of trauma, deprivation and lack, experienced by way of successively more realistic and limited fantasies. It starts with birth and expulsion from the womb, the prototype of all later deprivation; continues with a breast continually offered and withdrawn, and therefore experienced as two breasts, a good and a bad; moves to the anxious realisation that there is only one mother, at once reassuring and persecutory; moves to the realisation that there are parts of the body (the faeces) that can be detached by voluntary act and exercise of power; moves finally to a powerful fantasy of the loss of the penis.

It is as a means of defence against these experiences that the structure of the self – ego, superego and id – is built up; a stable set of inner objects is constructed in fantasy to detach the self from reliance on the unstable world of external objects. As Anna Freud put it in the 1930s:

> According to the theory of the English school of analysis, introjection and projection, which in our view should be assigned to the period after the ego has been differentiated from the outside world, are the very processes by which the structure of the ego is developed and but for which differentiation would never have taken place. These differences of opinion bring home to us the fact that the chronology of psychic processes is still one of the most obscure fields of analytical theory. (*The Ego and the Mechanisms of Defence*, p.57)

For Anna Freud, ego-defences are built up much later. In any case, the need for defence persists in the adult. Anna Freud lists ten mechanisms of ego-defence: regression, repression, reaction-formation, isolation, undoing, projection, introjection, turning against the self, reversal, and sublimation. This approach seems to throw a great deal of light upon the development of adult character as well as upon clinical symptoms. A whole school of analysts, partly following Anna Freud's lead, have concentrated their practice on the analysis and strengthening of the ego, and the interpretation of its resistances.

I find this an interesting school, and there are fruitful interpretations of literature that can be based upon it, in which one sees works of literature as offering fantasised ego-defences. Norman Holland has produced an impressive account of this kind. (See Chapter 4 following.) Nor is it the case that everything in this school is at odds with everything in the work of Klein; though it is not for a literary theorist to suggest a synthesis.

To the outside observer, the problem is that there is an utter lack of reliable empirical evidence to decide between the two positions. Both sides rely on theory-based retrospective interpretation; Klein interprets children's play, which is an inherently highly speculative method; Anna Freud uses verbal evidence, which is slightly more reliable but comes from a much later period in the patient's life. What we actually need is direct evidence about babies, of the kind Bowlby[30] provides; and this leads us to a different kind of theory – briefly mentioned in Chapter 5.

Freud as scientist, imaginative writer – or fraud?

Anyone with the least interest in Freud as a scientific thinker must take account of the possibility that his work is a gigantic confidence trick, played as much on himself as on his followers, by which the personal vision of a great literary genius has been imposed on the world as science. Academic psychologists and literary Freudians alike will rejoice to concur with this view, which confirms the epistemological prejudices of both. For the academic psychologists, Freud's theories are intrinsically implausible and his hand-ling of evidence is quite unsatisfactory. For the literary Freudians, the whole notion of a science of the mind is a philosophical mistake: Freud is actually engaged in a form of humanist textual interpretation; the excel-lence of his writing and the depth of his interpretations only confirm this. To those who hold these views, Freud inevitably comes to seem like his late twentieth century follower Jacques Lacan: a guru pretending to be a scien-tist, shoring up his empty claims with rhetoric. I don't agree with this view myself – it seems to me to be false in fact and to rest on a narrow view of science – but I regard it as a duty to hold the possibility open, and to con-sider every claim in the Freudian system in the light of it. Freud also did not agree with this view, though he knew of it. He staked his own reputation on being a great scientist, not on being a great writer.

Freud thought, from the beginning to the end of his career, that he was a scientist. He started off as a neurologist, investigating aspects of the nervous system that is the physical basis of mind and behaviour. This is hard science in all the ordinary meanings of the word. Its subject matter is part of biology; its methods are experimental; it aims at objective description and causal explanation; and it advances by making hypotheses which it then subjects to test. It is science both in subject matter and methodology. Although Freud moved on from this early work, to neurological medicine and then psychology, he never repudiated it. He freely accepted the possib-ility that the psychoses might be cured by drugs; he welcomed the hormone theory.[31] Early in his career as a psychologist, he produced a 'Project for a Scientific Psychology', which is a speculative elaboration of neuron theory.[32] Reading it now, it seems like a bridge between mid-nineteenth century brain science – sometimes called 'brain mythology' – and late twentieth century computer simulations of neural operation – which also probably deserve the name brain mythology. There is no reason to suppose Freud would turn away from modern cognitive studies.

Freud began, then, as a biologist of the mind.[33] He had moments of uneasiness, when he made his first moves from scientific neurology to what at first he thought of as the novelistic, literary world of psychological case studies. Hysteria made him a psychologist – not his hysteria, but that of a whole succession of desperately distressed and baffling patients, Breuer's and his own, whose cases could be understood only by taking them as psychogenic. Hysteria is not a common diagnosis nowadays, and the various symptoms that once constituted it would often be reclassified under dif-ferent diagnostic labels; but they have not disappeared. At that time it presented a bewildering mixture of behavioural disturbances and physical symptoms, like local paralyses of an arm or leg that seemed to have no physical cause and responded to no physical treatment. Sometimes (and this is where a neurological training is vital) the psychogenetic nature of such a paralysis can be proved by the very telling circumstance that what is paralysed corresponds to the patient's idea of her arm or her leg, rather than the arm or leg as defined by anatomy and controlled by nerves. In such cases the patient is imitating a real paralysis rather than having one; but the imitation is unconscious and the reasons for doing it are unconscious. Such cases, Freud and Breuer found, or thought they found, could be cured only by offering a talking cure, a kind of chimney-sweeping of the mind.[34]

If, from that point on, Freud stayed on psychological ground rather than biological, and insisted that his followers did so too, it was not because he had rejected the notion of empirical science. To the end of his life he supposed that that was what he was practising. He merely thought that the empirical evidence often pointed to a psychological level of explanation rather than a physical one. He thought that enquiries, both into psychological facts and psychological explanations, were properly pursued by such powerful (if laborious) techniques as free association and psychoanalytic interpretation. He thought that these provided material enough even for abstract metapsychological speculations. But never, in the whole of his work, even at its speculative peaks in *Totem and Taboo* and *Civilisation and its Discontents*, does Freud abandon the idea of scientific explanation, and think of his life work as purely interpretative, humanist, or literary, and he utterly repudiated political or religious accounts of it.

In the final essay of the *New Introductory Lectures*, written in 1932 when he was 76, Freud explicitly repudiates the notion of psychoanalysis as a 'Weltanschauung', and situates it firmly among the sciences. He takes an objective realist view of these. The aim of science 'is to arrive at correspondence with reality – that is to say, with what exists outside us and independently of us, and, as experience has taught us, is decisive for the fulfilment or disappointment of our wishes. This correspondence with the real external world we call "truth"'.[35] The analyst 'discovers something new by observation . . . puts forward suppositions . . . brings up provisional constructions, and abandons them if they are not confirmed'.[36] Freud thus believes that psychoanalysis is investigating objective realities outside the investigator, even if they are psychic realities like unconscious erotic fantasies rather than physical ones like traumas; and is employing the normal hypothetico-deductive methods of science even though he uses case studies rather than experiments.

Unfortunately, examination of Freudian practice, and in particular of the case studies Freud himself published, does not support this claim. There are two reasons for this. The first turns on the Freudian concept of repression, and on the question of what kind of material actually gets repressed. Freud's initial hypothesis was that neurotics have invariably been subjected as children to what he called sexual seduction – what we should call child abuse. This is in principle a hypothesis that is testable for many individual cases. Rightly or wrongly, Freud became convinced that this hypothesis was untenable; not least because there simply couldn't be that much child seduction about – not among respectable people, anyway. Freud therefore asserted that the 'seductions' had taken place in fantasy: children spontaneously generate sexual fantasies, which are repressed but not lost; they persist in the unconscious, as strong as ever, and in the wrong circumstances may come to energise the neuroses. The practice of the analyst therefore comes to be one of uncovering the infantile sexual fantasies that, combined with immediate circumstances, have produced the neurosis – or are currently affecting the process of analysis. However, in the nature of the case, there can hardly be objective and independent confirmation that these fantasies have been at work; and there is every opportunity for the analyst, consciously or unconsciously, to suggest them to the patient.

Second, the analysts themselves hardly exhibit restraint and detachment about their theories or their interpretations, and don't easily allow them to be refuted. On the evidence of his own published cases, Freud himself is one of the worst. It is very easy to argue that in these cases Freud behaves much more like a man possessed, using any means to argue his own interpretations, against any resistance put up by the patient or the facts. One might describe the 'Dora' case in this way. The teenage Dora (Ida Bauer) became neurotic when her father (whose wife was still living with him) started an affair with her older best friend, Mrs K. K consoled himself by making advances to Dora, which disgusted her; but her father tacitly approved, effectively treating his daughter as an exchange offering for K's wife. When she complained to her father about this multiple betrayal, he referred her to Freud, who treated her disgust at K as a neurotic symptom rather than a legitimate or natural response; and tried to bully her, on evidence that wouldn't have justified squashing a fruit-fly, into admitting that she unconsciously loved K, and that it wouldn't be a bad idea to take him on, while her father kept on with Mrs K. Such a menage would have been counted immoral by the standards of most societies; and most later psychoanalysts would have made strong recommendations against it on mental health grounds.[37]

A fair description of this case would be that it was a tacit conspiracy between Freud and the father to pimp the daughter. A clearer example of psychiatric malpractice is difficult to imagine, and though Dora had the sense to get out of analysis after only three sessions, she remained a very damaged person. Now this case is universally regarded as one of the most theoretically productive of all: that is, it stimulated Freud to theoretical production. But that was not because it satisfied the requirements of objective scientific investigation. On the hostile view, it may have been because it required a good deal of fast thinking for Freud to find excuses for his own wickedness! This was not the worst case of malpractice in Freud's career – the worst was perhaps his complicity in covering up and excusing the malpractice of his friend Fliess, to whom he referred his patient Emma Eckstein for a wholly unnecessary nose operation. Fliess, in an operation of spectacular incompetence, left some yards of cotton packing inside her nose: she nearly bled to death. But again, this case was enormously productive, for the theory of wish-fulfilment; even if Freud did end by attributing Emma's bleeding to a wish to bleed![38]

Not all Freud's cases were as bad as that of Dora, or of Emma Eckstein, but other scientists – behaviorist psychologists, for example – were not impressed by any of them. For them, the conclusions of psychoanalysis were speculative and fantastic: they were of the kind that only the strongest of empirical evidence would compel us to believe, while the evidence available was actually very weak. The methods of enquiry used by psychoanalysts were, in their view, wholly unscientific: individual case-studies grossly over-interpreted and only anecdotally reported with the raw data in the analyst's notebook left unpublished; no clear published procedures that other scientists could duplicate, no way of eliminating suggestion as a mechanism by which the patient could be induced to confirm false theories, and a training procedure requiring a personal psychoanalysis which seems designed to brainwash young analysts into accepting the theory. These criticisms have intensified as the century has worn on. It is now unthinkable in most areas of medicine to employ any medical technique that has not been validated in controlled trials; but this seems impossible for psychoanalysis. What tests have been made – and there is a good deal of doubt about their validity – sometimes suggest analysis has no greater success rate than leaving neurotic illness untreated.[39]

The response to this from the later followers of Freud has often been to abandon the medical notion of cure (which Freud never quite abandoned), and sometimes to abandon all scientific claims, which as we have seen would have horrified him. For some Jungians, and for humanistic Freudians like Guntrip, the notion of a hard, objectifying science of the mind was abhorrent.[40] For phenomenological and existentialist psychoanalysts, and for philosophers like Habermas and Ricoeur, the move that Freud made from a purely causal analysis to one in terms of unconscious intentions arrived at by interpretation changes altogether the philosophical status of the discourse. The notion of psychoanalysis as an objective science of mind becomes a scientistic self-misunderstanding: there really can't be such a thing, and Freud ought to have known better.[41] For them, what Freud is doing is indeed reinterpreting experience and providing us with a new understanding of ourselves; but we can no more treat this as objective science than we can treat the work of Nietzsche – also a fine psychologist – as objective science. There is a detailed analysis and demolition of these views in Grünbaum, 1984.

Notes and references

Suggestions for further reading are on page 212.

1. For a popular survey of criticisms of Freud as scientist, produced by a literary critic, see **Frederick Crews**, *The Memory Wars* (1995).
2. Such arguments have been deployed by philosophers ranging from behaviorist to phenomenological positions, and are still deployed – e.g. in the latest explanation of *Why Freud was Wrong* by **Richard Webster** (1996: pp.250–2 and Chap. 6 *passim*).
3. See Chapter 8.
4. **E. Husserl**, 1950.
5. **Sigmund Freud** (trans Mosbacher and Strachey, 1954), *The Origins of Psychoanalysis: Letters to Wilhelm Fliess* (1887–1902) p.261.
6. **Joseph Breuer and Sigmund Freud**, *Studies on Hysteria* (1893) S.E. 2; Penguin Freud 3.
7. Freud regularly used hypnotism, hysteria and dissociation of personality as evidence for the unconscious: e.g. 'A Note on the Unconscious in Psychoanalysis' (1912) S.E. 12, pp.255–66; Penguin 11, pp.45–58.
8. **R. Aldridge-Morris** for critique. **Morton Prince**, *The Dissociation of a Personality* (1905). (The 'Miss Beauchamp' case.)
9. **Ellenberger** 1970, Chaps 3 and 6 and *passim*.
10. **R.J. Sternberg** p.212; **Orne**, 1959; **Gray, Bowers and Fenz**, 1970; **Aldridge-Morris**.
11. Freud's determinism is illustrated particularly by his procedures in *The Psychopathology of Everyday Life*, where the least hesitation or malapropism must be given its cause. There is a general discussion of the issue in **Ernest Jones**, 'Free Will and Determinism' (1924) in **Ernest Jones**, *Psycho-Myth, Psycho-History: Essays in Applied Psychoanalysis* (1974).
12. **Donald Davidson**, 'Freedom to Act' in *Essays on Actions and Events* (1980) p.63. Quoted **Gay**, *Reading Freud: Explorations and Entertainments* (1990), Chap. 3 'Freud and Freedom' p.74.
13. **Christopher Caudwell**, *The Crisis in Physics* (1939), Chap. 12 – in **Caudwell** 1938, 1948, 1949.
14. **Sigmund Freud**, *The Psychopathology of Everyday Life* (1901).
15. **Sigmund Freud**, *The Interpretation of Dreams* (1900), Chap. VII E. and *passim*.

16. See **Fisher and Greenberg**, 1996 for an adverse scientific view of the dream theory, based on a rather crude version of it.

17. **Crews**, 1995; **Wakefield and Underwager**, 1994; **Ofshe and Watters**, 1995.

18. **Abraham**, 1927, 1955.

19. Freud's writings on sexuality, including *Three Essays*, are conveniently gathered together in the Penguin Freud Vol. 7, *On Sexuality*. A rather tendentious account of the controversy between Freud and 'feminist' psychoanalysts like Ernest Jones, Karen Horney, etc., can be found in the **Mitchell and Rose** reader, *Feminine Sexuality*.

20. **Sigmund Freud**, 'On the Universal Tendency to Debasement in the Sphere of Love' (1912), Penguin Freud Vol. 7, p.243.

21. **Sigmund Freud**, 'Fetishism' (1927), in Freud, *On Sexuality*, Penguin Freud 7.

22. See **Kline**, *Fact and Fantasy in Freudian Theory* (1981). But there is an excellent survey of empirical investigations, **Fisher and Greenberg**, *Freud Scientifically Reappraised* (1996), which offers support for the reality of the oral and anal character types, many aspects of the Oedipal stage, and even penis envy.

23. For discussion, see: **Eysenck and Wilson**, 1973; **Kline**, 1972, 1981; **Luborsky** in **Crews**, 1995, p.102. The definitive summary is in **Fisher and Greenberg**, 1996.

24. **Horney**, 1926; **Klein**, 1921–45. But see the evidence for penis envy in **Fisher and Greenberg**, 1996, pp.146–155.

25. **Mitchell**, 1974, pp.xv–xvi.

26. **Mitchell and Rose**, 1982.

27. **Sigmund Freud**, *Three Essays on the Theory of Sexuality* (1905) p.84.

28. **Sigmund Freud**, 'Formulations on the Two Principles of Mental Functioning' (1911) S.E. 12; Freud 'Beyond the Pleasure Principle' (1920) S.E. 18, Penguin Freud 12.

29. The classic publication here is perhaps **Klein, Heimann and Money-Kyrle**, *New Directions in Psychoanalysis: The Significance of Infant Conflict in Adult Behaviour* (1955) – see, for example, Chap. 10, **Heimann**: A Combination of Defence Mechanisms in Paranoid States.

30. **Bowlby**, 1969, 1973, 1980: *Attachment and Loss*.

31. S.E. 2, p.198.

32. S.E. 1.

33. **Sulloway**, 1979.

34. **Sigmund Freud and J. Breuer**, *Studies on Hysteria* (1895).

35. S.E. 2, p.218.

36. S.E. 2, p.223.

37. **Freud**, 'Fragment of an Analysis of a Case of Hysteria' (1905) S.E. VII; **Marcus**, 1984 pp.42–87; **Jacobus**, 1986, pp.137–96; **Appignanesi and Forrester**, 1992, pp.146–170.

38. **Appignanesi and Forrester**, 1992, pp.133–141.

39. **Eysenck and Wilson**, 1973; **Eysenck**, 1985. But see **Fisher and Greenberg**, 1996, for rebuttal.

40. **Guntrip**, 1968.

41. **Habermas**, 1971; **Ricoeur**, 1970; for critique see **Grünbaum**, 1984.

Chapter 4

Art as fantasy and defence

THE BASIC PSYCHOANALYTIC THEORY OF ART
AND LITERATURE

Summary

Early and late Freudian theory are hardly distinguishable from literature itself; and throughout the century most great critics have used Freudian insights opportunistically and in an essentially literary way. They did not 'apply' a science; their view of human beings was transformed by Freud, and this flowed into their criticism. Literary techniques of analysis have also been applied to Freud's own writings, which were recognised as important contributions to literature from an early period, and would remain so even if the whole system were rejected as science.

But the classical theory can be treated as a science, applicable to literature in at least five distinct ways. It offers a theory of literary creation, on the model of the dream-work; a corresponding theory of literary interpretation; a theory of reader-response; a general theory of human nature; and a theory of individual characters, types, neuroses, cases etc., which can be applied to authors, readers and characters in literary works. It therefore opens up a whole world of explanation and interpretation, the central point of which is that in art, as in the transference, unconscious fantasy speaks to unconscious fantasy at the same time as the surface of the art-work engages with the surface of the mind.

Freudian theory and literary criticism

There is something rather odd, as critics since Felman 1977 have recognised, in talking about psychoanalytic theories of literature as 'applications' of an independent science of psychoanalysis. For one thing, this is too petty and technical a way to put it. Freud changed the whole way we think about the human mind; great critics wrote on the basis of the new way of thinking. When Edmund Wilson wrote about Henry James[1] he wasn't 'applying Freudian theory'; he was making an honest attempt to come to terms with Henry James, drawing on psychoanalytic and even Marxist insights because they had become a part of him.

Most of the analyses and interpretations of literature put forward in the twentieth century have been informed by Freudian insights, and many of them have never been superseded or surpassed. It would be an appalling loss to literary discourse if we didn't have them. What we need to do with these insights is not abandon them as obsolete or unfashionable, but put them on a new basis, that is compatible with the new view of human nature emerging from cognitive psychology and behavioral ecology, but doesn't lose the essential insights of dynamic psychology. For cognitive science by itself is in danger of offering a model of human beings that is arid and shallow, and that makes no room for the creation of literature – or for any other complex human performance.

Much of psychoanalysis actually came in the first place from literature or literary theory. The concept of catharsis came from the theory of tragedy. The principle of interpreting symptoms by finding a meaningful narrative in which they are embedded goes back to tribal witch-doctoring,[2] but the interpretive method is literary. Literature gives us not only the basic concept, but many of the most subtle details, and the most brilliant fictional illustrations, of the theory of unconscious mind. The Oedipus myth Freud took direct from the play to define his central complex and the core of the neuroses.

The cathartic method of treating neuroses derives directly from Aristotle's concept of the curative effects of tragedy.[3] It was an attempt to get hysterics to re-enact traumatic episodes – not necessarily tragic ones – from their past, in the hope that this would have a cathartic effect, purging or purifying their emotions. Of course, the very existence of this clinical method then throws a new light on Aristotle's venerable conjecture about tragedy. It looks as if the human mind is so constructed that it can come to terms with traumatic experiences by rehearsing imaginary prototypes of them. It may well be that that is what literature is for: to enable us to come to terms with traumatic experience in fantasy, before or after we have to cope with the real thing.

It is a commonplace – starting from repeated observations by Freud himself – that the concept of the unconscious mind, and many of the functions Freud explored, were familiar to imaginative writers. One might look particularly at the history of romanticism here. One very striking example –

I am not suggesting it particularly influenced Freud – is Wagner's music-drama *Tristan*. It is, through and through, a celebration of the world of night (the unconscious) as the world of authentic feeling, and a denigration of day (the conscious world, or the world of the ego) as a phantasmatic world of inauthenticity. Almost the last word the soprano sings, at the end of the most ecstatically orgasmic aria in all music, is the word *unbewüsst*. Isolde dies, that is, celebrating her entry into the unconscious. In a culture such as this, one doesn't need psychoanalytic theory to introduce the concept of unconscious thought and feeling to art. It is entirely the other way around.

Similarly, to call Freud's interpretation of the Oedipus legend an application of his theory would be a mistake; this interpretation is more like the nuclear core from which psychoanalysis itself arose. It occurs in 1897 in a letter to Fliess, and recurs again in *The Interpretation of Dreams*, and turns up again and again throughout the work of Freud and every follower. It is not that psychoanalysis helps us to understand the Oedipus play; rather, that the Oedipus play is what enables psychoanalysts to understand human psychology. It was certainly what enabled Freud to perform the self-analysis on which he founded psychoanalysis. Taking everything together, early Freudian theory borrows so much from literature and literary studies that it is hardly possible to think of it as a free-standing science.

Late Freudian theory is in much the same case. Whatever Lacanian theory is, it is not science (though a great deal of it is more or less conscious pseudo-science), and it was sensible for Felman and others[4] to refuse to treat it as a master discourse which could provide explanations of literary works. There can be more than one opinion about how profitable it is to let Freudian texts and literary texts freely interrogate each other – which sometimes seems to mean making endless reinterpretations of The Purloined Letter[5] – but the enterprise is not a nonsensical one. Nor is it entirely nonsensical to do what is now most fashionable – to go one stage further and treat literary criticism as the master discourse, with which one interrogates and analyses the Freudian texts.

But there was a time between – stretching, let us say, from about 1910 to 1970 – when Freudian theory was defensible as the best scientific theory of the full complexities of the human mind that we had; and many of the analyses of the mind developed in that period have not been superseded by anything in modern cognitive theory. I am thinking in particular of analyses of types of ego defence. In that time it seemed possible to treat Freudian theory as offering something like a scientific explanation of the way literature works, including the way it is created, and the way it is read; and to treat Freudian literary criticism as an application of a genuinely independent science.

Five applications of Freudian theory to literature

Classical Freudian theory appears to be relevant to the theory of literature in at least five ways. It suggests a theory of **literary creation**, on the lines of dream and symptom formation, in which underlying fantasies are combined with daily experience and with material from the literary tradition, by processes of condensation, displacement, the use of concrete imagery, and the use of pre-existing symbols. This in turn suggests a process of **literary interpretation**, applied to texts, which attempts to get back to the underlying unconscious material. The two processes taken together suggest a theory of **writing and reader-response**, which tells us a great deal about how literature functions and what it is for – how it deals with traumatic material, for example. It also provides a theory of **universal human nature**, in its account of the structure of the mind and the contents of the unconscious; and of the vagaries of **individual character**, in its extensive library of case studies. This may be the full range of possibilities for explanatory theory. Modern post-Lacanians don't generally offer new literary applications of Freudian theory; as we shall see in Chapter 7, they study the interimplications of Freudian and non-Freudian texts. Theirs is not a scientific but a rhetorical enterprise, though it can be a very difficult one.

The dream-work and literary creation

Let me give a slightly fuller account of Freud's theory of dream-formation. A night-dream – like a day-dream – is a representation of the fulfilment of a wish. In the more interesting cases – those of distorted and apparently senseless dreams – it is the disguised representation of a repressed wish. The process by which this disguised representation is formed is called the **dream-work**, and it is the dream-work that forms an analogy to the process of artistic creation.

The wishes that underlie dreams may be straightforward biological ones – the wish to satisfy hunger or thirst, or to urinate – or they may be deeply repressed wishes about personal life – for example the wish to end one's marriage, or never to have married at all – or they may even be powerful infantile wishes, associated with deeply buried complexes of thought and emotion that date from early childhood – for example, the Oedipal fantasy of killing the father and marrying the mother. If these wishes are sufficiently powerfully repressed, it will be impossible for them to enter consciousness; it is as if there is a vigilant censor always on watch to prevent them; and even in sleep, he only becomes slightly drowsy. But the censor is prepared to let pass a transformation of the underlying thoughts, provided that it is sufficiently unrecognisable. ('The censor' is replaced in later theory by a complex set of ego-defences.)

Freud calls dreams the royal road to the unconscious; interpreting them takes one back through the dream-work that made them to the kind of thinking that goes on on the other side of the repression-barrier. Freud called this primary-process thinking, the implication being that it is more primitive or elementary than normal conscious thinking. If we compare it with conscious thinking, we find that it is marked by a tendency to translate abstract thoughts into visual images; to replace abstract connections, like causation, by simple concrete ones – thus, instead of one proposition following from another in the logical sense, we will find a picture representing one proposition following a picture representing another proposition in a procession. Concrete external features of language, like similarities of sound, will be seized upon, rather than abstract reasoning. The unconscious loves poetry and puns. Primary-process thinking thus represents the underlying wishes by a kind of charade, or allegory, made out of images drawn from scraps of recent waking experience; and it is already half-way to art or literature! The surrealists based a whole aesthetic on these properties.

If we take conscious thinking as our standard, primary-process thinking appears as a distortion or at least a translation of our wishes and perceptions. But it might make more sense to put it the other way round, and say that primary-process constitutes our thinking about the world in a raw state, before it is processed into language. A languageless animal would have no difficulty in understanding the literal sense in which a dog follows a hare. It is secondary-process thinking, in the sense of rational thought, supported by language, which turns this concrete image into the abstract notion where a conclusion can be said to 'follow' from an argument. The effective poet, notoriously, is the one who prefers the image to the abstract word: it has often been observed – most notably in Macaulay's essay on Milton – that poets are closer to primitive thought than philosophers.

Any idea present in primary-process thinking will be partially disguised when it is translated into secondary-process form. But this degree of distortion is not yet sufficient to disguise the more dangerous material. Before what Freud calls the latent dream-thoughts can cross the barrier of repression, and become manifest dream-thoughts, two further processes must intervene. The first is called condensation. Many latent dream-thoughts become focused on, or represented by, one or two manifest dream-elements; so that the dream appears poverty-stricken and fragmentary by comparison with the thoughts which underlie it, and which can be recovered by the analyst's method of pursuing mental associations. The second is called displacement. Matters that in the latent dream are of great emotional importance appear in the actual dream rather dull and pointless; while trivial details of the actual manifest dream are bathed in powerful, inexplicable feeling, that has been displaced onto them from the places where it originated. (In the latent dream I may wish to kill my father; in the manifest dream, a powerful current of feeling will seize me while I am chopping down a tree.)

Even these two processes of distortion are not sufficient by themselves to get all the primary-process material past the censor, or the ego-defences. Certain items – one's parents, one's own body, above all, the sexual organs – will appear translated into symbols. A wide range of long and pointed objects may stand for the phallus; a wide range of enclosing ones for the vagina or the womb; giants, for the parents; a house, for the body; going up a staircase, for the act of sexual intercourse. The 'dream-like' quality of dreams arises from the action of these four influences: primary-process thinking, with its concentration on concrete imagery; condensation; displacement of feeling; and the presence of a range of disguised sexual symbols.

But dreams are not wholly 'dream-like'. A further process of elaboration and even rationalisation takes place; if the dream contains the ascent of a staircase, some often quite implausible story is found to justify this. This final process Freud calls 'secondary elaboration'. (It is not clear from his account how far secondary elaboration occurs while dreaming, and how far while reporting the dream to the analyst; perhaps it happens in both stages.)

Freud argues carefully and at length that the processes going on in the dream-work are exactly analogous to those that underlie slips of the tongue and similar errors – parapraxes – and neurotic symptoms. He does not argue the case for works of art in general, or works of literature in particular, in anything like the same detail, save for one rather specialised art form: jokes. But in a sense the case makes itself. Most people who care about the arts have the sense that works of art spring from, and put us in touch with, sources of very deep feeling, which it is not easy to trace by the analysis of surface form. All critics agree that works of art 'dramatise' or 'embody' abstract concepts in visual or other concrete forms of imagery. Most critics agree that artistic creation has a non-rational, or 'inspirational' element – the artist does not fully understand what he is producing. (This view goes back to Socrates.[6]) All agree that there is a good deal of conscious construction (secondary elaboration) needed to bring the basic *données* of a work of art into its final artistic form. The Freudian picture of dream-formation needs adjustment in detail before it will serve as a model of artistic creation; the astonishing thing is that that is all that it needs.

This model, and the corresponding interpretative one, require a great deal of development in the light of later systems of psychoanalysis – in particular, of Kleinian and object-relations theory, with their account of the way in which external objects of the psyche are introjected into the psyche to produce an inner world of object relationships; and ego-psychology with its account of mechanisms of ego-defence. Mechanisms of defence are there to transform either underlying fantasy material in the id, or disturbing material from the external world, or even inner feelings of guilt produced by the action of the superego, and make them acceptable to the ego. Thus, by a process of **projection**, internal feelings of hostility are attributed to the object of hostility: an unconscious 'I hate him' becomes 'He hates me'. Or, by a process of **identification with the aggressor**, 'he is attacking me' becomes 'we are attacking . . . some common object of dislike'. In this way a subjective world is created with which the ego feels able to cope; though where defences are neurotic, this subjective world will be a distorted version of reality and may make behaviour less effective.

An account of some aspects of this process was given by Joan Riviere in her papers: 'The Unconscious Phantasy of an Inner World Reflected in Examples from Literature', and 'The Inner World in Ibsen's *Master Builder*'. Riviere, it must be said, is not trying to explain how literature works; she is using literature to show that phantasies of our containing other persons inside ourselves, though deeply unconscious, do exist. She thus draws on a seventeenth century poem:

> *By absence, this good means I gain*
> *That I can catch her*
> *Where none can watch her*
> *In some close corner of my brain:*
> *There I embrace and kiss her,*
> *And so enjoy her, and none miss her.*

A self-conscious conceit like this is not good evidence for deeply uncon-scious fantasy. But, once that fantasy is admitted, it provides an excellent explanation for the poem; and not only that poem, but all the novels and the dramas of the world. Our need for objects is such that, if we cannot have them in reality, we introject them, and have them in our private minds. That mechanism exists, independently of literature. But it is the existence of that mechanism that enables us to introject the imaginary objects provided by works of art and literature.[7] It is not only basic introjection that is called upon by literary works. Every mechanism of defence that is used unconsciously by people in their ordinary lives is available to writers in the unconscious processes that underlie composition, and to readers when they follow a work. A work of literature can therefore at once enact unconscious wishes, and provide defences against becoming conscious of them. The difference between these processes as they act in art and as they act in life is that in art there are fewer reality-checks. Projection of hostile internal feelings can be made just as well onto a wholly imaginary character as onto a real one; in both cases a vicious character will be created from whom evil actions may be expected; in art we will have a fictional story of really evil actions; in life we will have a paranoid interpretation of the actions of a real person. Art thus enables us to live out in fantasy unconscious wishes and fears, and also to construct elaborate ego-defences against them which, within the work of art, are reinforced by a contrived success in the denouement.

It will not surprise us if many of the surface features of works of art, and in particular many of the features that give most pleasure, in psychoanalytic terms correspond to ego-defence mechanisms. One of the most frequent of these – to be found in most novels – is the robust, rational, often ironic tone of some narrator, who presents the whole story, with all its internal disturbances, from the point of view of someone detached and in control. The ego of both writer and reader is expected to identify with this point of view, and one might say that in a curious sense an ideal ego is being constructed by the text for both writer and reader to identify with. Identification with the narrator is probably a far more common response to novels than identification with the hero or heroine, though it is possible to do both, and to do both at the same time. Perhaps the most powerful influence of novels upon real life is in giving novel readers the ability to rise above their own lives, and see them in the perspective of a Jane Austen or an E.M. Forster, with understanding and sympathy.[8]

This point is taken up below, in connection with the psychoanalytic reader-response theory of Norman Holland.

Literary interpretation and the trap of author-psychology

Freudian theory was born from Freudian interpretation, of dreams, of symptoms and of symbols. It is therefore natural to expect it to provide a good basis for an account of literary interpretation. The obvious approach is to reverse the process of composition, and go from the surface of the work back to the materials from which it was constructed – carefully to dismantle the ego-defences that provide reassurance, and get back to the deep unconscious material that gives it its emotional power. But there are traps here. Freudian analysis is intended to provide a basis on which the individual patient can understand and interpret his own life: can indeed, not merely learn about the unconscious conflicts which have been paralysing him, but take that unconscious material into his own ego, so that it becomes subject to conscious decision and control. 'Where **it** was' (runs a correct translation of the famous aphorism) 'there shall **I** be'.

A literary critical interpretation has something of that flavour: we are in a sense 'taking possession' of the inner meaning of the work, just as the patient is taking possession of the inner meaning of his own life. But neither the author nor the reader is actually a patient. In neither case are we using the work (as the psychoanalyst necessarily uses dreams) simply as a way station to the patient's unconscious. A literary seminar is not (or should not be) a place where people sit on couches and free-associate. The work is an impersonal thing; we don't know who the next reader will be, and we may not know who the author was. A critical statement, even based on a psychoanalytic theory, can only be true in this impersonal context: that is, it can only be true of a book, and of people in general.

A great deal of 'Freudian' discussion of literature ignores this obvious point. Most people who are interested in literature are interested in gossip; and gossip about authors is an especially fascinating form of this. In such gossip, a work of art can be treated as a gigantic symptom; and Freudian theory can be employed to diagnose the author, and reveal his personal conflicts. Notoriously Shakespeare, Jane Austen and D.H. Lawrence have been treated in this way. More recently Jacques Lacan[9] celebrated his extension of Freudian theory to cover psychosis by diagnosing James Joyce, on the basis of his early 'Epiphanies', as a pre-psychotic who avoided psychosis by writing *Ulysses* and *Finnegans Wake*. (A Joycean 'epiphany' – an appearance of God – is a tiny fragment of closely observed life claimed to embody intense meaning. Psychotics do have such experiences; a literary representation is found in Virginia Woolf's portrait of Septimus Warren Smith in *Mrs Dalloway*.[10])

These analyses may well be true. But there are two obvious absurdities in the general approach. In the first place, the author isn't there; we don't have his free associations to elements in his work; and he isn't a patient wanting a cure. The elementary basis of the psychoanalytic situation does not exist. In the second place, to approach the work in this way, we have to write off the process of conscious artistic composition as a process of secondary elaboration of no great interest. But to do this is to abolish the work of art altogether. Consider the effect of this procedure if the art we are concerned with is that of music. If writing the actual notes is a matter of mere secondary elaboration, what is there left to talk about? Sometimes Freudian analysis of this kind is a way of **not** talking about the work of art.

But the very generality of Freud's theory offers a way of approach to art in general. We can always ask: what powerful underlying forces are there, in the human personality, that are embodied in this work, and that could thus have led the author to create it, as they lead the reader to respond to it? We are thus led toward human universals. We can also ask: what are the forces that lead to this particular variety of secondary elaboration (artistic treatment) and what sort of response do readers have to it? We are thus led toward artistic detail and particular responses by the reader. The Freudian approach is thus compatible with a profound criticism that ranges from issues of great generality to matters of tiny detail, and never degenerates into gossip about authors. And the detail can be very tiny indeed. Freudian theory, as I have said, includes a theory of the significance of slips of the tongue, of elementary mistakes and of jokes. The analyst trained in these has already achieved a better skill in close reading than most grammarians could give him.

It is here that we find an answer to the common criticism that Freudian interpretations are necessarily reductive: that they limit the significance of works of art (which are, after all, complex products of civilisations) by reducing them, always and all the time, to the same limited set of primary instinctual conflicts. One part of this accusation is clearly true. Freudian theory **is** reductive: any theory which aims at explanatory force has to be reductive. That is what scientific explanation **is**: the reduction of complex surface phenomena to simpler underlying order. Freudian theory is only reductive when you work down from the complexities of civilisation to the powerful instinctual conflicts that are said to underlie them. It becomes constructive as soon as you start working up again, and trace the intricate ways in which the instinctual is mapped into the social and personal.

It was Freud's view throughout most of his life that the whole of human civilisation was based on the sublimation of the sexual instinct. But to say this is a very long way from saying that civilisation does not exist, or that sexuality is not, or ought not to be, sublimated, or that instinctual gratification ever could be immediate in any possible order of society. We accept deferred gratification for our instinctual needs as a necessary part of that accommodation with reality which is the condition for our continuing to satisfy those needs in the end. The intricate construction of a work of art on the basis of a simple underlying phantasy is a parallel for the intricate construction of the whole world of human culture on the basis of simple underlying phantasy.

Universal human nature: the place of the Oedipus complex

One major strength of Freudian theory, both in general and in its relation to literary theory, is that it makes precise claims about what the most important instinctual fantasies are. The Freudian critic, analysing particular works of art, is at the same time putting to the test a whole theory of human nature, and what is central to it. To be specific, if Freud is right, the Oedipus complex is the most important feature of human personality, and we should expect to find it hidden behind any human artefact of strong emotional force: behind the work of Homer and Aeschylus, Dante and Shakespeare, Beethoven and Wagner, Mills and Boon.[11]

We note immediately that there is a curious paradox about the theory. *Oedipus Rex* is a very fine play; it may well be the greatest of all Greek tragedies, or even the greatest of tragedies. But it is not the only one. In the Electra plays a daughter helps kill her mother, in order to avenge her father; this can readily be accommodated as a simple inversion, an equivalent of the Oedipus complex for women; and Jung indeed referred to the Electra complex. But Electra plays are also always Orestes plays[12] – Orestes killed his mother to avenge his father. Why do we not have an Orestes complex? In Greek tragedy, as in modern detective stories, every possibility of family slaughter is explored. Agamemnon sacrificed his daughter Iphigeneia to gain favourable winds for his military expedition. Ten years later, his wife Clytemnestra killed Agamemnon in revenge, and also because she had a lover. In *The Bacchae*, Agave the queen kills her son Pentheus under the influence of Dionysiac fury. In the *Medea*, Medea kills her own children out of fury at her lover Jason marrying someone else. In the *Alcestis*, Alcestis sacrifices herself for her worthless husband – though she is brought back from the underworld by the sympathetic demi-god Hercules. Why do we not speak of the Agamemnon–Iphigeneia complex, the Clytemnestra complex, the Agave complex, the Medea complex, the Alcestis complex? Presumably because psychoanalysis claims that the Oedipus complex is clinically observed and the other ones aren't. But we have seen that the way clinical research is carried out in psychoanalysis cannot give that kind of confidence in it. And there is certainly no literary reason for thinking *Oedipus Rex* more striking, more harrowing, more profound, or more central than any of the others. (Far the most moving, to a modern audience, is Agamemnon's sacrifice of his daughter in *Iphigeneia in Aulis*. I have been in an audience that was reduced to tears by this.)

On the face of it, Freud's theory predicts that every tragedy will be Oedipal in character: critics have hastened to extend Freud's work by finding the Oedipal conflict in *Hamlet*. But the same argument applies again. Why pick on Hamlet rather than Lear? Why is there not a Lear complex, which harps on the response of senile fathers to disobedient daughters? Or an Othello complex, or a Cleopatra complex, or a Bertrand complex whose symptoms are that one is quite unprepared to marry a lower-middle class bluestocking cleverer than oneself even if the king demands it?[13] Of course there is a simple answer: the Oedipus complex just is central to human nature and the others are not. So we explain *Hamlet*, *Henry IV*, etc. as directly Oedipal, and the others, with a little ingenuity, as *indirectly* Oedipal.

If we concerned ourselves solely with the literary evidence, and were not armed with a prior conviction that the Oedipal situation is the one that has universal human significance, we would, I think, regard each and every one of these plays as representing a striking complex of unconscious feeling based upon the conjunction of human instincts – principally sexuality – and family relationships. But I do not think we would want to privilege the Oedipus complex at all. The more seriously we take the literary and artistic evidence, the more likely we are to move toward the position of Jung, who tried to use literature and art themselves to guide us to what are the fundamental **archetypes** – wise old man, devouring mother, etc. – around which we build our personal **complexes**. It is not that we should defend the specific archetypes Jung claimed to find. The point is that Jung recognised a plurality of archetypal patterns; Freud recognises only one major one; and the evidence of literature and art here favours Jung.

Reader-response theory and the mechanisms of defence

One reason why Freudian approaches to literature may have seemed reductive is that we have been applying a rather early form of the theory, and looking only at the basic procedures of creation and interpretation. If we look at the problem of accounting for the response of the reader; and if we move to a slightly later and more sophisticated version of the basic theory, which includes an account of the structure of the ego and, more particularly, its mechanisms of defence, we find that the theory becomes both more complex and less reductive.

The reader of a work of literature is in the position of an interpreter of dreams rather than a dreamer; a substantial process of interpretation is required before he can get back to the primary fantasy material from which the work is constructed. Such an interpretative process is usually unconscious; because of the censor, operating alike in writer and reader, it may be necessary to be unconscious of the fantasy one is entertaining in order to enjoy it. The writer, too, may be unconscious of the primary fantasy with which he is operating. But he is not like a dreamer, producing freely and without conscious control. On the contrary, he is doing a great deal of careful conscious work. How then does he keep control of his material – how does he keep it as a transformation of a particular underlying fantasy, when he is not consciously aware of what that fantasy is? Presumably, he does this by rereading it, as each conscious change is made, and checking whether it feels right. This circular process, of writing and reading, changing the text and rereading, without ever applying conscious criteria to show whether the changes are for the better, is a common feature of the way writers work. Writers are active readers, who change the story they are reading, to make it feel better to them.

If we apply Freud's later theory of the self, as in Holland, 1968, we can see the full complexity of such a process. In the later theory, the underlying fantasy is a production of the id; if taken into the ego in anything near its original form, it would arouse censure from the superego. So it is transformed by unconscious ego-defences into a form acceptable to the conscious parts of the ego – i.e. not attracting attack from the superego and not too implausibly far from external reality. An example of such an ego-defence is projection. A person with sexual desires which they find unacceptable may project them, and the corresponding guilt, onto some suitable other. In ordinary life, a man who feels lasciviously about women, but whose superego prevents him acknowledging that feeling, will denounce women as lascivious. The writer of a work of literature, employing the same defence, will construct a character who is a lascivious temptress, and who gets her come-uppance through violence as a result. The reader can thus enjoy fantasies both of sex and of violence without guilt. This is the formula of a great deal of thriller-fiction; its basis in underlying fantasy is analysed further in Chapter 8.

A literary example of projection, mentioned in Holland, is that work of literature which is perhaps most basic to Freudian theory as a whole: *Oedipus Rex*. As many critics have pointed out, and as most undergraduates quickly see, whoever in literature has an unresolved Oedipus complex, Oedipus has not. There is no reason from the play to suppose that he knew he had killed his father and was bedding his mother; he has spent his adult life trying to avoid doing just that, and it takes all the power of the gods to make him fail. *Oedipus Rex* may appeal to an unresolved Oedipus complex in the author or the audience; it doesn't picture one in the protagonist.

If we assume that 'the censor' is actually a name for a set of unconscious ego-defences, one of which is projection, we will look at the matter in a slightly different way. On this view the underlying fantasy is still the Oedipal one, which gives pleasure in its old infantile way: in the unconscious, all men wish to kill their fathers and lie with their mothers. But such a fantasy, let loose, would be very disturbing to the ego. The unconscious defence of projection therefore operates on this fantasy. The desire that Oedipus should kill his father and lie with his mother is projected onto the gods; they are guilty, not Oedipus. The ego can thus have the pleasure of identifying with Oedipus, who has achieved this fearful fantasy, without guilt. What guilt remains, is absorbed by Oedipus's punishment: when this happens, we have the pleasure of identifying with the superego, which is the internal punisher.

The full procedure of reading or writing now looks very complicated indeed. The reader (who may in another phase be writing) uses a process of interpretation on the text to produce an underlying fantasy. By another process of interpretation, he finds defences to help him manage and control this fantasy. It is this whole process, rather than the mere entertainment of a fantasy, that gives pleasure. The writer works by unconscious methods on his own unconscious fantasies and produces a text in which those fantasies are successfully defended against. As reader, he checks to see that this has happened. As writer, modifies; as reader, checks again. In the course of this he may be playing quite complicated games with the transformed fantasy; identifying with all the characters and their interrelationships, for example. In the course of such identification, he may engage in all sorts of processes of projection, denial, etc. It is in these circumstances that the text may seem to take on a deep life out of the control of the author's conscious mind, and beyond the rational understanding of the reader.

It has often been remarked that there is a similarity between the relation a reader has to the text, and the transference in therapy. Skura, in 1981, discussed literature as case history, fantasy, dream and transference. We might usefully turn this upside down, and explain the transference in therapy as a variety of literary response. Patient and therapist are colluding to construct an unconscious narrative fantasy in which, for example, the therapist stands in for the patient's father in infancy, and infantile feelings are projected on him. This is a reminder that narrative and drama are much older, more widespread, and more flexible methods of therapy than psychoanalysis is, though they have the same ambiguous quality of sometimes making neurosis worse.

The psychology of character

The most obvious application of a theory of psychology – any theory of psychology – to literature comes in my fifth category. A great deal of literature – most of it, in fact – appears to be about human behaviour, human character, human mental processes, etc. That is, literature seems to offer a more or less realistic representation of human psychology, within the limits imposed by the demands of literary form. But the science of psychology also aims to do this, and to provide some general explanations into the bargain. We naturally expect a fairly close affinity between the two: and are usually gravely disappointed. Apart from the psychoanalytic schools, most branches of psychology have nothing whatever of interest for the student of literature. Neurophysiology, psycholinguistics, cognitive psychology in general, learning theory, personality studies so far as they are conducted by questionnaires statistically processed, have nothing of interest. Most non-analytic accounts, even of processes like early learning (as in Piaget), have very little.

The analytic schools, on the other hand, have almost too much literary interest for their own good as sciences. They are overflowing with clinical accounts of neurotic and psychotic cases, all of them very much like novels. They offer colourful and exciting explanations, which either read like mythology (as in the case of the conflicts between the ego, the superego, and the id) or actually are mythology (as in the case of the Oedipus complex or Jung's archetypes). And every successful analysis (as well as many unsuccessful ones) constitutes a tremendous psychodrama, which can be made into an excellent novel simply by providing a competent précis. At the same time, some of the best literary work of our own century cries out for Freudian study. *Sons and Lovers* is a case study in the Oedipus complex, exactly as it stands (though Lawrence thought the Oedipal theory a half-truth; he himself had told the whole truth). *The Trial* is already a Freudian dream. 'Stream of consciousness' technique insistently provokes the question: is this **really** how the mind works? – and we look to dynamic psychology for the answer. Certain fundamental ideas, like that of the unconscious, were commonplaces of literature before ever Freud took them up.

For all the obvious promise of this approach, it is potentially almost as big a trap as the Freudian analysis of authors. The point is, that only in certain art forms – late Shakespearean plays, serious novels, etc. – are characters designed to have a complex internal psychological structure. Quite often, characters have a purely representative function, and no interiority at all. The heroes of Ariosto, Venus in Shakespeare's *Venus and Adonis*, the allegorical characters of Spenser or Bunyan, comic types like Horner in Wycherley or Thwackum in Fielding[14] simply do not have the interior space to be psychoanalysed. But that does not mean that their representative function in their works of art cannot be analysed psychoanalytically. Shakespeare's Venus, for example, and various Spenserian characters, are direct representations of types of desire (as opposed to being direct representations of people who have those desires). Horner claims falsely that surgery to remove venereal disease has rendered him impotent. His friends therefore trust him with their wives – whom he debauches. This is almost the ultimate joke about the castration complex; but it would be idiotic even to discuss whether Horner had a castration complex or no. He isn't complex enough to have any kind of complex. The castration fears that the play arouses are those of the men in the audience; and it is those that both the men and the women in the audience laugh at. The same is true for the sadism of Thwackum. In all these cases, it is the work that needs to be the primary focus of psychoanalytic examination; the characters in the work have psychoanalytically interesting features that derive from the work as a whole.

Even in those novels where interiority exists, and it therefore seems to make sense to discuss the motivation of the characters, a Freudian analysis of them may not be the best Freudian approach to the work of art. Richardson virtually invented psychological interiority as a feature of the English novel. In *Pamela*, using epistolary technique, he fastens us for hundreds of pages inside the mind of a fifteen-year-old servant girl under sexual siege. That girl is constantly using the thought of her parents to keep her virtuous; she has many unconscious stirrings of desire for her persecutor which the reader notices long before she does. In a sense, she is an open and shut case for psychoanalytic examination. But if you look at the way Richardson conceived her, it will be seen that she is primarily a moralistic rather than a psychological invention – an ideal type of womanly virtue whose virtue is proof against all assault; and she is naturalistically improbable, despite Richardson's often brilliant naturalistic writing. The character of Pamela is a man's construction of a social ideal, though it was very acceptable to his initial audience of women, as reassurance that the social ideal was a possible one.

What is of psychoanalytic interest in this novel, at a first approximation, is not the interiority of the character but the two fantasies simultaneously played out: the Cinderella fantasy of women, and the rape fantasy of men. And these are not inside the character of Pamela, but in the mind of the reader. What is of psychoanalytic interest, at the second approximation, is again not inside the character of Pamela, but in the defences which Richardson erects in order to enable his female readers to indulge in the Cinderella fantasy, and his male ones in the rape fantasy. The major defence in both cases is a moral one: both sets of readers are invited to join with their own superegos in moral applause of the conduct of Pamela, faithful to her principles whatever the pressures and whatever the temptations, and moral condemnation of the conduct of Squire B – till he reforms and marries her. Only at a third level of approximation, I believe, after dealing with more important matters, would it be appropriate to note that Pamela is sexually attracted by Squire B's very persistence and activity, his phallic quality, and is partly unconscious of that attraction. And I don't think one would want to look at the character of Squire B at all. It is easy enough to fit the basic Oedipal pattern to him, of the young man, over-impressed by his mother, who can only be sexually attracted to servant girls. But there really isn't enough interiority in him to find a complex; he is a conventional character, which means he is a convention rather than a character.[15]

Psychoanalytic criticism in action: some examples

The Oedipal pattern: Hamlet *and* Sons and Lovers

A great deal of early psychoanalytic literary criticism was little more than a trawl through literature to find further exemplifications of the Oedipal pattern of experience. Freud readily recognised that *Hamlet* offered a Shakespearean parallel, and Ernest Jones developed this into what is still perhaps the most fully argued Oedipal interpretation of any work of literature. Jones uses literary-historical arguments to show that Hamlet's delay in carrying out his revenge – inexplicable to Hamlet himself and to many readers – has been recognised by most critics as the most striking feature of the play. He diagnoses Hamlet (the character) as suffering, not from some generalised inadequacy, but from a 'specific aboulia' – an inability to perform just the duty of revenge that the ghost of his father lays on him – to kill his uncle. And this inability, he argues, stems from the Oedipus complex.

Hamlet's uncle has done more than kill Hamlet's father; he has married Hamlet's mother, and thus replaced Hamlet's father. Hamlet is thus left in the classic Oedipal situation. He has been vividly reminded of his mother's still active sexuality, and as the text shows, is bitterly, obscenely jealous of it. In the circumstances, for Hamlet to kill Claudius would be for Hamlet to live out the Oedipal fantasy of killing his father for sexual jealousy of his mother. He cannot do this; so, to his own surprise, he does nothing, even when he has clear opportunities to kill the king; and he invents obviously spurious reasons for not killing him, just like the hypnotic subject who invents obviously spurious reasons for opening a window, not knowing she is under a post-hypnotic instruction.

The concept of the unconscious is more than earning its living in this interpretation. Neither Shakespeare nor his original audiences knew about Freudian theory, and Hamlet, as a mere collection of lines, can hardly be said to have an unconscious mind. Yet we have no difficulty in accepting that the character, Hamlet, has been given an unconscious motive by Shakespeare; that Shakespeare was able to do this partly because Shakespeare had the same motive in his own unconscious; and that the audience could respond to the play because they had the same motive in their unconscious minds. Unconscious fantasies in the writer are here unconsciously written into the text; they form the unconscious of a character; and are responded to unconsciously by an audience which has the same patterns in the unconscious. The exciting thing about this approach is that it begins to show us how literature in general may produce profound feelings which are inexplicable by analyses that limit themselves to the conscious level. Literature is a mode of unconscious communication. Note that in this case we are perfectly justified in engaging in psychoanalytic character-analysis: Shakespeare has gone to some pains to give Hamlet sufficient interiority for us to analyse him. But the analysis of the character, Hamlet, is only a part of the analysis of the play.

D.H. Lawrence wrote *Sons and Lovers* in 1912; he had learnt something about the Oedipus complex from his new wife Frieda, in the later stages of writing the book, but the main body of it was simply autobiographical. The psychoanalysts were quick to realise that he had provided an almost perfect Oedipal case study; Kuttner wrote about it in 1916.[16] In the book a mother takes her sons as lovers (emotionally, not physically) and they are unable to form mature relationships with other women. Paul, the younger son, suffers from the classic split described in Freud's paper 'The Most Prevalent form of Degradation in the Erotic Life'.[17] Young men who consulted Freud often showed roughly the following symptoms: impotence with wife, but potency with lower class girl or prostitute. Freud always diagnosed an unresolved Oedipus complex; the affectional parts of the sexual instinct are still bound up with the mother, who is sexually taboo, and the sensual ones are directed at a somewhat degraded object. Paul showed the analogue of this; his affair with his friend and spiritual companion, Miriam, was physically unsatisfactory, while that with the mildly raffish Clara – feminist, separated from her husband – was physically passionate. Other relationships in the book also show Freudian features. The book was thus a gift to the psychoanalysts.

Lawrence himself was less sure. In his view 'the scientists' had only half a truth; the novelist gave a whole truth. Lawrence here probably means emotional truth; but there is also an alternative, social realist truth. It is fairly easy to construct a non-psychoanalytic account of the way in which young men of the time – and later times – come to divide women into virgins whom they respect and whores whom they use. The explanation is based on economics and on class factors. At the beginning of the twentieth century, with birth control unavailable to respectable young women, having a baby would spell social and economic ruin for them; they therefore had strictly to control their sexual feelings, and would thus through an acquired frigidity, become poor sexual partners even after marriage. For some poor young women, on the other hand, a liaison with a well-off young man might make economic sense even if it did not lead to marriage. Such young women were far less likely to train themselves into sexual anaesthesia, and made better partners. A young man thus doesn't need to be suffering from a complex of any kind to view the two kinds of women differently: merely realistic. And his expectations would account for his different performances.

It is one of the defects of Freudian critics that they don't systematically look for alternative non-Freudian accounts of the works they consider. This is not true in the classic case of *Hamlet*, where Ernest Jones made a survey of all criticism up to his own time which was unparalleled in its range and depth, and puts most literary scholars to shame. But it is true of Lawrence, where orthodox Freudian treatment of the sexual side of his work coexists with social commentary, and with exposition of his own strange sexual doctrines, without ever being brought into confrontation. I have never seen this social realist account of the madonna–whore complex pointed to as a clear alternative to the Freudian one, or a necessary complement to it. (It won't account for everything in *Sons and Lovers*, of course; no doubt the Freudian interpretation is correct here.)

The castration complex: nine-fingered Frodo

It is not difficult to find other Freudian patterns scattered throughout literature. I remember noticing, sometime in the 1960s, that J.R.R. Tolkien's escapist fantasy novel, *The Lord of the Rings*, is an extended treatment of the castration complex. We can be quite certain, given Tolkien's ultra-conservative nature and published opinions, that this was not intentional, and that it is an interpretation that would have been contemptuously rejected if it had been suggested to the author. But the textual evidence is about as unequivocal as it can ever get. It comes, *inter alia*, from the climactic scene of the whole novel – the one that provides its emotional resolution.

Frodo, a hobbit (a diminutive creature to whom the reader responds with affection, as to a child) carries a ring which could make him all-powerful, but would corrupt him morally and make him the equivalent of the evil Lord of the Rings who originally manufactured it. Instead, our hero is dedicated to destroying the evil thing in the original volcanic forge where it was made; but as he gets nearer to this, he is plagued by a continually increasing temptation to put it on and claim it for his own. He is followed by Gollum, an evil counterpart of himself, who has previously worn the ring, and already been corrupted into hopeless desire for it. When Frodo attempts to throw the ring into the gulf, he cannot do so; his will has been sapped, and he has to claim the ring for his own. But Gollum desperately throws himself at the new ringlord, struggles with him, swaying on the edge of the fiery gulf, and then **bites off Frodo's finger, with the ring on it**, jumps with joy, falls into the fiery gulf and is destroyed. So too is the old ringlord Sauron and all his works: his great black tower collapses and falls to the ground; and Frodo and his friend Sam wake up to a world in which everything bad has unhappened; and in due course they, with other hobbity playmates, restore even their own exquisite and childish little civilisation in their native land of the Shire.

It seems to me that the imagery here is about as clearly Freudian as one could ever hope to get. If this scene is **not** a reference to the castration complex, then there is no reference to castration anywhere in literature, except possibly in *The Country Wife, Tristram Shandy, Sarrasine* and the works of Origen.[18] Indeed if this imagery is not Freudian, there is no warrant for interpreting any works of literature at all in Freudian terms. Furthermore, the recognition of this characteristic seemed to me to solve a number of critical problems about the book, including problems about its social meaning. In its social meaning, the evil that encroaches on the Shire, and dominates Sauron's land of Mordor, and the domains of his imitator Saruman, is the evil of technology; and when it is dissipated, an innocent agricultural and feudal world re-emerges. What the Freudian interpretation does is to make agricultural innocence the metaphorical equivalent of sexual innocence. Frodo's struggle not to put on the ring – i.e. not to adopt the demonised magical technology which will make him Lord of the World, or destroy him – is thus equated unconsciously with a struggle against sex (in terms of childish experience, against masturbation) and his decision to put on the ring and claim his rights – represented in the book as a conscious and deliberate, though irresistible, decision – is his fall into adult sexuality.

Most readers of *The Lord of the Rings* struggle violently against an interpretation of this kind, and they do so with good reason: when you read it, the book doesn't feel in the least sexual; indeed, it must be one of the least sexual books in literature. Freudians would say, of course, that this is an effect of the creative process that produced it: specifically it is the effect of the process of **displacement**, which we have met in our account of the dream-work. Sexual feeling, present in the latent thoughts, the underlying phantasy, has been displaced onto landscape, which is why the book makes us feel so strongly about landscape and its destruction. Indeed (a Freudian would say) the entire point of the book (which is directed emotionally to thirteen-to-fifteen-year-olds, or to older people emotionally fixated at that level) is to provide a massive displacement of sexual feeling so that it colours a whole imaginary world of boyish adventure, and is not redirected toward an adult sexual object. And for this purpose the book **celebrates** castration! 'Nine-fingered Frodo' has ballads written about him, and the whole world is recovered through his digital loss.

This interpretation solved a number of critical problems which rather bothered me in the 1950s. I fell in love with Tolkien's earlier book, *The Hobbit*, when I was a child (it is aimed, I suppose, at nine-year-olds). As an adult, I admire it; it is the story of a quest in a group where the hobbit begins as the humblest and clumsiest member of an expedition in which numerous perils are met, and eventually grows into being the real leader: it is thus an allegory of growing up, and very useful to help a child cope psychologically with the difficult process of growing up. (The magical or monstrous challenges that the hero meets are a good allegory of the child's experience of the world; the moral problems and the problems of working with a group actually are the problems that real children meet.) When I started reading *The Lord of the Rings* at twenty, I was rather dismayed to find it less mature than *The Hobbit*, though it claimed to be for grown-ups. This was true, for example, of its vision of evil and danger – in *The Hobbit*, there are many dangers and evils, and they are largely independent of each other, and there are many mixed cases of evil and good, just as in life. In *The Lord of the Rings*, there is a paranoid vision of all evil emanating from a single source, and the hero is not one small person who happened to get mixed up in adventures but the one person who can save the world.

All this can be explained by the observation that *The Hobbit* belongs to the latency period in which sex is not perceived as a threat, but suffuses the whole experienced world; *The Lord of the Rings* belongs to adolescence, when the emergence of sexuality is, in any civilisation, the greatest threat to the integrity of the personality that there can be, and one that it is urgently necessary to bring under control. A mature response to this threat is provided by the Mills and Boon romance, which offers a fixation on a particular object: at the highest level of literature, by the ultimate adolescent romance, *Romeo and Juliet*. An immature and panicky response is that of Origen: 'Cut the thing off and get control of yourself again'. That is the response metaphorically provided by *The Lord of the Rings*.

To ensure that the castration option feels right, the book is stuffed with father figures. Virtually every adult male in the book – including a dwarf, an elf, several men, an incarnate angel, an earth-spirit and a very long-lived tree-creature – has at one point or another the emotional relationship of a father to one or more of the hobbits. The menacing, castrating side of the father is concentrated in Sauron, the Lord of the Rings; Frodo's decision to put on the ring is seen as a challenge to him, and (since Frodo cannot possibly match him) a disastrous one, from which he is saved only by losing ring and finger. This promptly removes the menacing father from the scene.

But all the reassuring fathers are left behind, unanimously honouring and praising Frodo for his achievement.

In the 1970s, when I was interviewing students for admission to read literature, I would always ask them what they read for pleasure; and it was nearly always *The Lord of the Rings*. These were students full of the fashionable opinions of the day: they lived in communes, were anti-racist, and were in favour of Marxist revolution and free love. I would ask them why their favourite reading should be a book about a largely racial war, favouring feudal politics, jam-full of father figures, and entirely devoid of sex. They never knew the answer. I wasn't sure; but I would put it down to the fact that the very lives they led and thoughts they consciously had, as young adults emerging into autonomy, presented an enormous unconscious threat. The unconscious fantasy of castration removed that threat; but it had to be unconscious. It was and is a very important part of the appeal of *The Lord of the Rings* that its greatest *aficionados* are quite incapable of noticing what it says. Come to think of it, what psychoanalysis suggests is that it is a very important part of the appeal of all literature that its *aficionados* are quite incapable of noticing what it says!

Conscious genital symbolism: the poisoned valley

Tolkien was an unconscious and driven writer, for all his constant and obsessive rewritings; but many writers are highly self-conscious artists, using erotic symbolism in a quite deliberate way. Lawrence, notoriously, is both at once; the works wrote themselves while he watched and discovered; but he rewrote again and again to get them right. In *Sons and Lovers* two lovers take a walk on the steep and dangerous banks above a rushing river into which they seem in danger of slipping; they do drop a small parcel, which is rapidly swept away. The symbolism of being swept away by passion is obvious enough, and this symbolism has to bear the whole burden of conveying their feelings when they do actually find a place to make love.

Elizabeth Smart's *By Grand Central Station I Sat Down and Wept* is at once one of the most intense, and one of the most literary and contrived pieces of poetic prose ever written. Smart invented many of the elaborate images before she wrote the book, and slotted them into an appropriate place. They are used, with baroque elaboration, to show the intensity of the inner, emotional reality of an adulterous love affair, and joined organically with fragments of plainer prose to indicate its outer, and rather sordid, social appearance. For all the extravagance of the prose, the wild Californian landscape is described with minute naturalistic accuracy that does not stop its being a continuous metaphor of erotic feeling and a prophecy of disaster if the affair takes place. For all that they are wild and beautiful, there are some places it is impossible for human beings to go: 'poison oak grows over the path and over all the banks, and it is impossible to go into the damp overhung valley without being poisoned'. Poison oak is a real feature of the local flora and can seriously damage your health; and no doubt that damp overhung valley has a real counterpart as well as its obvious metaphorical one. But in case we miss the metaphor, we are told 'Later in the year it flushes scarlet, both warning of and recording fatality'.[19]

I have taught this novel repeatedly to first year students, who are probably reasonably representative of ordinary intelligent late-twentieth century readers. Do they consciously recognise the damp overhung valley as female genitals? Yes and no. Everybody who understands the book at all notices the erotic nature of the scene as a whole; those who are accustomed to Freudian interpretations point out the symbol; nobody denies this meaning of the image, but many find the passage better – more erotic, for one thing – when this meaning is sunk in the general erotic atmosphere along with all the other sexual associations. One can't, at least with contemporary students, describe the sexual meaning of the image as 'repressed' in the clinical sense, and it requires no special analytic or hypnotic skill to make them conscious of it.

Now this is not a refutation of Freudian theory; it is precisely what one would expect from it. According to Freud, pretty well all culture and adult personality is a transformation of sexuality; in literature, you would expect sexual energy to be spread throughout the whole of a text, by processes akin to those which build up the adult personality. The critical process of picking out a specific image as a Freudian symbol, far from being a part of normal response to the text, may be a distraction from that response; it employs the adult critical intelligence to draw attention to the genitals, but pointing out the genitals is an infantile activity. An infantile sensibility is therefore evoked in the critic, and the erotic feeling of the passage as a whole, which is young-adult, collapses. It is factors like this which make Freudian criticism feel reductive; but that does not prove that Freudian theory is false. It might well be, however, that one principal benefit of Freudian theory for readers of literature is to explain why it is inadvisable to make conscious Freudian interpretations while reading.

The phallus as weapon: the smile of Ortheris

We can make a useful distinction between Freudian and non-Freudian symbolism in literature by looking at a short story by Kipling: 'On Greenhow Hill' (*Life's Handicap*, 1891). The main story is a melancholy first person account of a Yorkshire lad's hopeless love – hopeless, because (i) he had an educated Methodist preacher as rival and (ii) his intended was consumptive; Learoyd, the narrator, solved his problem by signing on for the army, and is found in India telling his story to his friends: Mulvaney, who had just as cursed a love-life, and Ortheris, who has a different love:

> His was an almost passionate devotion to his rifle, whom, by barrack-room report, he was supposed to kiss every night before turning in.

There is a framing story: a native deserter is prowling outside the lines calling for his fellow tribesmen to join him and fight against the British: Learoyd's story is told while the other two wait for the marksman, Ortheris, to kill him, with a single long and marvellous shot: this happens, naturally, at the story's end. Learoyd shows fellow feeling with the deserter: 'Happen there was a lass tewed up wi' him too,' said he. But

> Ortheris did not reply. He was staring across the valley, with the smile of the artist who looks on the completed work.

Ortheris is an artist, or at least a first class craftsman who has achieved a great feat. Kipling means us to admire him, and at the same time be horrified, and at the same time recognise the necessary murder which keeps an empire in being and enables those who care about art to be civilised. (We artists at home can exist only because of Ortheris's art in India.) At the same time, we are invited to reverse the symbolism, and see that the artist – Kipling himself, perhaps – has the impersonality of the rifleman pinning down his target. All these non-Freudian symbolic equivalences were doubtless clear to Kipling himself; he was a very self-conscious artist.

One of my students, commenting on this passage, said 'Ortheris, who has never had a woman . . . ' There is no real evidence of that, but it fits well enough. The obvious Freudian interpretation of this is that the rifle is a 'phallic symbol' and military murder – not necessarily in Ortheris's mind alone, but in the whole culture – is the product of frustrated sexuality. This goes well with Learoyd's story, the plain meaning of which is that army life has replaced normal married life. Here it was death – the imminent death of his intended – that drove Learoyd to renounce love, join up and become a killer. The phallic image of the rifle, and the never explicitly stated equation of murder with orgasm brings all these themes together in the last page.

Would Kipling have rejected this as an obscene travesty of his intention, and of the facts of empire, which require soldiers on economic, not sexual, grounds? He would probably have found the blank Freudian symbol much cruder than his own carefully constructed symbolic equivalence, but it would be nonsense to suggest he didn't know about the sexual significance of the rifle; on his account, the whole barrack room knew, and made obscene jokes about it. In fact, he was entirely conscious of the way he was balancing the themes of death and of sexual love: he explains this in a poem at the beginning of the story, in which Love and Death are personified and the puzzle is that the attractions of death are stronger. It is perhaps unfair to say that if Kipling had read Freud he would not have learned much; while if Freud had read Kipling he might have got onto the theory of Eros and Thanatos twenty years earlier.

Regressive desublimation: Death in Venice

In the novella of 1911, *Death in Venice*, the approach of death unlocks a lifetime's sublimation and releases in Thomas Mann's elderly great writer, Aschenbach, a homosexual passion for a beautiful adolescent boy. Aschenbach has built his art, and his life, on classical restraint; on a principled repression of psychological insight and of the compassion that might stem from that; on the Germanic virtues of work, endurance and respectability, which had built a weak constitution and a slight talent into a set of major works; on a celebration of the militaristic Prussian heritage of Frederick the Great. It is not a political story; but the psychological roots of two world wars are present here. What chiefly matters, however, is what this lifetime has done to Aschenbach. The damage is realised in images: that of the beautiful boy St Sebastian, pierced with arrows, which represents his art and his soul; that of the fetid wild swamp, patrolled by tigers, which represents his desires – desires that he realises, as best he can, in that final holiday in Venice (a city which is, it will be remembered, a set of palaces built on a swamp).

There are no characters in *Death in Venice* save Aschenbach himself; there is an outward story, but the drama is an inner one. Figures loom out of a murk and embody stages in his inner disintegration. At first they are figures of death: a man seen by a cemetery; an old man on a cruise with young companions, made up grotesquely to look young; a sinister Gondolier who conveys him over the water to death. Then beauty: the unknown boy Tadzio for whom he abandons all dignity, following him all over Venice, himself wearing young make-up to disguise his age. And for whom also he abandons all moral positions, preferring that Tadzio should die of cholera in Venice rather than leave it to go where Aschenbach cannot see him.

Few stories are more psychoanalytic in flavour than *Death in Venice*, which might well be described as a study of the death instinct in operation, as it disassembles the structures of inner reality which it has taken a lifetime to build up. If we do call it that we have to note that Freud did not introduce the death instinct till 1920. This story is not an adaptation of Freud, any more than the Kipling story is. It is, rather, a parallel phenomenon; something which is common form in modernist writing: a story constructed to symbolise inner reality. It is in fact one of those subtle psychological works invoking the compassion that the fictional Aschenbach had made it a principle to reject. We see how the Germanic hero is formed by reaction-formation against weakness; an insight as much Adlerian as Freudian. When, with the approach of death, weakness comes again, we see the return of the repressed.

Nothing is easier than to describe a story like this in terms of one psychoanalytic school or another. But in fact it does not need to be so described; and it is not an orthodox case-study of any school. What it shares with psychoanalysis is the perception that each of us builds up an ego and a set of defences as much to control inner impulses as to cope with external reality.

Norman Holland and ego-defences: *Dover Beach* and the primal scene

By the sixties, psychoanalysis was well established as a model for literary criticism, and also, in the minds of many, as the best available science of mind. A psychoanalytic critic like Norman Holland, writing in this era, shows enormous confidence in psychoanalysis as a science, and regards its scientific status as a reason for thinking of psychoanalytic interpretations as peculiarly privileged. Furthermore, since sciences can reasonably be taken as progressive disciplines, it seems proper to base psychoanalytic interpretation on the very latest science. This, for Holland, was the American version of psychoanalysis which concentrated on ego-defences. Holland's book of 1968, *The Dynamics of Literary Response*, can in many ways be seen as marking the supreme peak of scientific self-confidence in the psychoanalytic theory of literature. Much later in Holland's productive career, there is a book, *The Critical I*, 1992, which recognises just how very much things have not gone Holland's way: how cognitive studies has taken over the scientific psychological ground from psychoanalysis, while literary criticism has whored off with a scientifically quite implausible French metaphysics. We can thus tell much of the history of the field through the work of Holland.

For Holland in 1968 psychoanalysis is a science firmly based on clinical evidence which the literary theorist, *qua* literary theorist, does not question; on the basis of that science it is possible to propose a scientific theory of reader-response. The essence of that theory is that there is a finite set of basic fantasies: Holland provides a provisional dictionary of them. These fantasies are formed into literature by literary techniques which correspond to ego-defences. Holland describes a number of them. The various types of affect that works of literature have can be explained by the interaction of the basic fantasies and the defences against them. Holland provides classified charts of different types of literary affect, along with the fantasies and defences that account for them. If these charts were satisfactory, Holland would have established a periodic table of literature,[20] and founded a psychoanalytic science of literature, which explains how literature works and why we have it.

A dictionary of fantasies

Holland classifies the basic fantasies according to an extended list of phases of childhood sexual development. He extends the usual three phases of development – oral, anal and genital – into a nominal seven (actually eight). The oral phase is split into two. The first is the oral-dependent, corresponding to the earliest dependent stage when self–object boundaries are being worked out, and characterised by fantasies of fusion with the world – fantasies of being engulfed, overwhelmed, drowned, devoured, buried alive; or more benevolently, of blissful merger and fusion. Literary fantasy offers fusion; so does love; so does the oceanic feeling of the mystic. Disturbance at this very early level characterises the malingerer, the addict, the alcoholic. The second sub-phase is oral-sadistic, corresponding to a more active sucking or biting stage when the fantasy is that of incorporating parts of the world – a fantasy that leads in due course to the psychological processes of introjection and identification. The characteristic fantasies here are of devouring and being devoured; emptying the mother's body by devouring threatening objects out of it; incorporating threatening objects into the self; or building up a wall of fat against the threatening world, like Falstaff. Other fantasies align with this. Seeing – feasting one's eyes – is an oral aggressive act which may lead to guilt. Speaking – putting words out of the mouth – can be a defence against such fantasy. The roots of literature and literary response are in orality – we depend on the work as for nourishment. Holland even describes our desire for rhyme, and for plot closure, as 'hungry expectation'.

The anal phase also Holland splits into two, naming them separately as anal and urethral. Defecation seems to be about giving up part of oneself, or even giving birth. The anal phase centres on elimination and retention, which evolve into control and moral demand, a world of laws and rules. The active–passive dichotomy of the first phases become defiance and submission, and habits about rage are formed. Fantasies of engulfment by excrement – of dirt, smell, fog, the roots of realism – alternate with fantasies of mist, light, pure air and the logos – the roots of idealism. The beginnings of both realism and idealism thus lie in this phase. This is followed by the urethral phase, with fantasies of wetting, drowning and fire, and this, strangely, is said to be associated with the ability to wait, to conceptualise consequences. (Presumably from bladder control.)

The last four phases of this system are phallic, Oedipal, latent and genital. The erect phallus is identified with standing, acting, talking, seeing, learning; it becomes the symbol of autonomy and capability. To be without the phallus is to be feminised, helpless, liable to be overwhelmed – which would be a form of castration, as also would be torture, mutilation, blinding. Fear of castration represents a later form of oral fears of engulfment or anal fears of loss of body. The whole body symbolises the phallus, and a quest fantasy in literature is the phallus entering some fearful place. 'The single most common fantasy-structure in literature is phallic assertiveness balanced against oral engulfment' (Holland, 1968, p.44). There are complicating factors in these fantasies, arising from the child's animism, his feeling of the omnipotence of thought leading to guilt at injuries done by his thoughts. One traumatic fantasy is the primal scene: a child seeing the sexual act as struggle followed by death-like sleep: the child regards the father's phallus as a weapon that wounds the mother. Later sexual fantasy, by recalling the trauma of the primal scene, is thus a source of anxiety.

The Oedipal phase succeeds, with its well-known imagery and fantasies, which structure all later development: every woman is a mother, and every man a father. A variety of images of the basic triangle proliferate throughout literature; and roughly speaking everything that deals with more than two persons, or makes us feel realistic versions of adult love and hate, is Oedipal. In the Oedipal complex in life, the little boy wants to kill or castrate the father and possess the mother; but under pressure of castration fears, gives up, and identifies with the father. In literature, the boy longs to become the father and make a child in the mother; the girl to take mother's place and have a child by the father. The wish to become the father inspires rescue fantasies, obscure birth fantasies ('he's not really my father . . .'). The mother emerges as untouchable, unattainable, pure, taboo, virgin – or a slut, common, fickle and available to anyone. Incest fantasies translate into brother–sister, uncle–niece, or even racial taboos.

The castration complex leads into latency and then to the final phase of genitality. Holland says little about these; it is as if the development of fantasy stops at the Oedipal level. For Holland, the most important fantasies in literature are pre-Oedipal; these give it depth.

A list of ego-defences

In the dream-work, latent dream-thoughts include not only underlying infantile phantasies, represented in primary-process thinking by concrete imagery and symbols, but residues of daily experience: these are brought together to form the manifest dream by a process of condensation, and in the manifest dream the weight of emotional experience is shifted from one item to another by a process of displacement. In the work of art, presumably, the part of residues of daily experience is taken by another kind of material: bits of Scottish history, for example, in the case of *Macbeth*. The underlying fantasy in this particular play, according to Holland, is that of the primal scene; and a good deal of the imagery of the play is derived from this: it is a play about dark deeds at night. (The dark deeds in question are murders rather than sexual encounters: but in psychoanalytic terms, that is accounted for by displacement: our emotional response to the underlying primal scene phantasy is displaced onto the murders, and that accounts for the peculiar affective tone they carry. That literature involves condensation and displacement is, I take it, a general Freudian position, not peculiar to Holland, nor dependent on this particular play-interpretation.)

'A defence', says Holland, 'is an unconscious process of the ego which the ego puts into action automatically at a signal of danger from the external world, the id, or the super-ego' (pp.57–8). The distinguishing mark of Holland's theory is that he makes a central place for ego-defences, and he regards these as different varieties of displacement: the value, or cathexis, placed on one object is shifted to another. Holland is rather brisk in establishing this notion. Repression, for example, is the most obvious Freudian example of a defence against threats from within, as denial is against threats from without; and these are apparent counter-examples to the theory that defence is always a variety of displacement. But Holland calls repression (and presumably denial) limiting cases: displacement onto nothing!

Here is the list of ego-defences that Holland claims to be operating when we respond to literature: repression, denial, reversal, reaction-formation, undoing, projection, introjection, identification with the aggressor, turning against the self, regression, splitting, symbolisation; they operate unconsciously against unconscious impulses or perceptions. Whether we can usefully describe them all as forms of 'displacement' seems doubtful to me; Holland's purpose, of course, is to maintain the parallel with Freud's account of the dream-work; but it might make more sense if we recognised that the notion of displacement was a rather crude one, and this list of ego-defences gives a much more precise notion of the ways in which unconscious desires can be transformed.

We have considered repression and denial. In reversal, the object of a wish takes the opposite form: the censor, whose underlying wish is to see pornography, reverses it into a wish to stop others seeing pornography. In reaction formation, the aim of the wish is reversed: the classic example of this would be the anal-erotic man who becomes very tidy because of his reaction-formation against a desire to wallow in dirt. Holland offers the case of the Player-Queen's protestations of fidelity: 'The Lady doth protest too much, methinks', remarks Gertrude diagnostically. Undoing – ritual action to undo an event or impulse – is said to be akin to reversal or reaction-formation.

Projection is a displacement from oneself to the outside world – in *Oedipus Rex*, as we have seen, the hero has no desire to kill his father and mother; that desire is projected onto the gods. In introjection, there is displacement from the outside world into the self: where the perception 'He hates me' is felt to be unhandleable, it is brought into the self as 'I hate me'. Introjection, remarks Holland, is very close to the classic defence of identification with the aggressor. Regression is displacement to an earlier time; splitting is the breaking up of one object into several (which gives us the multiple characters exploring different aspects of a theme, so characteristic of complex works of art). Symbolisation too – defined here as displacement from one thing to another based on some similarity between them – is a key defence, and leads to the non-neurotic defence of sublimation.

This complex system of ego-defences can be, rather loosely, equated with a range of literary devices, some linguistic, some plot-shaping. 'Irony looks like reversal or reaction-formation; omission looks like repression or denial; improbable causality in a story resembles projection; pointing a moral seems like rationalisation, and so on' (p.58). Other defences of some significance include what Holland calls the 'displacement to language', in which some of the fantasy conflicts are played out at the level of sound. More grandly, meaning itself can be a defence. It can be a transformation or sublimation of the unconscious fantasy embodied in the work; it can also be a disguise. We can be persuaded that we are engaged in a respectable intellectual exercise rather than a disgraceful indulgence in fantasy.

Recognising that not only the form, but the very meaning of a work may be no more than a psychological defence against the underlying fantasy embodied in it transforms our notion of what art is. But in psychoanalytic terms it is nothing that has not been implicit in the theory from a very early stage. Almost the whole of cultural life is, in psychoanalytic terms, a sublimation of sexual desire. That has always been recognised. But when we look at the Holland theory, we are looking at a plausible mechanism – the interaction of desire and defence – by which the process of sublimation can be carried out.

Holland makes no special mention of it, but it seems obvious that literary criticism too consists essentially of a system of ego-defences, mobilised against the impact of literature. Literary criticism is a more or less conscious system by which we transform our inchoate and often infantile responses to literature into something socially and ideologically acceptable in our particular society.

The basis of literary effect

Fantasy and form interact in literature in very complex ways. Early oral fantasy – the fantasy of oral fusion, of being dependent and sustained – has a very special role: it provides our basic attitude to literature itself, a temporary regression toward an unquestioning oral dependency that we sometimes call 'the willing suspension of disbelief'. This attitude is particularly marked when we are consuming popular or fantasy literature, and it has a role in our attitude to mythical structures whenever we recognise them in literature and see them as archetypal (Chapter 5). It is an effect of this oral attitude that we introject literature, so that its narratives appear to take place inside our own minds. But the fantasy structures so introjected are not themselves necessarily oral. They may be anal or Oedipal. And we do not lose higher ego functions – the ability to think and feel as adults about what we are reading – though our capacity to act physically is suspended.

Literary form mostly provides defence. Holland doesn't claim there is a one-to-one relationship between ego-defences and literary techniques; what he does claim is something more plausible and interesting: that the literary techniques exist in order to enable the reader to employ psychological defences to manage the fantasy material aroused by the work. A work of literature, when read, offers a managed fantasy – perhaps, more accurately, a complex of managed fantasies. Its final effect is not that of the simple underlying fantasies, but that of those fantasies defended against in complex ways. (*The Lord of the Rings* is a good example here.)

Literary effect will therefore vary, not only according to the fantasies that underlie a work, but to the strong or weak defences that are brought against them. Fantasies themselves are of more than one kind. Some, like oral fusion, or sexual gratification, or sadism, are drive-gratifying: they give pleasure in themselves, though they may arouse adverse reactions in the superego. (Anyone whose literary sensibility was formed by F.R. Leavis will have a built-in literary superego that reproaches him every time he takes simple pleasure in any of these, and takes much of the pleasure away. This is an example of the way in which literary criticism involves ego-defences that reduce the effect of literature.) The general point here is that strong ego-defences reduce the pleasure of drive-gratifying fantasies.

If a drive-gratifying fantasy is only weakly defended against, the pleasure of the work will be the pleasure proper to the drive itself. Thus, in pornography, images of sexual gratification are offered with little or no defence against them; and the result is straightforward erotic arousal. Similar sexual images embedded in a serious novel would bring into play all sorts of defences; arousal would be less. Similarly, as psychological experiments have shown, violence in films produces aggressive arousal. But violence in films that is justified by a plot structure, or the moral order of the work, and hence defended against, produces only muted aggressive arousal. I would add that in a thriller, the violence of male characters against female ones may offer a defence to the reader against erotic involvement, and become invisible. Pornography, representing consensual sex, is often denounced as violence against women; thrillers, in which women are torn to pieces by crazed killers, rarely are. Here, projection is at work. (See Chapter 8.)

Other fantasies, like the primal scene (the parents having intercourse) are for Holland anxiety-producing. Weak defences here would reduce the anxiety somewhat; strong ones can produce a positive effect, of what Holland calls 'reassurance through disillusion'. The effect of heavy defences against the disturbing fantasy may well end by providing a positive, reassuring effect. (This is the explanation, within Holland's system, for the ancient observation that when we read literature we may enjoy events that in life would be horrible. Such works over-defend against anxiety-producing fantasies.)

Holland accepts that the text does not and cannot completely manage the response of the reader. That is why the same piece may carry very different affect for different, equally competent readers. Readers may bring to bear personal defences of their own; if they dislike a film they may shut their eyes, or shut their mental eyes, however much the camera insists on seeing.

Transformations of the primal scene

Psychoanalytic interpretations are often thought of as whimsical and arbitrary. We need to ask, what are the grounds for postulating a particular fantasy underlying a particular work? They are in fact very similar to the grounds for postulating unconscious material on the basis of a patient's discourse. One postulates unconscious material when the discourse contains inexplicable gaps: when one cannot make sense out of what the patient says without it. This is what happens in the classic Freud/Ernest Jones interpretation of *Hamlet*. As Jones shows at enormous length, no one before in the whole history of criticism had understood *Hamlet*; but psychoanalysis did.

Our thesis must be that very often you cannot analyse a work, or grasp its coherence, until you realise what underlying fantasy is being defended against, and what psychological defences are being mobilised against that fantasy. Holland offers two examples of works which he claims are based on the primal scene fantasy. One example seems to me to work much better than the other. Holland quotes the soliloquy from *Macbeth*:

> Tomorrow, and tomorrow, and tomorrow
> Creeps on his petty pace from day to day,
> To the last syllable of recorded time,
> And all our yesterdays have lighted fools
> The way to dusty death. Out, out, brief candle.
> Life's but a walking shadow, a poor player
> Who struts and frets his hour upon the stage
> And then is heard no more. It is a tale
> Told by an idiot, full of sound and fury,
> Signifying nothing.

And he gives us John Crowe Ransom's argument that it is metaphysically incoherent. The speech moves illogically from metaphor to metaphor: '. . . the tomorrows creep along till they have crept far enough, and bring up against – what? A syllable; remarkable barrier. After the tomorrows, in the whirling sub-logical mind of this harried speaker, the yesterdays . . . Dramatically, this speech may be both natural and powerful; so I am told. Metaphysically, it is nothing.' Holland accepts this argument, and tries to show that the speech becomes a coherent poem once one reads it in terms of the primal-scene myth it defends against (Chap. 4, pp.106–14).

Obviously, this argument is less convincing if, like me, one finds this soliloquy to be a rigorously logical argument, translated into brilliant imagery. Macbeth's is a rational despair, not a neurotic one: by his own actions, full of sound and fury, he has constructed a life that signifies nothing, in which every tomorrow in an infinite succession up to the last syllable of the record of time will resemble every yesterday, and each of these will merely have been one day's light on the road to death. My analysis here is just a paraphrase of the original, because the literal meaning of the original already conveys most of the despair. The in-joke that compares the emptiness of Macbeth's life with that of a player – like Shakespeare himself or one of the actors – adds a wry bitterness that it would be insulting to call post-structuralist, though it is certainly self-referential.

It makes the play ludicrous to suggest that this speech is a defence, for character or reader, against a memory of Mummy and Daddy half-seen copulating. The poetry is in this case better without the Freudian interpretation.

Holland has, to my taste, far more success with a similar interpretation of Matthew Arnold's poem, *Dover Beach*. Here again we have an obviously very good, even very great, poem that seems at first sight to have colossal faults. The overt meaning of this poem is perfectly clear. It claims that with the loss of religious faith, all over the world, we are left without any stable moral basis for living; we must rely on personal fidelity in love. But if we put this schematic claim against Arnold's imagery, we might find the imagery mostly romantic afflatus, and the poem might seem bad.

> The *sea is calm tonight.*
> *The tide is full, the moon lies fair*
> *Upon the straits; – on the French coast, the light*
> *Gleams and is gone; the cliffs of England stand*
> *Glimmering and vast, out in the tranquil bay.*
> *Come to the window, sweet is the night air!*
> *Only, from the long line of spray*
> *Where the sea meets the moon-blanch'd land,*
> *Listen! You hear the grating roar*
> *Of pebbles which the waves draw back, and fling,*
> *At their return, up the high strand,*
> *Begin, and cease, and then again begin,*
> *With tremulous cadence slow, and bring*
> *The eternal note of sadness in.*
>
> *Sophocles long ago*
> *Heard it on the Aegean, and it brought*
> *Into his mind the turbid ebb and flow*
> *Of human misery; we*
> *Find also in the sound a thought,*
> *Hearing it by this distant northern sea.*
>
> *The Sea of Faith*
> *Was once, too, at the full, and round earth's shore*
> *Lay like the folds of a bright girdle furl'd.*
> *But now I only hear*
> *Its melancholy, long, withdrawing roar,*
> *Retreating, to the breath*
> *Of the night-wind, down the vast edges drear*
> *And naked shingles of the world.*

Ah, love, let us be true
To one another! for the world, which seems
To lie before us like a land of dreams
So various, so beautiful, so new,
Hath really neither joy, nor love, nor light,
Nor certitude, nor peace, nor help for pain;
And we are here as on a darkling plain
Swept with confused alarms of struggle and flight,
Where ignorant armies clash by night.

If we concentrate on the tremendous imagery we shall find at once a great horror and a great vision:

Its melancholy, long, withdrawing roar,
Retreating, to the breath
Of the night-wind, down the vast edges drear
And naked shingles of the world.

but we might find that the connection of this with the decline of Christianity in the period between the renaissance and the nineteenth century was purely intellectual, and the lines would become sentimental or theatrical. The poem would then illustrate rather well the kind of disconnection between intellect and feeling that Eliot called a 'dissociation of sensibility'.

But when we read the poem without trying to fix the meaning it seems both powerful and emotionally unified; one wouldn't change a word. Why is this? I take as my starting point Holland's superb psychoanalytic interpretation.[21] For Holland, as for me, this is a 'tremendously peaceful, gently melancholy' poem, which gives 'a feeling of almost sensual satisfaction' although it is about 'disillusionment, loss of faith, and despair'. The reason is that the poem offers a massive set of psychological defences. In each stanza, such a defence precedes, and neutralises, the psychological disturbance. The peace and beauty of the night, in which, it appears, two lovers are looking from a window out to France, and to the great cliffs of Dover bay, neutralise the 'eternal note of sadness' heard in the slow rhythm of the sea drawing back the pebbles and flinging them up the beach again and again. This note is distanced by the comparison with the very remote figure of Sophocles, at the same time as 'sadness' is strengthened to 'human misery'.

In the next stanza, in a superb leap of imagination (which Holland finds allegorical and schematic) this image is applied to the decline of religious belief. The bright enclosing fullness of the sea of faith offers a defence, surely inadequate, against the retreat where 'in the most pathetic lines of the poem he lets it roll off the edge of the earth in long slow vowels'. The full defence against this loss of faith is offered next: that the lovers should be true to one another; this is all that remains in a world which offers no real joy, love, light, certitude, peace or help for pain, and can only be compared with the most terrible and confused of military disasters. (Arnold had in mind the night battle in the Athenian war in Sicily, though he doesn't make this explicit.)

In my summary the poem sounds disjointed; it is united by its tone, and by underlying sexual imagery. Holland sees the cliffs as vast breasts and the sea and air as nurturing fluids. 'The bright girdle is removed and we are left with naked shingles . . . the "Begin and cease, and then again begin" has become a naked clash by night.' For Holland, in this poem, the central focus of neurotic disturbance is an unconscious primal scene fantasy: 'heard but not seen naked fighting by night'; and it is this threat that is managed by the rhetorical defences that the poem supplies. It would be easy to argue that Holland goes way beyond his evidence here; it is Holland, not Arnold, who makes the clash by night 'naked' or 'sexual'. But I am perfectly prepared to believe his claim. The theory Holland is using predicts that any such reference would be deeply concealed. This interpretation makes the poem into a unified study of love and sexuality instead of an inconsequent darting about between landscape, religion and war, and goes some way to explain its power.

What is unsatisfactory, I think, is something that belongs to Freudian theory itself, with its obsessive concentration on infantile fantasy. The conception of the primal scene here is that of the uncomprehending infant's view of the father and mother coupling, which in the theory leads to vast neurotic disturbances. I doubt very strongly that any species could have evolved in which such a natural sight led inevitably to later dysfunctions. On the other hand, when there are complex culturally produced taboos on sexuality, as in Victorian and most other times, such early experiences may be viewed with a peculiar retrospective horror. What I am suggesting here is that it is not merely the unconscious memory of infantile fantasies about sexuality once observed but not understood that is being evoked in the last lines of the poem. It is sexual intercourse itself.

What the last three lines of the poem say, at the overt level which Arnold and his first readers would have recognised, is that being alive is like a confused and disastrous night operation. On the unconscious level it is sexual intercourse which is like being 'on a darkling plain/swept by confused alarms of struggle and flight/where ignorant armies clash by night'. (The comparison of sexual intercourse to combat with weapons by night is immemorially old; the comparison of the body of the beloved to an army with banners goes back to *The Song of Songs*.) Arnold's lines are, unconsciously, an account of the emotions accompanying sexual intercourse, where fidelity is not assured. They strike me as an accurate metaphorical description, at least of our sexual fears, and certainly of the sexual experience of many women and some men. At the conscious level, the fidelity of lovers is a small but brave consolation for the confused instability of the world. At the unconscious level, the fidelity of lovers is a real remedy against the neurotic fears surrounding sexual intercourse.

Holland submerged in a post-structuralist flood

For all its occasional clumsiness of detail, *The Dynamics of Literary Response* still seems to me the best psychoanalytic account ever given of how works of literature work on the reader. In its complexity, its detail and its confidence, the system clearly belongs to an age in which one could still be confident in psychoanalysis as an empirical science; and Holland went on, as in what Kuhn called 'normal science', to do empirical research in reader response, as in his book, *5 Readers Reading*. If psychoanalysis were a genuine empirical science, and his branch of literary theory an application of it, one would have expected serious progress over the next thirty years. In science, certain knowledge is not to be had; the most elaborate and satisfactory theories remain ultimately merely our best current conjecture. On the other hand, an established scientific theory is not lightly to be overthrown. It is more than a bright idea, and different from a metaphysical position. It is something which already accounts for a great deal of the relevant data; and one will only abandon it if one has a better theory that accounts for more. In scientific terms, one would expect some psychoanalytic theory like that of Holland to dominate the field nowadays – if psychoanalysis were a science.

There is therefore considerable pathos in Holland's book of 1992, *The Critical I*, in which he both pays his respects to modern cognitive theory, and does his best to take account of the mainstream of modern post-structuralist criticism, even adopting a very mild version of post-structuralist literary form. One of his targets is the pervasive literary formalism of these newest of New Critics ('New Cryptics', he calls them) in which texts are said to read or interact with other texts, as if without the intervention of any human mind: an approach which of course obviates the need for any psychological theory at all. He blames this approach partly on the adoption of Saussure's model of language, in which signifier and signified hold together without a mind to exist in. He is rightly appalled by the way in which literary critics, faced with a linguistics dominated by Chomsky, retreat 70 years to the ideas of Saussure. But the central problem that he has is that the field he is working in is, on the whole, not engaged in scientific activity of any kind.

Holland does what he can with a world in which the majority of critics reject the scientific paradigm altogether, and those critics who use psychoanalytic terminology are influenced mainly by French rhetorical philosophy. But since his arguments are, in the last resort, scientific ones, based on evidence, he has little hope of carrying conviction in a world of loud-mouthed mystics.

What is to be done with the traditional Freudian theory of literature?

It would be easy to fill this book, as many books have been filled, with psychoanalytic interpretations based on classical theories of psychoanalysis. That is not the problem. The problem is that every time one offers a psycho-analytic interpretation of a work of literature, one is making a tacit commit-ment to some version of psychoanalysis. But as we have seen, it is getting increasingly difficult to believe that psychoanalysis is true. For a hundred years psychoanalysts have been in business, but the theories still seem to rest on ideological interpretations of inadequately published case studies by people with a prior commitment to the theories concerned. Meanwhile, academic psychology, in its new guise as cognitive studies, is providing steadily more convincing alternative explanations of mental activities. The honest literary critic has to ask himself: what happens if I come to believe in none of the claims of psychoanalysis? What is the status of a psychoanalytic literary critical interpretation then?

There is a large class of critics for whom this will pose no problem at all. These are the critics who believe in an infinite plurality of interpretations, and make no claim that any interpretation is true. For them, a psychoanalytic interpretation is simply a bit of twentieth century writing which draws on certain classic twentieth century texts – the texts of psychoanalysis – and bounces them off other texts – the texts under interpretation. No factual claims are being made – particularly not claims about the universal features of the human mind. We are dealing with an intertextual phenomenon. On the same principles, one doesn't need to make Marxist claims when one is offering a Marxist interpretation. One is simply bouncing a literary text off a text by Marx. On the same principles one could offer criticism of the school of Jung or W.B. Yeats or Nostradamus, or Christian or Islamic inter-pretations – there are many of them – or on the principles of Leavis or Addison or Hitler or Malcolm X. There is nothing wrong with any of these approaches – how could there possibly be? – and no sound argument against using them. Let a million flowers bloom.

The only objection to this approach is that literary theory as an enter-prise collapses. The point of literary theory is not to generate endless interpretations. It is to explain the nature and functioning of works of literature. Why does literature exist? What is its relation to other human institutions, like religion or marriage? How does a work of literature affect a reader? Whether you call these questions scientific or not, they all have one thing in common. They all relate literature to something other than literature – the mind, the economy, general anthropology, or whatever. They can't be answered simply by bouncing one text off another to produce yet another interpretation. The million flowers approach may look liberal, welcoming and humanistic to some; and radical, revolutionary and anti-humanist to others. I find it obfuscatory. Psychoanalytic theories of literature are interesting because they claim to explain how, at a very deep level of mental functioning, literature works. Million flowers people are not interested in such explanations; or at least, not interested in determining whether they are true. Psychoanalytic interpretations are interesting because they bear on the truth of psychoanalytic claims about the human mind. Million flowers people have nothing very interesting to say about the human mind except that it should be called the subject, and that it has been decentred.

An alternative conclusion, which seems to me much more interesting and honest, is to say that if psychoanalysis is false, psychoanalytic interpretations are of no interest and we should stop making them. After all, even in the hey-day of psychoanalysis, most literary critics did not use it as an approach. The overwhelming majority of interpretations, even of *Hamlet*, are non-psychoanalytic. The study of literature will not cease just because psychoanalysis is untrue. This position is not only honest: it is also theoretically productive. For it provokes us to ask: are we really willing to do without psychoanalytic interpretations? I could easily live without the interpretation of Macbeth as a complex disguise for a vision of the primal scene. But I would not in fact be happy to lose the Oedipal interpretation of *Hamlet* – not, at any rate, unless I found another general theory that better explained the critical history Jones discusses. I would not in fact be happy to rely solely on the sociological account of Paul Morel's problems: I think this novel is a study of the psychological effects of a mother taking her sons as, metaphorically, lovers: and so, come to think of it, did Lawrence. I think a psychoanalytic account – even if not exactly Holland's version – captures perfectly the evasion of sexuality that is at the heart of Arnold's poem. Neither Kipling nor Thomas Mann need Freud to tell them about concealed sexual symbolism. But they powerfully confirm his insights into sexuality. And, once having noticed it, I cannot imagine the strength of critical argument needed to make me give up the account of *The Lord of the Rings* as a castration fantasy.

If it really is the case that we cannot do without some psychoanalytic interpretations, then this has important consequences for the theory. The main consequence is, that it is overwhelmingly likely that the theory itself contains some truth. Literary interpretations, responsibly made, are actually evidence for Freudian theory. Indeed, since a literary interpretation is a matter of public debate, by people uncommitted to the theory as well as people committed to it, it provides better evidence for the theory than clinical interpretations do – for clinical interpretations are provided on the basis of a one-to-one relationship that is not a matter of public record, and are made by people who have been brainwashed for life into believing the theory, and who would have to resign from their professional associations if they came to disbelieve in it. We literary critics have no professional commitment whatever to any form of psychoanalysis; so if we can't do without it, maybe there is something in it. It seems very odd, after a hundred years of clinical work, that we might have to rest the case for psychoanalysis on Hamlet's words to his mother, on Frodo's nine fingers, and on the smile of Ortheris. But that may be the way of it.

Of course, even this we cannot do without looking at alternative theories of dynamic psychology that might account better for the literary evidence. High on the candidate list are the works of Jung and Lacan.

Notes and references

Suggestions for further reading are on page 213.

1. **Wilson**, 1952. See Chapter 7 below for post-structuralist discussion by Felman, and for questions about the notion of 'applying' Freudian theory by Spivak.
2. Cf **Ellenberger**, 1970, Chap. I.
3. **Aristotle**, 4th century BCa.
4. **Felman**, 1977a, 1980. See Chapter 7 below.
5. The first, I think, was a rather biologistic one by Marie Bonaparte in her study *Edgar Poe, Sa Vie – Son Oeuvre* in 1933. This is part of the subtext of Lacan's and Derrida's contributions. The whole issue is studied in **Muller and Richardson**, 1988, who reprint much of all three.
6. Five Platonic dialogues that bear on poetic inspiration are *Ion, Symposium, Meno, Phaedo, Phaedrus* (collected in **Plato** 'a'). On the Socratic question – which doctrines are those of Socrates, which are Plato's doctrines put in Socrates' mouth – start with **Ferguson**, 1970.
7. See **Klein, Heimann and Money-Kyrle**, Chaps 14 and 15 and **H.J.C. Grierson**, *Metaphysical Lyrics and Poems of the Seventeenth Century* (1921) (Oxford: O.U.P.) for John Hoskins' poem.
8. As one might expect, post-structuralists are hostile to this valuable quality of mainstream realist novels. For the case against, see **Roland Barthes**, 1970, *S/Z*; **Catherine Belsey**, 1980, *Critical Practice*.

9. *Seminaire XXIII, Le sinthome*, 1975–6. See **Nobus** (ed.) pp.64–70 (by **Russell Grigg**) and pp.156–7 (by **Luke Thurston**).

10. London: Hogarth Press, p.88.

11. Mills and Boon – a publishing firm which has achieved legendary status for escapist romances for women.

12. Orestes and Electra are brother and sister: Orestes avenges his father Agamemnon by killing his mother Clytemnestra and her lover Aegisthus; Electra helps him.

13. *All's Well that Ends Well.*

14. **Ariosto**, *Orlando Furioso* (Harington's translation is best fun); **Edmund Spenser**, *The Faerie Queene*; **William Shakespeare**, *Venus and Adonis*; **Wycherley**, *The Country Wife*; **Fielding**, *Tom Jones*.

15. This is not true of all eighteenth century works. There is more interior space in Lovelace in *Clarissa*. And the hero of **Goldsmith's** *She Stoops to Conquer* is virtually a case study in the 'young man who is only potent with serving girls' from Freud's paper 'The Commonest Source of Degradation in the Erotic Life' – save that we don't meet his mother.

16. **A.B. Kuttner**, 1916.

17. **Sigmund Freud**, 1912; in Penguin Freud Vol. 7, *On Sexuality*, under title: 'On the Universal Tendency to Debasement in the Sphere of Love'. The other title, which I prefer, comes from Joan Riviere's translation in the 'Collected Papers', 1925.

18. I.e. except in literal references to castration. **Wycherley's** Horner is mentioned above; **Lawrence Sterne's** *Tristram Shandy*, in the novel of that name, has a window fall on the relevant part, at least circumcising him; **Honoré de Balzac's** short story *Sarrasine* is about the castrato, La Zambinella; Origen the Christian father, worried by sexual temptation, took the most obvious means to end it.

19. **Elizabeth Smart**, 1991, p.19 (London: Paladin).

20. The periodic table in chemistry is a two-dimensional table on which the chemical elements are arranged roughly in order of atomic weight (precisely, in order of atomic number) in a repeating, or periodic, fashion; the chemical properties of each element correspond very accurately to its position in the table, and if an element is missing from the table, as some were when it was first constructed, it is possible to predict its properties. The emergence of the periodic table was one of the greatest triumphs of nineteenth century chemical theory. Later on, it led to an understanding of atomic structure. Holland's tables, if his theory were true, would belong in a predictive science of this hard kind.

21. **Holland**, 1968, pp.115–33.

Chapter 5

Instinct, archetype and symbol

Summary

Jung is widely seen as an uncontrolled religious speculator, but can easily be rescued for cognitive science. Following commentators like Anthony Stevens and perhaps Andrew Samuels rather than anti-scientists like James Hillman, one can interpret the 'collective unconscious' as the biological basis of mind, and the archetypes as human instincts which structure our responses to the world and our actions in it. Archetypal images correspond to the 'specific releasers' in lower species which, ethologists say, trigger 'fixed action patterns'. In human beings they trigger archetypal patterns either of action or fantasy. The emotional effect of literature thus arises because it supplies images that trigger archetypal fantasy. This version of Jung fits better with cognitive studies than Freud does.

Jung himself made extensive explorations of literature and mythology, as well as some picturesque non-literary writing like the work of the alchemists, to produce a vast but unsystematic catalogue of archetypes identified by images and mythological figures. Jungian criticism is strong at the biological and the mythological level, but weak at history and politics. It works by identifying archetypal content not merely in openly mythical work like that of the romantics, but in disguised form in apparently realist novels. I here consider an archetypal account of works of literature in general, and look at the special case of hero-myths.

Archetypes, stereotypes and complexes: rethinking Jung

The great strength of Jungian theory is that it is rooted both in biology and in mythology. Its great weakness is that it sometimes confuses the two.

We hear from Jung of a 'collective unconscious' filled with archetypes inherited from the dawn of human culture, and represented by mythological figures. Whatever this is, it does not sound much like psychological science. Yet it can in fact be reformulated to provide a much more satisfactory hard scientific framework for psychology than that of Freud.

Jungian biology

Modern Jungian theory is, or can be, rooted in biology, because its basic concepts, the archetype and the archetypal image, are the subjective correlates of the fundamental concepts of the science of animal behaviour, ethology. Lower animals – wasps, or leaf-cutting insects, to use Jung's own example – display fixed patterns of behaviour, which are elicited by a specific stimulus. So fixed is a wasp's behaviour, that if it is disturbed in the middle of building a nest, it has to go back to the beginning and start again. Animals higher up the evolutionary ladder show much more variation within a more generalised action pattern; they can learn to do things differently, and they can start again in the middle of a sequence; and they can recognise a wider variety of stimuli as specific releasers. At the highest levels, animals like lions or dogs do not merely behave, they act intelligently: they spend time thinking what to do; a stimulus leads directly not to action but to fantasy – imagined action – which in turn may lead to real action.

Human beings are obviously more versatile than any other animal; they not only formulate possible actions in fantasy before performing them, but can describe them in language and discuss them with others. Jung knew nothing of modern linguistic science, but language illustrates rather well the distinction between the biological, cultural and individual levels of behaviour. Language acquisition is a biological instinct peculiar to human beings; if you are born human, you have it, if you are born a chimpanzee, with a very similar genome, you don't. It is much more than an unstructured drive to speak: it amounts to a tacit knowledge that in order to speak one must put together items of vocabulary according to the principles of rules of grammar. Specifications of the universal features common to all possible human languages appear to be inscribed in the brain, and that is what makes it possible for children to pick up languages so quickly. In neo-Jungian terms, one might say that we all possess the archetype of language.[1]

An individual language, however, is not a biological but a social fact; a set of vocabulary items and grammatical principles which have to be learnt from earlier speakers by an astonishing process in which the child unconsciously infers what grammatical principles his elders are using from the things they say. A young child, possessing, or being possessed by, the archetype of language, has no difficulty in picking up one or even several of these complex systems, which then become the foundation of the child's own spontaneous discourse. An individual person can then express himself freely, making up entirely new expressions in any language that he knows, and be immediately understood by any speaker of that language, since those new expressions will be constructed on familiar principles. The principles of construction of the language enable him to construct representations of complex concepts; others who know these principles of construction can decode these representations; so the complex concepts can become public property and part of the culture.

It is possible to argue that this is a perfectly general case, covering all human behaviour. Whether we are dealing with hunting, fighting, sex, child-rearing or whatever, we expect to see in-built instinctual or archetypal structures, which act as a framework for socially defined learnt practices, which in turn make possible free human action.

The archetype, on this interpretation, is a generalised action pattern. The archetypal image, where it exists, corresponds to the 'specific releaser' for that pattern – that is, to the stimulus, specified by the animal's nervous system, which sets that action pattern going. To take the least controversial case and put it in behaviorist terms: the baby, at the mother's breast, produces appetitive behaviour it has never learnt, for which the breast is a specific releaser. But this behaviorist language is not very appropriate for human beings, because it misses out subjective and emotional elements. A Jungian way to say this might be to say that the baby is born possessing the archetype of the great mother which the real mother then embodies; and the breast is the archetypal image. Cultural learning then sets in; and this will determine the final form the concept of the mother and the breast will take within the culture.

In behaviourist terms again, the mother responds to the baby at the breast with a repertory of caring behaviour she has never learnt (as well as a great deal she has). This description again pointedly ignores the subjective side, and the emotional side, of the mother's 'behaviour'. A Jungian way to say this might be to say that she already carries within her an archetypal system for recognising her baby and responding appropriately to it; the real baby's form and behaviour triggers off this system, since it corresponds to the pre-existing generalised image of a baby which is specified by the archetype. Of course, an immense amount of cultural learning has already taken place which affects the mother's concept of her baby.

To be biologically satisfactory, a full-scale Jungian system has to specify archetypes and archetypal images that correspond to the major instinctual patterns found in human beings, and also to specify the stages of life at which those instincts develop. (The instincts of a baby are not the same as those of an adult mother; they have to be complementary in order to mesh together in a working mother–baby system.) One possible major set of these is the **five major affectional systems**, proposed by the Harlows in 1965 for non-human primates, quoted sympathetically for human beings by the psychoanalytic child development specialist John Bowlby, 1969, and repeated by Anthony Stevens, a biologically oriented Jungian, in 1982.[2] In addition to the two systems mentioned above – the **infant–mother** system, which integrates the baby's responses to the mother, and the **maternal** system which integrates the mother's responses to the baby – they suggest there is a **peer** system, in which affectional bonds are developed – it involves much exploratory behaviour, and may involve promiscuity – a **heterosexual** system, whose success may depend on the success of earlier bonds, and a **paternal** system.

It is an interesting characteristic of these instinctive affectional systems that, though clearly distinguishable analytically, they also interact with each other; for example, gestures from the infant–mother and maternal systems will turn up as indications of fondness in the heterosexual system. Lovers 'baby' each other. Equally, if one extends the peer system into adult life as the dominance–hierarchy system, then gestures of dominance and submission turn up as indications of power relationships – invariably the power of male over female – in the heterosexual system. Men bully women, and women meekly give way to men. Furthermore, gestures from sexual behaviour – e.g. mounting – are found in the dominance system. Dominant males in male assemblies (like human prisons) often treat other males as female, by sodomising them.

If we accept that there are archetypes and archetypal images corresponding to each instinctual system, we would expect to see a complex interaction of these, providing a basic instinctually given vocabulary for quite complex animal and human experiences – indeed, providing a specification for the full range of possible instinctually given experiences. Complex social experience – whether or not elaborated through language – will necessarily be built upon this archetypal base, and the possibilities of complex social experience will be limited by the archetypes in innumerable ways, which will not necessarily be available to conscious introspection. Whether we like it or not, we all live in worlds defined by the archetypes; we are conscious of the world through them, though we are not conscious of the archetypes themselves.

Jung himself did not build his system on biological research, though he was well aware of it. His own proposals for the archetypes are based on purely psychological evidence; he inferred the archetypes from their images in experience (which are indeed the only way in which we can become conscious of them as they function) and sometimes wrote as if the archetype and the archetypal image are the same. In the next section, I give a brief account of the system of archetypes that can be extracted from Jung's work; it has to be said that it is fairly extensive, obviously incomplete, not particularly systematic, and I don't defend it in detail.

But whatever one thinks of the detail of Jung's own system, his fundamental concepts, interpreted in a biological way, complete the work of the ethologist and weld *homo sapiens* firmly into the natural order. The theory enables one to think of human beings as animals driven by instincts to perform (or to fantasise) within a limited set of generalised action patterns, just like all the other animals save in having greater intelligence and the use of language. At the same time it fully recognises the subjective nature of the instincts, and their feeling-tone, and the possibility of fulfilling instinctual pressures not in action, but in fantasy, by going through some rudimentary narrative in the head. It thus provides a foundation for a theory of the primary processes – that is, of the pre-verbal, pre-rational processes – of human thought, and makes certain types of fiction a natural part of these processes. That is what any theory of the arts needs as a foundation; nothing else will do.

Jungian mythology

It is the special mark of a Jungian theory to be rooted in mythology as well as in biology. A Jungian theory is rooted in mythology because the basic therapeutic process that is peculiar to Jungians is a process of **active imagination**, in which the fragmentary images from dreams or elsewhere are filled out from the vast mythological store of the world. The archetype, for Jungians, is abstract and ungraspable, since it is what we grasp the world through.[3] The archetypal image is concrete and mythological; it is what we are conscious of, and what we infer the archetype from. It is easy to see why the archetypal image should be concrete. For any animal, the releaser for a fixed action pattern must be something which is encountered in ordinary experience, and which the animal is wired up to recognise as the appropriate object for instinctual behaviour. Thus it is easy to understand why the archetypal image for the male sexual instinct should be the female body, or some isolated secondary sexual characteristic such as large breasts, or the whole female offering gestures of invitation, while that for male aggression is that of another male in aggressive action as enemy or friend.

But why should the image be mythological? Why should it be Venus or Mars? The answer seems to be because human beings, in all societies and in all periods, are innate fantasisers. They are also innate craftsmen. They imagine the ideal sexual object long before, and very much more often than, they meet a real woman who embodies it. They make representations of the ideal sexual object, in stone, in celluloid, in song and in words; they do this in all human societies which do not make strong laws against it; and they have done so since the palaeolithic era. When, in late Roman times, Venus disappears from the official pantheon of the West, she remains for fifteen hundred years as an essential poetic fiction. When in the twentieth century she disappears altogether from the culture of the uneducated, she is replaced by a changing pantheon of film stars and pop-stars, who retain her essentially mythological quality. A similar story could be told of the warrior hero, who has evolved from similar divine or legendary figures into a similar pop pantheon of Bonds and Rambos.[4]

It seems to be an innate property of human beings, when they dream about aggressive action or sex, to do so by identification with the actions of fantasy figures.

Mythology, for the Jungian, is a fairly direct product of the collective unconscious – which, on the scientific interpretation of Jungian theory, means that it is a fairly direct product of the biologically determined structure of the brain. This means that it ought to be possible to identify at least elements of the myths with specific instinctual patterns of human action or development. But mythology is also the raw material of the world's literature and art. Jungian theory thus provides the foundation for a plausible naturalistic theory of much of the basic material of literature and the arts. Whether this extends to a full theory of artistically finished works is another matter. It clearly leaves out the whole complex interaction with society and culture which is a major part of the genesis of each work and of the history of the arts as a whole – and indeed, as we shall see, a major part of the genesis of mythology itself.

Jungians would certainly accept that culture is responsible for most of the superficial social properties of every human being, including many aspects of the masculine and feminine roles. But the distinctive contribution of the theory is to say very firmly that collective consciousness is rooted in the collective unconscious; and that collective consciousness is veined through and through with the products of the collective unconscious, of which mythological motifs, as the representatives of the archetypes, are not the least important part. It thus represents not a contradiction of ordinary cultural theory, but a fundamental critique and transformation of it. Modern cultural theory is often desperately shallow. It is cut off at once from biology and from the universal significance of mythology. Cultural theory in a Jungian framework has greater depth.

On the other hand there are obvious defects in a psychological theory with so little interest in the detailed life of current society, and so great an interest in mythology, folk-tale and legend. The picture of human life that it provides is often that of an archaic but highly coloured pageant, in which individuals who have no significant historical location or economic function enact timeless roles as hero, trickster, divine child, maiden, wise old man, and so forth. A modern man or woman – whether a patient in real life, or a character in a realist novel – is thus transformed into a whole set of characters from a fairy-tale. Jungian therapy indeed can work on precisely this basis; the patient may enter into collusive play with the analyst to see himself in just such fairy-tale roles, rather than the boring and commonplace social ones – middle manager, suburban husband – that he enacts in real life.

One can call this 'actualising the archetypes within'; and this may actually be true, if Jungian theory is true: therapy may be achieved by reconnecting the individual with the archetypes, which are the subjective aspect of his own instincts, and thus represent the only teleology, the only purpose in life, that he can have. One might, on the other hand, think of this as a way of escaping from contemporary realities, into a world of regressive fantasy. And one might think of literary criticism based on this approach as a way of escaping from the realist text, and constructing a bad romantic one in its stead; again, of turning literature into regressive fantasy.

What casts doubt upon the Jungian view that the archetypes are timeless is that it seems to be a product of Jung's ahistorical approach to mythology. Religions – including the pagan religions that are the original source of mythologies – often claim to embody and reveal timeless truths; but they are actually cultural phenomena deeply rooted in the life of particular societies at particular periods. In *The Greek Myths*, Robert Graves puts the point sharply: '. . . the historical and anthropological approach is the only reasonable one: the theory that Chimaera, Sphinx, Gorgon, Centaurs, Satyrs, and the like are blind uprushes of the collective unconscious, to which no precise meaning had ever, or could ever, have been attached is demonstrably unsound. The Bronze and Early Iron Ages in Greece were not the childhood of mankind, as Dr Jung suggests.' And Graves goes on to point out that even an apparently extravagant myth like the birth of Athene from Zeus's head has a political meaning: the Achaean conquerors suppressed the cult of Metis, Goddess of Wisdom, but tolerated that of Athene, her daughter, provided it was recognised as subordinate to that of their own God, Zeus.[5]

I have already spoken of Venus as if she were the timeless product of a collective imagination; and she is indeed the most obvious example of a direct metaphor for a timeless instinct: sex. But she could just as well be seen as an obvious example of historical change. Aphrodite, in Ancient Greece, was a genuine Goddess with temples, rituals, priests and priestesses; her literary appearances – her drive-on part in *The Iliad*, and the force of her presence in the *Hippolytus*, for example – were minor aspects of her being. Venus, in Roman times, was a more artificial and literary figure, though still a real Goddess, and supposed to be a version of Aphrodite; educated Romans had adopted the principle that their own pantheon ought to be a version of the Greek pantheon, though their original religious customs were rather different from those of the Greeks. In the later, Christian phase of the Roman Empire and in the Middle Ages, Venus was no longer a goddess and ought to have become a demon – instead, she became a figure of speech, an allegory of sexual desire; the dependence of love on sexuality was shown by the myth that the God of love, Cupid, was her son. (And the capriciousness of love was shown by his being a blind archer, shooting arrows at random.) In modern times, Venus has disappeared altogether, save as a character in old books, and been replaced in her role of erotic ideal by a scattered showbiz iconography.

On the other hand, one cannot deny that there is a continuity-in-difference in the use of myth throughout history. Literature of all periods, from pretty well all societies, is seamed through and through with mythological and legendary references, which often play a deep structural role. It isn't merely a matter of openly mythological works, like *Paradise Lost* or Wagner's *Ring*. At the height of bourgeois realism, we have a Henry James carefully letting us know which of his characters we should regard as a princess,[6] or a wise old king reigning in Gardencourt.[7] T.S. Eliot based *The Waste Land* on the myth of the impotent king and his barren land, and left endnotes explaining what he'd done; Lawrence based *Lady Chatterley's Lover* on the same myth without explaining it. Eliot thought Joyce's use of myth in Ulysses had the force of a scientific discovery!

There is nothing regressive or escapist about any of these works, and the mythic dimension seems in each case to be offering something profound or even numinous. It is not at all obvious that it is biological. Most authors think of their mythical references as essentially cultural ones. In the study of literature it would be possible to regard all uses of myth, however deep, as intertextual reference and cultural metaphor, going back eventually to bodies of ancient mythology investigated by the methods Graves recommends. What this doesn't explain, and Jungian theory may, is the evocative and intellectual powers of the the myths themselves. The question to be answered, after all, is not 'What is the connection between the myth shared by *The Waste Land* and *Lady Chatterley's Lover* and ancient vegetation rites?' It is 'Why has the myth survived down all these centuries when the ancient vegetation rites have not?' Or possibly: 'Why are we moved nowadays by literature built around this ancient myth?' The answer that Jungian theory gives is that the origin and the appeal of the myth are to be found in the same place: in the structure of the human mind. And the myth has survived down the centuries and the millennia because in each generation it has meshed with the same mental structure. Myth tells us the fundamental structure of the human mind. It is a large, and as yet undetermined, but not irrational, claim.

The system of Carl Jung

Archetypes and the collective unconscious; complexes and the individual unconscious

The major part of the mind is not only unconscious but common to all human beings; it consists of **archetypes** – essentially general frameworks for the reception, production and analysis of experience, and action upon it. An archetype is – on the harder, more scientific interpretation of Jung's work – the subjective side of a biological instinct. (On the less scientific view it is the deposit of immemorial cultural and historical experience – but this would commit one to Lamarckian inheritance theory.) Around these archetypes develop clusters of ideas developed from individual experiences, and largely unconscious. Jung called these **complexes**. A complex may have a large degree of independence; it can sometimes behave like an inner sub-personality.

Because the archetypes are the general framework of experience itself, we cannot directly experience them. Nor can we directly experience the complexes built round them, since these are what make up parts of the mind that does the experiencing. But we can discern these complexes by their effects. For example, in some of Jung's earliest work, he devised a word association test. A long hesitation time on particular words in the test gave a clue to the presence of a **feeling-toned complex of ideas**, which was influencing response, unknown to the conscious ego.

A more general way of getting in touch with complexes and the archetypes underlying them is through characteristic images, mediated to us below the rational level of analysis, in dreams and also in mythology. Jung did not distinguish sharply between an archetype and the associated images till quite late in his work – 1946 – but the distinction is obviously theoretically essential; the archetype is a way of processing experience which we all inherit; an image is the way an individual becomes conscious of the operation of an archetype; it is, as it were, specified by the archetype. Archetypes may also emerge into the individual life in two other ways: an individual may be possessed by some archetype, and experience it intensely as part of his self. Or the archetype may be projected onto some other individual or entity. The notions of possession by an archetype and projection of an archetype are important in explaining everything from joining the Nazi party to falling in love.

Comment: Jung's basic claim has something in common with the positions of Plato, and of Kant. It is very difficult to disagree with it from a modern cognitive viewpoint. It is tempting to say 'How else could one possibly design a mind?' It can't be a blank sheet; it has to have preprocessing systems and preset action sequences built in by evolution before it starts learning, and the nature of these will characterise all later experience, all learning and all actions. Thus the basic Chomskian claim is simply that the mind contains an archetype of language, which in this case would be a set of general principles for the construction of linguistic expressions, to which any object recognisable as a language must conform. One would also expect the mind to contain some archetype of the material world, specifying ways of treating material objects; and archetypes of human others, perhaps specialised into mother and father archetypes, specifying responses to them. Without these bits of built-in preprogramming, it is difficult to see how human babies get so variously competent as quickly as they do.

There is, however, a considerable gulf between many of these cognitive archetypes which form the necessary nuts-and-bolts of mind, and the romantic images in which Jung trades. If a Jungian were asked what he would expect to find as the archetypal image of language, he would probably exercise a process of active imagination, trawl through the mythology of the world, and come up with the god Hermes – simply because the Greeks, at one particular stage in the history of the world, assigned the language function to him. A scientific psycholinguist would find this a queer way to look for a specific releaser for the in-built language acquisition device, and would be tempted to ignore the notion of archetypal image altogether. But in fact there **are** specific releasers for language acquisition. The human voice is one; communicative gestures are another. And if you reread literature and mythology in the light of that observation, you do indeed find that the voice is a world-wide symbol of thought and language. Much of the philosophy of Derrida is devoted to deploring various metaphysical delusions which he supposes to flow from this phenomenon, which he has christened 'phonocentrism'.[8] (I wonder if Derrida would be amused to find himself enrolled as a supporter of Jung.)

It seems likely that other cognitive frameworks which are in-built into the mind – Kant's favourite, three-dimensional space, for example – also develop in response to specific experiences: in this case, to the experience of physical objects. The emotional life too requires the presence of human objects, or perhaps part-objects. The archetypal image that releases one of the baby's earliest behaviour patterns is the breast; and there is nothing implausible in the Freudian and Kleinian attempts to show how funda-mental structures of feeling are first built up around this image.

There is an obvious gap in Jung's theory. The archetype is a biological inheritance; the complex an individual acquisition. Where do we put the social? Many systems of ideas and feelings are derived from typical situ-ations in our society; they are not individual, and feel universal. But observa-tions of other societies show that they are not biological. Because Jung does not work seriously with this category, he is always tempted to call things archetypes which are actually social or cultural stereotypes. This makes the theory politically conservative, since changes in these stereotypes – for example, in the stereotype of men and women – would be impossible if they were biologically given archetypes. In my view the only way to make Jungian theory a viable system would be to incorporate the category of cul-tural **stereotype** explicitly, to fall between genuinely universal archetype and individual complex. But this has not been done.

Specific archetypes

The empirical strength or weakness of any archetype theory turns on its claims for what the archetypes are, and what particular features of human perception and behaviour they explain. The following list is taken from Hopcke, 1989, checked against Jung, and slightly rearranged for my con-venience. A hostile critic will notice that there is a good deal of redundancy and overlapping, and the boundaries between archetypes are often unclear. I wouldn't disagree.

Ego, shadow, persona and self

There are several archetypes concerned directly with the organisation of the self. There is an archetype of wholeness as an organising principle, which Jung labels the **self**; in principle it presumably corresponds to the whole set of complexes that make up the mind, along with a directed purposefulness that unifies them, and makes possible a process of individuation (see below). There is also for each individual a complex of self-representations. Jung calls this the **ego**. There are unpleasant or immoral aspects of the self, which are repressed or denied. They form the **shadow**. There is a part of the personality which acts as mediator or mask; it is developed specifically for playing parts – roles – in the outer world: the **persona**.

Logos and Eros; masculine and feminine; animus and anima

Logos and **Eros** are the **masculine** principle of knowledge and the **feminine** principle of relatedness respectively. One of the useful effects of feminism has been to show that this is an arbitrary association, not a God-given identity. (As Hopcke points out, mythology doesn't support Jung here: Eros is a god, and Sophia, the logos as wisdom, is a goddess.) We clearly have social stereotyping at work. On the face of it, it continues strongly in the **syzygy archetype, animus/anima**. Each sex is supposed to have a secondary complex built of the qualities it has rejected: in men, the repressed feminine functions form the **anima**; in women, the repressed masculine functions form the **animus**. When one reads one of the classic accounts of animus/ anima – for example Emma Jung's[9] – it appears entirely bound by the social values of the day. The man possessed by his anima is illogical and confused; the woman possessed by her animus is obsessive and argumentative. In fact, however, the theory can readily be given a feminist rereading. On this view, animus and anima are socially created when each sex is compelled to repress qualities which conventionally belong to the other. Jung, encouraging patients of each sex to become acquainted with the qualities they have suppressed, is reversing this conventionalising social process. He's a feminist.

Mother and father; puer aeternus/divine child and kore/maiden; hero, trickster and wise old man

The archetypal image of the **mother** is one that Jung constantly works over, as if, Hopcke suggests, to compensate for the patriarchal emphasis of our culture, or perhaps of Freud. She is present in earth mothers, sky mothers, fertility goddesses, dark mothers who 'swallow, clutch, devour and restrict'. By comparison, Jung says little about the **father**. Freud had given a very rich account – father as superego, as God, as Oedipal rival. Jung also wrote little about the **puer aeternus**, the child-figure within us, the divine child which is a perpetual source of freshness and light, but his followers have produced rich studies.[10] Identification with the divine child is the core of a neurosis: refusal to grow up. **Kore**, the maiden, is the feminine counterpart of the puer; she is also a figure of the anima.

The **hero** is a ubiquitous figure in mythology and art; a fuller analysis is given in the next section, departing slightly from Jung, and adopting a literary-mythological orientation. For Jungians, he usually symbolises emerging ego consciousness and is essential to differentiating the self from the mother. The hero is an essentially masculine figure, of divine birth, who descends into the underworld, battles with monsters, performs dangerous tasks; he is assisted by helpful companions, male, female or animal. (In Freud's reductive imagery, he would be a phallic figure.) Identification with the hero-archetype, however, could lead to a great inflation of the ego: to neurosis. The **trickster**, on the other hand, is a clever fool; at once source of tricks and victim; he overturns hierarchies and 'continually upsets the balance of our ego-dominated consciousness'. We find him from American Indian mythology to, presumably, Shakespearean fools and the television programme 'Beadle's About'. Jung points out that Jahweh in the Old Testament has some trickster characteristics, as has the devil: consider Mephistopheles in Marlowe and in Goethe.

The final figure, the **wise old man**, represents knowledge, reflection, insight, wisdom, cleverness and intuition. He also, clearly, by a process of inflation to which Jungians make no objection, represents Jung himself. Obviously, God (and Jehovah at his best) are versions of the wise old man. He is, finally, the wholeness of the self. Feminists will certainly regard him as an avatar of patriarchy.

Comment: I have rearranged these archetypes from Hopcke to show them as a connected set: anthropologically, they seem to combine three types of distinction: family relationships, age gradings, and contrasting roles. Once one does this it raises all sorts of questions about completeness. If there is a hero, why is there no heroine? And why is there no villain? The trickster figure comes nearest, but is actually closer to the *puer aeternus*. Why only a wise old man? Why no wise old woman? Or silly old man? As soon as one breaks the archetypes down into their defining characteristics, it is obvious that these characteristics could be combined in quite other ways to form different archetypes. Why aren't they?

There are two answers to these questions, both of them empirical. The first is that basic thinking is not, in fact, conducted with componential systems of analysis, but with prototype figures combining several features. The second is that these are in fact the specific features found in Jungian research. There is a hero archetype but no heroine archetype. Hopcke remarks that 'for women, the animus, or unconscious masculine side, often fits the archetypal mold of a heroic figure struggling toward consciousness and effectiveness' (p.115). It seems rather hard on women that they can't be heroines without calling on their masculine side: Euripides, in the *Alcestis*, knew better. (And biologically, in all mammals, no creature is as brave as a female with young to defend.)

There is an alternative possibility. Some Jungians hold that there is no limit to the number of possible archetypes. For Hillman, anything that is numinous is archetypal. Modern popular Jungians happily invent a new archetype any time they wish to allegorise some new aspect of personality for their latest book. Thus we have not only the Great Goddess but *The Horned God: Feminism and Men as Wounding and Healing*;[11] we have the *Witch and the Clown, Two Archetypes of Human Sexuality*;[12] we have the archetypes of the mature masculine: *King, Warrior, Magician, Lover*.[13] This is obviously a game that can be played by literary people like Northrop Frye quite as well as by analysts; it will be seen that the word 'archetype' here has come to mean something like 'evocative stereotypical romantic image'. I offer my own contribution to the archetype hunt in Chapter 8.

Symbols, religions, dreams and active imagination

Archetypes can be apprehended only by images that act as **symbols**. The notion of symbols started in religious thought. There are supposed to be certain realities, like Heaven, or the nature of God, which transcend human understanding and can't be stated literally. They can only be apprehended in symbols. For Freud, on the other hand, symbolism usually is more like allegory, with a statable sexual meaning – as in the long list of possible phallic symbols. Jung's attitude to symbolism is closer to that of traditional religions than to that of Freud. Symbolic language is for him the only language in which the truth can be spoken about certain things. The tendency of Jungianism – this is openly accepted by later Jungians – is to become a modern alternative religion, without churches or dogmas, which celebrates the myriad symbolic forms of those truths.

Symbols are the language of the unconscious; and that language is spoken freely by **dreams**. There is for Jung no Freudian censorship, forcing the unconscious to engage in a complicated dream-work to construct a cunning allegory of current experiences and infantile fantasies. The dream is indeed not talking about the past so much as the present or the future; and we can understand what it says by reading its symbolism, and finding its unique meaning (almost, we might say, its purpose) for the dreamer. For this we engage in a process not of interpretation but of **amplification**. We do ask the dreamer to produce associations to the dream-symbols, but we don't stop there; we look also for mythological parallels. (This is a valid procedure presumably because the archetypes are universal.) The patient is also encouraged in a process of **active imagination**, dreaming the dream onwards, in order to face consciously the unconscious directions of our inner life.

Hillman takes this a step further: he rejects the word 'symbol' and requires us to speak of 'image'. He rejects the notion of a fixed set of archetypes and speaks of finding the archetypal in the image. Psychology is 'revisioned' essentially as the search for archetypal images – which means images with archetypal force – that will remake our souls.[14] One can respect Hillman because he is actively trying for an alternative to the scientific approach, and knows it.

Comment: This approach to the unconscious is one of the most appealing features of Jung's system: especially for the healthy person who does not have one of the crippling neuroses Freud describes, does not have very disturbing material violently repressed, and is looking for what amounts to a new religion, which will give meaning to life.

But it is very worrying if treated as a kind of scholarship about mythology and symbolism. The problem is that it regards the unconscious mind as timeless and universal, and abstracts away completely from the social and historical roots of myth and symbol. Yet as we have seen, any actual mythology is totally rooted in a particular society, and historically constructed. What are known as 'the Greek myths' for example, are often abstracts of the plots of a few plays written in Athens in the fifth century BC, and very concerned with topical problems. The central Christian symbol, the cross, is a memorial of one specific historical event. An analytical treatment of Native American trickster mythology would in the first instance relate it closely to the historical anthropology of certain Native American tribes.

As Graves would put it, none of these was produced by some timeless human unconscious in the dream-time of sleeping humanity. But such an unconscious is precisely what Jung's procedures imply. One result of this is that much of Jung's treatment of mythology is not only unhistorical, but boring and repetitive, since it is only the similarities in the myths he accounts for, not the historically mediated differences. It is also dated. The only consciousness in which Hermes, half of Jahweh, and Native American trickster myths, all read unhistorically, can happily co-exist is that of a mid-twentieth century educated European with syncretic religious interests – like Jung or the more intelligent of his patients and followers. It is just this kind of 'wise old man' that Jungian therapy aims at producing, and just this syncretic religion which some forms of Jungian analysis finally became.

Psyche/soul and libido

Jung saw the psyche as something broader than the ego-identified self; it encompasses both consciousness and unconsciousness, and there is not only an individual psyche, but a collective one. He preferred the word soul to psyche: there is individual soul, world-soul and transpersonal soul, the objective psyche beyond human understanding. Rational individual self-consciousness therefore occupies a small part of the territory of psyche as a whole. Psyche stretches down toward lower levels, which Jung calls psychoid, heavily infiltrated with instinctual libido.

The concept of **libido** has great historical importance. For Freud it was the sexual energy which was the basis of virtually all other manifestations of human behaviour. In the transformations of sexual libido we see the animal becoming human. Jung refused to accept the purely sexual nature of libido, and gave the name to a general psychic energy. This was a major factor leading to the break between them; Freud thought Jung was being cowardly.

Comment: On soul – Jung's position would sound a great deal less mystical if we could rechristen the collective soul as 'human culture'. But this would not square with his own mystical views. On libido – nowadays we prefer an information-processing model of the mind to an energy-transforming one; and we can make more sense of the notion of specific instincts like sexuality or hunger than of a generalised 'psychic energy'. Jung seems to me to do little of value with the concept of libido.

Psychological types

Jung's contributions to character typology strike an odd note among his more mystical interests; his categorial model is part of the ancestry of a rather down-to-earth questionnaire-based form of academic psychology, associated with hostile figures like Eysenck, who in general had even less time for Jung than for his *bête noire*, Freud.

Jung divides people by attitude type, and cross-classifies these divisions by function type, giving eight categories. There are two attitude types: extroverted, in which orientation is to the outer world, and introverted, with orientation to the inner world. There are four function types; two rational, in the sense of using criteria of some sort, and two irrational, in the sense of providing immediate irrefragable experience. The two rational functions are thinking and feeling; they are rational in the sense that we make judgements, of truth or of value. The two irrational ones are intuition and sensation: both put experience first, but the experience to which the sensation type attends is that of the concrete, physical world; that to which the intuitive type attends is that of the inner world of symbols and images. What makes for difference of character type is which of the four functions is dominant.

Comment: Despite the tradition of quantitative investigation both by Jungians and non-Jungians, Jung's own interests are very different: he engages in a series of literary biographical studies, contrasting Plato with Aristotle, Schiller with Goethe. His distinction between extrovert and introvert was a way of making sense of the different approaches of Freud and himself. I am doubtful about the four functions, but feel that the distinction between extroversion – attention to the external world – and introversion – attention to the internal world – is very important.

I would put it this way. There is a world of outer reality – of rocks and trees and tables, of animals and other people, of social institutions and so forth; and a world of inner reality – of archetypes, stereotypes and complexes existing in our minds. The phenomena that fill our consciousness refer to the world of outer reality which we perceive in them, but they are produced by the interaction with that outer reality of the archetypes, stereotypes and complexes within us. Phenomenal experience is our perception of outer reality and our symbol of inner reality. The extrovert is the person who tends to see phenomenal experience as the gateway to outer, objective reality. The introvert is the person who tends to see phenomenal experience as the gateway to inner reality.

In Chapter 8 I offer a contrast of the outer and inner reality of human sexuality, as described by modern objective studies and by categories I have derived from the Jungian tradition, though they are not Jung's own.

Individuation, psychotherapy, the transference and the conjunctio

Individuation – a concept which in Jung applies more to the middle period of life than to childhood – is the process of coming into a psychic balance in which one holds together the unconscious and conscious levels of existence, the individual ego complex and the archetype of the self, a sense of one's unique individuality and one's connection to the larger experience of human existence: these are all supposed to be aspects of the same balance, though they sound rather different. Jung often talks of psychotherapy as if it were indistinguishable from the individuation process. In his view of the transference, Jung resembles Freud; but thinks the transference may contain archetypal material and is not necessarily pathological. In his essay 'On the Psychology of the Transference' Jung speaks of the union of opposites, and in particular of male and female, making use of the alchemical image of the *conjunctio*. (Jung consistently uses alchemy as a kind of supplementary mythology rather than a failed science.)

Comment: It could be argued – would certainly be argued by postmodernists with a taste for fragmentation, irony and schizophrenia – that individuation is an ideological requirement rather than an innate aspect of psychic health. Among Jungians, Hillman – who favours polytheism rather than monotheism – seems slightly hostile to it. He is also dubious about psychotherapy, at least if it is thought of as a technical and definable task. On the other hand, some goal is necessary for any variety of psychotherapy; it might well be that every great ideological system recognises some ideal personal goal or destiny for its agents which is the analogue of what Jung is symbolising here, though the terms in which a Dogmatic Rationalist, a Jungian, a Catholic Christian and a passionate follower of Hitler might describe that state would be very different. Each of them would have an ideal which the other three would regard as pathological.

Archetypal theories of literature

The basis of archetypal theories of literature is set out in Jung's article: 'On the Relation of Analytical Psychology to Poetic Art'[15], and the approach was developed at some length by Maud Bodkin in *Archetypal Patterns in Poetry*, as long ago as 1934. For Bodkin and Jung, romantics both, some poems have a special emotional significance going beyond any definite meaning conveyed; and this is attributed to 'the stirring in the reader's mind, within or beneath his conscious response, of unconscious forces which he [Jung] terms "primordial images" or archetypes' (p.1). It will be seen that this definition inherits all the confusions of Jung's own thought in this period: unconscious forces are identified with primordial images and these with archetypes. This confusion is not Bodkin's fault, but it does damage her theory. How would one put the point more precisely, respecting the distinction between unconscious force, image and archetype, and, incidentally, generalising the theory from poetry to art as a whole?

What a work of art presents may be an image – obviously a painting presents an image – or as in most poems, a linguistic or logical structure relating together a whole set of images, or a narrative, or even an abstract formal structure in some sensuous modality, as in most music. There is no special reason to limit the relevance of archetypal theory to only one of these. What makes a work of art an embodiment of an archetypal image is that it functions to trigger an archetype – the innate unconscious phantasy of an instinctual pattern of behaviour. Now it may well be that in some cases the triggering of an archetype will be subjectively apparent through a certain romantic suggestiveness surrounding traditional romantic imagery. But in the most important, most obvious, most blatant cases where archetypes are at work, there need be no romantic suggestiveness at all.

A routine popular thriller, for example, which holds a firm grip on its audience, works by combining fighting and sex. Both of these are archetypes. That is, human beings are equipped with a basic instinctual pattern that determines how they fight and they are equipped with a basic instinctual pattern that determines how they court; and the popular thriller offers a formal structure of narrative which repeatedly produces imaginative realisations of these archetypes. It is because it does this that it holds such a grip on the imagination of the reader. Fighting and courting are two activities that human beings are naturally equipped to concentrate on.

This, as I said, is something obvious: any reader could tell you, and I am sure any Jungian would admit the point. The puzzle is why Jungian theorists don't pay much attention to it; why they concentrate on the archetypes faintly evoked by the romantic suggestiveness of decorative imagery, and ignore the archetypes blatantly evoked by the main storyline. The reason, I suggest, is the generally religious, romantic and other-worldly orientation of Jung and his followers. If we want a down-to-earth explanatory theory, the first thing to do is to rescue the Jungian tradition from romanticism. I have tried to do this in Chapter 8.

'These archetypes' Bodkin continues 'he describes as "psychic residua of numberless experiences of the same type", experiences which have happened not to the individual but to his ancestors, and of which the results are inherited in the structure of the brain, *a priori* determinants of individual experience.' Here we have a worse theoretical disaster. Jung appears to be committed, as Freud often is, to a Lamarckian theory of inheritance, in which individual experiences modify the germ plasm, rather than to the standard Mendelian/natural-selection theory, according to which natural selection operates on random genetic change to preserve favourable genetic features. Indeed it seems likely that Jung did often commit himself to such a theory, though he was not an exact enough expositor of his own ideas to make this certain.

Archetypal theory as such, however, is not dependent on Lamarckian inheritance. General archetypal structures, like, for example, the narrative structures of the courting behaviour of the stickleback or of *homo sapiens*, not only can be but clearly are inherited. Archetypal images – taken here as general specifications of the form of a specific releaser – clearly are inherited, and do act as *a priori* determinants of individual experience – as when the stickleback recognises another stickleback as a sexual object, or when a human being recognises another human being as a sexual object. Natural selection and Mendelian inheritance are all that is necessary to fix such archetypal patterns of behaviour and patterns of recognition in the genes; and we can be very sure that if these patterns were not fixed in the genes, sticklebacks and human beings would die out, since they would literally not know, and would not be able to learn, how to reproduce themselves.

There is an important implication of this account of inheritance mechanisms. It is clear that very little evolution has taken place in historical times. The reason for this is not that, with the coming of history, natural selection stopped. It is that the length of human history is very short on an evolutionary scale. Basically, modern human beings have the same genetic inheritance as Cro-magnon Man, say thirty thousand years ago. They have a slightly different genetic inheritance from Neanderthal Man. (Say 70,000 years ago and upward; and not quite on the same line of development as *homo sapiens sapiens.*) But history cannot possibly be stretched beyond 10,000 years. It follows that throughout recorded history the same archetypes have existed, and all cultural forms ever recorded must fall within them.

Working within Jung's framework, clinicians have developed a characteristic clinical method for dealing with putative archetypal images derived, for example, from dreams; and this method may be transferred directly to literature. It is the method of **amplification**. One trawls through all the literature and mythology of the world, one looks also at discourses like those of astrology, alchemy, magic and religion, in the hope of getting nearer to the elusive archetype. Subjectively this can provide a very strong feeling that one is gaining in wisdom and understanding; though it can also seem immensely tedious and pointless. It has often been pointed out that this is not a very good way of providing an explanatory theory of anything. You don't really explain the effect of *Hamlet* by pointing out its parallels to the myth of Orestes; you simply provide yourself with two things to explain rather than one.

But one can make scientific sense of this method by suggesting that it is not really a way of providing scientific explanation at all; it is a way of setting out the data to be explained by archetype theory. If it is true that all human cultures, however various they may have been, have developed within the constraints provided by a fixed set of archetypes, then we must expect significant repetitions of theme and motive between cultural artefacts from widely separated cultures that have not necessarily influenced each other. And, conversely, if we find such significant repetitions and cannot account for them by the ordinary processes of cultural history, then we are entitled to count them as good evidence for the existence of transcultural archetypes. Not merely good evidence, but the best evidence; better, for example, than clinical data from an individual patient, or even a group of patients, since this might be evidence merely of social stereotypes from the society they lived in, or indoctrination by the analyst.

If this method is a valid one, it clearly offers a type of psychological enquiry that goes beyond anything either academic psychology of the early twentieth century, or modern cognitive studies, can offer. As Bodkin puts it (p.3):

> We might almost say that academic psychologists have been routed by the attack of those medical writers [Freud and Jung] who claim access to the deeper layers of the mind, just because the demand for exact verifiable results has held academic psychologists to the mere outworks or surfaces of the mind they set out to study. If inexactness of thought or one-sided emphasis has characterised the medical writers, this can be established only by following them along the obscure paths they have opened into the concrete human psyche, and bringing to bear, if possible, a wider ranging interest and a more exact and cautious scrutiny.

Bodkin seems to me right in principle though I am not in the least satisfied with her book. By basing archetypal theory mainly on the arts, we are at once bringing a wider ranging interest and making possible a more exact and cautious scrutiny.

Before we can do this, it seems worth while to examine one of these mythological archetypes that can be said at one and the same time to represent basic instinctual patterns and to underlie complex works of literature and explain their appeal. I will take as my example the myth of the hero.

The archetype of the hero

The study of myths and legends didn't begin in the nineteenth century. It is nearly, but not quite, as old as the myths and legends themselves. Myths begin as religion, and legends as recent history; when the myths are no longer quite believed, and the history has retreated into legend, both are retold with advantages as folk-tale and art. The systematising scholar follows on this stage. So at least it was in ancient Greece, when mythography began, probably among the pre-Socratic philosophers of Ionia, though it flourished most in later, Hellenistic times. Nineteenth century mythography, like classical mythography, was pursued in large part for nationalistic reasons: it seemed to give an insight into the ancient identity of a people. But at least since the romantic period there were two other reasons, which have remained current: the quest for an alternative religion, made up from the detritus of old religions; and the quest for a deeper insight into the constitution of the human mind.

Psychoanalytic mythography began in the early 1900s, well before the split between Freud and Jung. These were the days when mythographic theory was still dominated by the notion of the solar myth: the hero whose trajectory rises and falls like the sun, because he **is** a version of the sun. (Actually, many real careers are like this: one sardonic mythographer proved that Napoleon was a solar myth.) Just beginning was the next paradigm of mythography to dominate the twentieth century: the dying and reborn king of Sir James Frazer's *Golden Bough*, which was destined, in the work of Jane Harrison and others, to revolutionise classical studies, as well as casting a lurid comparative light on Christianity. The psychoanalysts did not aim to supersede these studies, on which they always remained dependent. What they offered were theoretical explanations of myth and fairy-tale, based on hypotheses about child development and the structure of the unconscious mind.

The second number of the series *Papers in Applied Psychology*, published under Freud's aegis in 1908, was devoted to Franz Riklin's *Wishfulfilment and Symbolism in Fairy-Tales*. Riklin was a colleague of Jung at Zurich. The fourth number of the same series was Karl Abraham's *Dreams and Myth*, 1909. The fifth, immediately following, was Otto Rank, *The Myth of the Birth of the Hero*. It is clear that for many of the pioneers of psychoanalysis, the explanation of myth was becoming almost as important as the explanation of neurosis. But of all the major figures of this period, no one went further than Jung. In his vast and rambling book *Wandlungen und Symbole der Libido*, 1912 (English translation: *Psychology of the Unconscious*, 1916 – which he revised almost into readability as *Symbols of Transformation*, Collected Works vol. 5) Jung spent several hundred pages of mythological amplification on a few short personal fantasies by a Miss Miller. To those who have the key, the book gives deep insight into Jung's personal psychology and near breakdown, as well as adumbrating many of the insights on which later Jungian theory is based.[16]

But to those with Freud's reductive view of psychoanalysis, it represents a theoretical disaster and a danger to psychoanalysis; the danger being that the theoretical concentration on sexuality will be lost, and psychoanalysis dissipated into the study of a wide range of semi-autonomous complexes, most of them non-sexual. This book therefore led to Jung's being forced out of all the psychoanalytic institutions of which he had once been crown prince and designated leader. And Freud himself started to publish speculations about anthropology and myth, with quite disastrous results. Those who have wondered how a great thinker can have produced *Totem and Taboo*, whose serial publication concluded in June 1913, should realise that it is a salvo against Jung: its purpose is to show that the most complex psychic, anthropological and mythological phenomena can be explained, while still recognising only one important complex – the Oedipus complex. Indeed they can, given sufficient freedom to transform one psychic content into another, and to invent, or select from unreliable sources, anthropology and prehistory ad lib – to construct, for example, a primitive history in which young men eat their father, later young men eat the totem of their tribe, and later ones still taboo it. Freud's arguments are far less responsible than those of Jung, if more readable. This is not scholarship about fairy-tales, but fairy-tale presented as scholarship.

The Jungian tradition – ever since Jung recovered from his breakdown – has been enormously stronger than the Freudian in its treatment of mythology; but that treatment still tends to be too easy and quick a reduction from attested mythological contents to specifically Jungian concerns. We jump from the hero of the myth to the ego, without a pause. There is something to be said for looking at the details of myths and legends, to see what universal features they actually offer, before closing down the identification to the ones that seem relevant to analytic psychology.

Vladimir Propp in 1928 compared a hundred versions of Russian folk-tales. Not entirely to his surprise (since the formal similarity of these tales is fairly obvious) he found that he could provide a common specification for all of them: it includes a list of thirty-one ordered 'plot-functions' (that is, mini-episodes) which folk-tales tend to have, of the type 'hero leaves home', 'hero is tested', 'hero gets magical weapon' and so forth. He had constructed something resembling a generative grammar of folk-tales – a kit of parts for constructing them. Working independently of Propp, Lord Raglan in 1936 offered a similar analysis of the hero-myth. In many ways his results are more impressive than Propp's; Propp was dealing with a deliberately restricted range of tales already intuitively much like each other and all from the same region. But Raglan took twenty-one of the basic hero-myths of the world, mostly classical, but including Old Testament, Nordic, Celtic, Javanese, and Upper Nilotic tales, and showed them to be essentially the same tale, with almost the same episodes in almost the same order.

Here is Raglan's grammar of the hero-myth:

(1) The hero's mother is a royal virgin;
(2) his father is a king, and
(3) often a near relative of his mother;
(4) the circumstances of his conception are unusual, and
(5) he is also reputed to be the son of a god.
(6) at birth an attempt is made, usually by his father or his maternal grandfather, to kill him, but
(7) he is spirited away, and
(8) reared by foster parents in a far country.
(9) We are told nothing of his childhood, but

(10) on reaching manhood he returns or goes to his future kingdom.

(11) After a victory over the king and/or a giant, dragon, or wild beast,

(12) he marries a princess, often the daughter of his predecessor and

(13) becomes king.

(14) For a time he reigns uneventfully, and

(15) prescribes laws, but

(16) later he loses favour with the gods and/or his subjects, and

(17) is driven from the throne and city, after which

(18) he meets with a mysterious death,

(19) often at the top of a hill.

(20) His children, if any, do not succeed him.

(21) His body is not buried, but nevertheless

(22) he has one or more holy sepuchres.

This is how it compares with the story of one of the major heroes, Oedipus:

His mother, Jocasta, is (1) a princess, and his father is (2) King Laius, who, like her, is (3) of the line of Cadmus. He has sworn to have no connection with her but (4) does so when drunk, probably (5) in the character of Dionysus. Laius (6) tries to kill Oedipus at birth, but (7) he is spirited away, and (8) reared by the king of Corinth. (9) We hear nothing of his childhood, but (10) on reaching manhood he returns to Thebes, after (11) gaining victories over his father and the Sphinx. He (12) marries Jocasta, and (13) becomes king. For some years he (14) reigns uneventfully, but (16) later comes to be regarded as the cause of a plague and (17) is deposed and driven into exile. He meets with (18) a mysterious death at (19) a place near Athens called (says Raglan) The Steep Pavement. He is succeeded by (20) Creon, through whom he was deposed, and though (21) the place of his burial is uncertain, he has (22) several holy sepulchres.

Oedipus gets 21 points of a possible 22. Raglan then proceeds in the same systematic way through another twenty cases, scoring them as follows: Theseus, 20 points; Romulus, 18; Heracles, 17; Perseus, 18; Jason, 15; Bellerophon, 16; Pelops, 13; Asclepios, 12; Dionysus, 19; Apollo, 11; Zeus, 15; Joseph, 12; Moses, 20; Elijah, 9; Watu Gunung (Javanese), 18; Nyikang (Shiluk tribe of the Upper Nile), 14; Siegfried, 11; Llew Llawgyffes (Welsh), 17; Arthur, 19; Robin Hood, 13. The case of Jesus Christ is pointedly ignored, but must jump to the mind of any European reader.

It is customary to refer to Propp and Raglan rather patronisingly as precursors of structuralism. This is distinctly misleading, as structuralism also started in 1928[17] and was flourishing in Prague in 1936; these thinkers are not precursors, but part of the same broad current of thought, though there is a gulf between continental literary formalism and British anthropology. More important, Propp and Raglan are far more original and interesting than the later French structuralists. Raglan's treatment of the Oedipus story establishes something fundamental and true: that it shares an archetypal structure with many other stories from a wide range of cultures, and this is something that needs a universalistic explanation. Lévi-Strauss's treatment of the same story offers a less balanced summary, subjects it to violent and arbitrary transformations, and comes up with an interpretation that is at once densely obscure and wholly banal: that the overrating of blood-relations is to the underrating of blood-relations as the attempt to escape autochthony is to the impossibility of succeeding in it.[18]

Raglan's observations are stunning: his theoretical treatment of them is distinctly disappointing. All he tries to do is to show that the hero-myths are not historical; they are, rather, stories based on ritual. It is a familiar argument in the British anthropology of the time; and it has elements of absurdity; for there is no more reason that stories based on religious rituals should survive in their original form, once those rituals have vanished, than that stories based on history should survive in their original form, once their original historical moment has passed; and there is no more reason why religious rituals should always have the same pattern, than there is why historical events should always have the same pattern. Raglan simply does not grapple with the problem he himself has posed: namely why there should be a vast range of stories (or, indeed, of rituals) from different cultures and periods, which all have the same essential structure. The only theory that can account for this is a universal psychological theory, like that of Freud or Jung.

There are two obvious questions to ask about Raglan's schema. The first is, what is its relation to any plausible Jungian archetype of the hero? It is obvious that the Raglan schema is far more complex. If archetypes are basic instincts, it is very likely that they have some kind of narrative structure; for an instinct, in wasp or man, is normally an instinct to perform some sequence of actions. But it beggars belief that we have built into us an instinct to go through Raglan's twenty-two mini-episodes, or Propp's thirty-one. It might be plausible to suggest that there is a basic instinctual structure built into human beings, of which 'hero slays monster' or 'hero slays villain', or 'hero hunts animal', or 'hero finds treasure' – i.e., some of the basic units of which a Raglanian hero-myth might be made up – are possible variants. But the full inclusive structure offered by Raglan or Propp, simple as it is by comparison with works of literature, looks like a complex combination of a set of mythologemes[19] each of which separately might represent a Jungian archetype.

Is there any special reason for believing that a mythologeme like 'hero hunts animal' has any significance outside narrative and myth studies? I think there is. *Homo sapiens* is an animal which actually has an evolutionary adaptation to hunting and gathering. We have no instinctual adaptation to agriculture or to industrial production, though our intelligence and our linguistic abilities enable us to sustain agricultural and industrial adaptations rather against our inclinations. (They both involve hard work under unnatural conditions, and damage human health.) But we have a direct adaptation to hunting–gathering life. And many of the basic mythologemes in hero-tales and folk-tales seem closely related to the hunting–gathering adaptation. A nomadic hunting–gathering animal is well adapted to journeys, to quests, to fights with animals and strangers; and well adapted, therefore, to fantasies about these things. The mythologemes of the hero-tale are the alphabet of heroic fantasy, and probably have an instinctive base in an adaptation to a specific mode of life.

Curiously enough, this is not the kind of instinct, nor the kind of archaic meaning, that Jungians say very much about when they are considering the meaning of a hero-myth. A Jungian is far more likely to consider the hero-tale as an allegory for an inner process; for the emergence of the ego, say. And there is no special reason to reject this view. Under hunter–gatherer conditions (which are the normal conditions of human life throughout most of the existence of *homo sapiens*) hunting and gathering activities are precisely the activities under which the ego does emerge. But few Jungians are interested in the possible instinctual basis of the hero myth; they are interested in its significance for the inner reality of a modern patient who is not likely to be a hunter–gatherer, but has certainly been a child. As Stevens puts it (in the usual radical metaphors adopted by Jungians, even biologically oriented ones), 'failure to overcome the dragon-monster signifies failure to get free of the mother; the hero languishes in her belly forever, ingested, engulfed, "absorbed", and the damsel (the Anima) is never liberated from the monster's clutches (jailed by the mother complex, she is trapped *in perpetuity* in the unconscious).'[20]

Picturesque allegory of this kind may well be the only way of approaching inner realities, which are otherwise irrepresentable. But it is not in any simple sense a direct representation of an instinctual pattern. Rather, a story with its roots in one pattern of behaviour – hunting and searching for food, nomadic travel, combat – has been adapted as an allegorical representation of an inner problem of a quite different type; a problem which is not even about the concrete difficulties of a child trying to overcome its actual mother, but about the difficulties of an adult in enabling his own inner representation of himself to overcome and escape from his own inner representation of his mother. Jungian theory draws on the whole vast mass of mythology for allegories of this kind; and it is precisely when it does this that mythological symbols are felt to be 'numinous'. The numinous symbol, in fact, is not so much the symbol that directly represents a biological instinct, as the one that on interpretation represents a conflict between figures of the inner world.

The second question to ask about Raglan's schema is how does it relate to actual works of literature? Our knowledge of Greek and Latin mythology is in most cases fairly directly taken from Greek and Latin literature, and for us, far from being something primitive out of which the literature is made, mythological stories are second order constructs made out of the literature. For most of us, the Oedipus story is something we have worked out from three of Sophocles' plays.[21] Once we have worked it out, of course, it is not identical with the Oedipus plays. Consider, for example, *Oedipus Rex*. This takes the story up to the self-blinding and exile of Oedipus, and casts back to the beginning of his story. But it does not tell that story, as it appears in Raglan's summary. On the contrary, the story that the play tells is how Oedipus found out that story, and what he did as a result of finding out. If the play itself embodies any archetype, it is the archetype of the quest. And the hypothetical process of making the play is a process in which the pre-existing story material, taken from mythology, is moulded into the form of this particular quest.

If I am right about this, we thus need to postulate levels of analysis above and below the mythology of the hero – or any other mythological story. Below mythology is the level of the mythologeme, which is also the level of the archetype. Somewhere above mythology is the level of psychiatric interpretation, in which the myths are worked on, and become the key to an inner world. And also somewhere above mythology, but not necessarily in the same place as psychiatric interpretation, is the level of art, in which again the myths are worked on, and become the key to a slightly different inner world: a collective inner world provided by general culture.

A comparison of Jungian and Freudian interpretations

There is a kind of writing that translates very readily into Jungian interpretations. It is the kind that we might call 'secondary mythical'. Examples are Spenser's *The Faerie Queene*, Milton's *Paradise Lost*, Wagner's *Ring*, and *Parsifal*, and a vast body of contemporary popular fantasy.[22] All of these are recycling ancient myths, and providing their own new meanings for these. In cases like this there may well be a conflict, or at least a disconnection, between the meaning intended by the artist, and perhaps accepted by the culture, and the meaning conveyed by the ancient archetypes. In fact it could be, and with an original artist usually is, a three-way split. There is the original archetype; the archetypal image, worked over by a long and complex cultural tradition, and carrying a great deal of social meaning over and beyond its archetypal meaning; and there is the new meaning found by the artist within his own new work.

But the effect is not necessarily one of conflict. What happens often is that the power of the ancient mythologeme is strengthened in the very process of applying it to say something new. Often the artist is using, as an essential part of his own technique, the very method of 'active imagination' – the piling up of mythological parallels – which Jungians claim as their own, and use in therapy. He is drawing on a wealth of intertextual reference and cultural suggestion, at the same time as using the symbol for its original purpose and his own.

Consider, for example, what the works listed above do with an archetypal image that occurs in all four of them: that of a man with a spear. The spear, which can be used for thrusting or throwing, is one of the oldest weapons; it goes back to the palaeolithic, and may have been used for hundreds of thousands of years, chiefly for hunting animals, but partly for killing people. In the modern world, it is an obsolete weapon, used only in the meaningless sport of javelin throwing.[23] But in literature it appears from *The Iliad* to present day fantasies and often carries impressive magical powers. All three of our writers inherit the image of the spear from the literary traditions in which they are working. Spenser is writing knightly romance, so he must use lances-in-rest. Milton is telling the Christian story as a classical epic, so Satan must become a classical warrior with a spear. Wagner's Wotan gets his spear from Germanic epic, and Parsifal his from knightly romance.

For a Freudian, this symbol is always phallic, and no Jungian could completely dismiss this view. Spenser, in a stunning symbolic coup, supplies his greatest spear – the one with magical powers which can never break and whose bearer can never be overthrown – to the female knight Britomart, who represents marriage. The ideological point is straightforward enough – it is Puritan propaganda for marriage and against adulterous romance – but the imaginative effect is extraordinary: a faithful wife becomes the bearer of the phallus. Britomart foreshadows Fidelio.

Milton employs the spear-image as an amplificatory device when he is building up the power of Satan.

> *His spear – to equal which the tallest pine*
> *Hewn on Norwegian hills, to be the mast*
> *Of some great ammiral, were but a wand*

(P.L. I. 293–295)

For the Freudian this is the ultimate big phallus, and establishes Satan as the ultimate male. The Jungian would be more likely to pick up the backward references to all the mighty heroes of mythology, with their great and magical spears. And, from a purely literary critical point of view, the Jungian is obviously right. Milton is here making a deliberate comparison of Satan with the heroes of *The Iliad*, and of *The Odyssey*, *The Aeneid* and the long series of epics and heroic romances to which he is consciously appending his own Christian epic. Milton does, in fact, characteristically work in a Jungian manner, by piling up mythological parallels to whatever he is talking about at the moment. There are moments in *Paradise Lost* when he sounds like a modern speculative mythographer, like Robert Graves, say, on *The Greek Myths*.[24]

But this is not altogether such a moment. A modern reader is tempted to treat the reference to 'some great ammiral' in the same mythological way, as an evocation of the archetypal quest-ship. But that would be a complete mis-reading of the feeling of the comparison. An ammiral is an admiral's flagship – the capital ship of a fleet. It is enormously large and consumes major national resources to build – for example, you have to import the mast from Norway. In any period of history, the capital ship is the largest and most formidable mobile weapons system on the planet. The British Empire in 1914 rested on 20–30 Dreadnought battleships. American power world-wide rests on a few aircraft carriers – any one of them bigger than Trafalgar Square. A capital ship of any period can destroy a city of the same period, unless it is heavily fortified; a U.S. aircraft carrier can destroy a country. Milton's point (which one can imagine without difficulty made by a modern Iranian preacher) is that the destructive power of Satan is much greater than that of the United States Sixth Fleet.

The spear-image in Wagner is, one might say, archetypally Jungian: its purpose seems wholly evocative. Indeed, this is a general truth about Wagner, as about other romantics like Yeats. It is their use of mythology, as a way of symbolising an inner reality, and inner conflicts, which is the model for Jung's world view. It is not surprising that one of the finest of all Jungian critiques is that of Robert Donington, *Wagner's Ring and its Symbols*. It is not that Wagner is Jungian; rather that Jung is Wagnerian. Yet to judge by his use of the spear-symbol, Wagner didn't (to put it fancifully) limit his reading to Freud and Jung. He had read Lacan as well. Wotan's spear is a symbol of the Law of the Father. He goes beyond Lacan, and gets as far as Nietzsche, when in *Siegfried* the Law of the Father is broken by the reforged Sword of the Son.[25]

Secondary myth is not the only kind of literature and art in the nineteenth century, nor even the main kind: this is the great age of realism. On the face of it, the central, even the defining feature of realist art is that it is not mythological; it relates to the everyday world of real men and women in which we all live, and not to a world of impalpable essences personified by items from legend and myth. It turns out, however, that this is not true. Realist novels often seem to drift in and out of myth. Mythical elements crop up in them. And this alerts us to the fact that we can give no satisfactory critical account of realist novels if we stay at the level of realism. It is the greatest merit of Jungian theory that it drives us to look at a realist novel and look for the underlying and sometimes unconscious myth.

Consider Henry James, in that triumph of his middle period, *Portrait of a Lady*. Isabel is a young lady of exceptional personal and intellectual qualities: a really interesting woman. We have to take these qualities rather on trust: they are not displayed in action, since James rather disapproves of women actually doing anything, and actually invents a vulgar journalistic friend for her, to show what intelligent women ought not to be like. A young man, dying of consumption and therefore unable to marry Isabel, persuades his dying father, a great banker, to leave her a huge sum of money instead: it will interest him to see how she chooses to use it. Inevitably, she makes a tragic mistake, marrying the most deathly of the suitors available to her, and being locked into the marriage by compassion for his natural daughter. The story is told in realist mode, though every now and then a proper name, a symbol, or merely something in the style of the narrative suggests that levels of fantasy are being evoked.

As indeed they are. This realist novel easily yields a Jungian interpretation. The first clue is the name of the old banker's home: Gardencourt. So he is a king, and a dying king; and his wife, like Isabel's fairy godmother, brings Isabel to his court. There his son Ralph is a dying prince: and this is the first twist to the myth, for the young prince usually stands mythically for rebirth and the new generation; and here the new generation is dying at birth. All our hope for the future is therefore concentrated on the heroine, with her vast new estate, who we recognise now as a princess. (In his later work, James seems to have become anxious lest his readers should miss points like these: in *The Wings of the Dove* he explicitly describes his young dying American heiress as a 'princess', leading that sturdy middle-class liberal Dr Leavis to ask what is so special about her.[26])

The princess must have appropriately mythical suitors, and so she does: three: a nobleman, a merchant, and the third? – on the literal level a slightly impoverished middle-aged art connoisseur who attracts her because of his fine perceptions, but then casts a blighting spell on her life – in the myth he is a wizard. Certainly, his friend, his unacknowledged mistress and mother of his child, who betrays, even enchants Isabel into marriage with him – she is a witch. His backward daughter has all the marks of a changeling. Once you have seen the pattern, everything realist in this great novel is absorbed into the fairy-tale. Even the vulgar journalist friend, of the earth earthy and successful in just the type of journalism James himself felt most embarrassed to produce – even she falls into the pattern of the vulgar honest servant-companion, the nurse to Phaedra, the Brangaene to Isolde, whose sensible advice is never taken, or if taken proves disastrous to the finer character.

What would this story be, on a Freudian interpretation? I do not think a Freudian analyst would want to deny these mythical patterns; but he would be committed to explaining them, by saying that they were transformations of the limited set of underlying archetypal patterns permitted by Freud. Somehow, everything must emanate from infantile or Oedipal fantasies, or defences against these. A world of unconscious meaning is thus lost. Yet one cannot rule out a purely Freudian level of interpretation, which does not correspond to anything in the fairy-tale, but matches a deep unconscious fantasy of the writer. At this level the whole novel is a voyeuristic fantasy of stripping a woman bare, combined with a sadistic fantasy of punishing her for her independent spirit: that is, for her intellectual and sexual challenge to the supremacy of men. (The vulgar journalist can safely be mocked for her challenge; a lady you respect has to be humiliated – symbolically raped.)

It seems to me that I need both the Jungian and Freudian levels of explanation, or I cannot understand this novel or see any real value in it. At the realist level, after all, I am expected to admire a detestable society and see it as a fine civilisation; to laugh at the only woman – almost the only person of either sex – who works for a living, and admire the fine mind of a lady who would not qualify for a modern BA in English. The mythical levels of analysis take me through to something that is worth being interested in; it needs the Freudian level to make the work accessible to an intelligent feminism.

Notes and references

Suggestions for further reading are on page 213.

1.   Compare **Chomsky's** view of language – see Chapter 2.
2.   **H.F. Harlow and M.K. Harlow**, 'The Affectional Systems' (1965) in **A.M. Schrier, H.F. Harlow and F. Stollnitz** (eds), *Behaviour of Non-human Primates*. London: Academic Press.
      J. Bowlby, *Attachment and Loss* (1969) Vol. I *Attachment*.
      Anthony Stevens, *Archetype: A Natural History of the Self* (1982) pp.144–5.

3. This does not preclude research into archetypes, any more than the fact that we have no direct grasp of the universals of grammar precludes research into those.

4. Warrior gods: Ares/Mars, Wotan; heroes: Achilles, Hector, Lancelot; modern films: James Bond, Rambo. I imagine the average man could recall fifty or so warrior figures in these categories without particular difficulty. What does this say about the mental furniture we carry around and the nature of our inner lives?

5. **Robert Graves**, *The Greek Myths* (1960) Vol. I, pp.20–1.

6. *The Wings of the Dove.*

7. *Portrait of a Lady.*

8. **Derrida**, 1967. For discussion, see **Jackson**, 1991.

9. **Emma Jung**, 1934–55.

10. **Hillman**, 1970, 1973, 1975, 1979; **Von Franz**, 1981.

11. **Rowan**, 1987.

12. **Ulanov and Ulanov**, 1989.

13. **Robert Moore and Douglas Gillette**, 1990.

14. **Hillman**, 1975, 1990.

15. In **Jung**, *Contributions to Analytical Psychology* (1928).

16. For discussion of this period, see **Kerr**, 1994, *A Most Dangerous Method: the story of Jung, Freud, and Sabina Spielrein.*

17. **Jakobson and Tynjanov**, 1928, in **Jakobson**, 1985.

18. For discussion, see **Jackson**, *The Poverty of Structuralism* (1991) pp.90–91.

19. A mythologeme is the minimum distinctive unit of narrative in a myth or folk-tale; the analogy is to the phoneme as the minimal distinctive unit of sound-structure in language. I make no strong theoretical claims for this unit.

20. **Stevens**, 1982, p.129.

21. *Oedipus Rex, Oedipus at Colonus, Antigone.*

22. Like the immense Bantam Press sagas of **David Eddings** – the *Belgariad*, the *Malloreon*, etc. – which were, as his book *The Rivan Codex* informs us, consciously designed around Jungian theory to capture an audience.

23. Meaningless because the javelin thrower tries merely for distance. Unlike the modern archer, he doesn't try to hit anything.

24. E.g. *P.L.* X, 578–84.

25. Actually grandson in the myth. But as son of both Wotan's son and his daughter, he will get a son's portion of Wotan's genes. And he is Nietzsche's superman.

26. **F.R. Leavis**, *The Common Pursuit* (1952) pp.229–30. Leavis is, of course, writing from a consciously anti-romantic point of view.

Chapter 6

The first post-structuralist

A COGNITIVIST CRITIQUE OF JACQUES LACAN

Summary

Jacques Lacan dominates modern psychoanalytic literary theory; and there are competent people – in the post-structuralist tradition that descends from his work – who regard him as the most important psychoanalyst of the twentieth century, after Freud himself: a philosophical sophisticate who introduced Freud to Hegel and Heidegger and saved him from mechanism and positivism; a grand unifying theoretician who brought together anthropology, psychoanalysis, and linguistics; and of course a spell-binding lecturer, who dazzled several generations of Parisian intellectuals. There are equally competent people – including, probably, most cognitive scientists – who agree with Noam Chomsky that he was a conscious charlatan, trying to see what he could put over on the Parisian public.[1] They complain that none of his theories work, or even make scientific sense; and that some of his claims are fraudulent.

In this chapter, I argue that at the heart of Lacan's work is a defensible cognitive theory: that the ego is only an imaginary representation of the self and that at least part of the unconscious is structured like a language. But in general Lacan uses theories not for their own sake but as metaphors for the analytic situation; he is not a scientist as Freud was, nor a credible philosopher. Nevertheless, the early Lacan makes an interesting philosophical critique of the ego-centred American version of psychoanalysis, based on a genuine understanding of Heidegger, and of his teacher Kojève's version of Hegel, and on a perfect knowledge of Freud's texts; and he makes interesting claims about the central place of speech in the cure.

His later work – a gnomic, extravagant and rhetorical rereading of Freud in the light of a very personal transformation of Saussure's linguistics which Saussure would have indignantly repudiated, of Lévi-Strauss's structuralist anthropology and of parodistic borrowings from algebra and topology – gestures at a thrilling unification of disciplines which never becomes a coherent scientific theory. It did, however, provide the model for the whole process of radical rereading, practised by Althusser on the texts of Marx and by Foucault, Derrida and others on almost any text – which became what we know as post-structuralism. Lacan was the first post-structuralist.

Lacan and the question of science

(a) Lacan as Zen Master

> The master breaks the silence with anything – with a sarcastic remark, with a kick-start.
> That is how a Buddhist master conducts his search for meaning, according to the technique of *Zen*.
>
> (*The Seminar of Jacques Lacan*, Book I (1953–4) p.1.)[2]

(b) Lacan as Fake Algebraic Formaliser

> Thus, by calculating that signification according to the algebraic method used here, namely:
>
> $$\frac{S(\text{signifier})}{s(\text{signified})} = s(\text{the statement}), \text{ with } S = (-I) \text{ produces } \sqrt{-I}$$
>
> This is what the subject lacks in order to think himself exhausted by his *cogito*, namely, that which is unthinkable for him.
>
> ('Subversion of the Subject . . .' (1960) *Ecrits* (1966a) p.317)

Coming to Lacan directly after Freud, the first thing one notices is the extraordinary difference of style and attitude. Freud writes a clear and beautiful scientific prose, comparable with that of Darwin. He treats his readers, even in elementary works of exposition, as respected colleagues to whom he is submitting his theories, which it is his duty to make as clear as the material allows. Lacan, by contrast, begins as a Zen master, even in the relatively clear and useful first volume of *The Seminar*, and is a charismatic bully in the later volumes and in the *Ecrits*. His style there is that of the leader of a cult, not a scientist.[3] It is intentionally difficult. It is often rhetorical, gongoresque and full of wordplay. Sometimes, as in the 'algebraic' formula above, or in the formulae in 'The Agency of the Letter . . .' (1957) in the same collection, it is manifest nonsense, neither obeying the ordinary formal rules of algebra, nor defining any alternative rules.

In such a style he obviously cannot present theories for scientific evaluation. What he can do is to present them as metaphors for the analytic experience; and one has to read all the theories he appropriates – Lévi-Straussian, Jakobsonian, algebraic, topological – in this loose, pictorial, metaphorical way. Thus at one point in the algebraic formula for metaphor in 'The Agency of the Letter . . .', a plus sign is said to signify not addition but the crossing of the bar between conscious and unconscious.[4] This is a naïvely pictorial interpretation where you expect a mathematical one; for Lacan if there is a cross on the page it means that you cross something! Lacan thus interprets his own formulae as if they were Freudian dreams; but this is hardly the way to construct a science.

The second thing that one notices is that Lacan is not normally presenting new hypotheses with supporting data, in the manner of a scientist. He is, rather, producing radical rereadings of Freud's original texts. His own positions are often widely different from those of Freud. But they are read back into the original texts as if they were always present in them. This is the approach of a rhetorician or even a theologian. His seminars, which continued throughout his life and drew all intellectual Paris to them, became impassioned sermons rereading Freud's sacred texts – like his teacher Kojève's famous rereading of Hegel,[5] but much wilder.

In these seminars he inaugurated the very practice of post-modern radical rereading – close, but arbitrary and highly metaphorical reading to bring out gaps, contradictions, and potentialities rather than any obvious sense – which was continued by Althusser, Foucault and Derrida, was applied first to Marx and then every other conceivable text, and has become the basic method of the whole discipline, virtually excluding older philosophical and scientific approaches. Naturally he himself provokes brilliant critical rereadings rather than evaluation as science. In this chapter I am reading him against the grain by trying to extract some basic scientific claims from their rhetorical surroundings in his seminars and writings.

True followers of Lacan try to make sense of the world within his own philosophical framework of the symbolic, the imaginary and the real. The question I am asking is: can one find, in the gnomic wordplay of Lacan's own texts, some ordinary scientific theory that might make a contribution to an objective science of mind? Such a question may be absurd – like trying to read Blake, or Leavis, or Heidegger, or Grock the clown as a scientist. But it is the question that obviously poses itself in a book that considers psychoanalysis alongside cognitive science. I have given particular attention to the gulf between Lacan's understanding of language and Saussure's.

The mirror stage and the imaginary nature of the ego

Lacan's first major innovation was to propose a new stage of child development, which implied a new and inferior status for the ego. His theory of
the mirror stage was first announced at the 15th International Congress of
Psychoanalysts in 1936, but made little impact – Ernest Jones cut off Lacan's
presentation under the ten-minute rule. Lacan repeated it in a new paper,
'The mirror stage as formative of the function of the I as revealed in
psychoanalytic experience', delivered at the congress thirteen years later, in
1949 (*Ecrits*, 1966a, Chap. I) when, he claimed, the idea had become more
or less established in the French group. The mirror stage, he said, offers an
imaginary unification of the self, a unification in fantasy on the model of
other people or the mirror image, before full motor control of the body is
established.

Lacan thus makes a distinction, within the structure of the psyche as
a whole, between the subject who speaks – and who, in the course of an
analysis as the early, Heideggerean Lacan conceives it, should be brought to
offer true or full speech – and the ego, which he sees as an objectified self-
image, constructed erroneously before the subject can speak. Freud did not
make this distinction.[6] For Freud, for Anna Freud, and even more for the
American ego-psychologists who continued Freud's work in Lacan's day, it
is the ego that speaks, though its speech is often interfered with by material
from the unconscious – from the id, the superego, or the ego-defences. But
for Lacan the ego is an imagined object, and it is as absurd to think of the
ego speaking as it is to think of a desk speaking: he expands this conceit at
length in his paper 'The Freudian Thing' (1955).[7]

It is indeed arguable that there are inconsistencies in Freud's conception
of the ego. In his metapsychological writings, the ego is an agent, originally
centred on the perception-consciousness system, whose primary purpose
is to deal with external reality, though it is surrounded and protected by
unconscious defence mechanisms that actually hide some aspects of both
inner and outer reality from it. In earlier writings by Freud, the ego is constructed by identifying with, and then internalising, lost objects of desire. It
is difficult to see how an object constructed like this can be more than that
agent's internal image of itself – and a false image at that. How can a process
of internalising images produce anything but an internal image? How can it
possibly produce an agent? We might as well expect a desk to speak as an
image to deal with reality.

Lacan does not think the ego is centred on the perception-consciousness
system, or organised by the reality principle. He rejects the reality principle
as 'the expression of a scientific prejudice most hostile to the dialectic of

knowledge'.[8] He also bitterly attacks American ego-psychology. For many analysts, particularly in the USA, the ego was a conflict-free zone in which reason could operate. A prime aim of therapy was to strengthen the ego, which Lacan thought usually meant remodelling it on the ego of the analyst. For Lacan, the ego is more like a neurotic symptom than a self, or 'subject', and the last thing you should do is strengthen it.[9] Lacanians start from the function of *méconnaissance* – misrecognition – which according to Lacan characterises the ego in all its structures. He refers to Anna Freud's account of ego-defences for examples of this.[10] But Anna Freud never equated the defences with all the ego's structures, and held quite orthodox views on the reality principle.

On the face of it, Lacan here falls into the same logical confusion as Freud. He too makes the ego, formed by a process of internalising images, into an agent rather than a mere false image; but it is an agent for lying and misrecognition. We thus have two logical problems instead of one. How can an image be an agent of any kind? And how can any agent be purely an agent of misrecognition? (One might as well train a dog to be disobedient – how would it know what disobedience was?) Surely some kind of accurate recognition is a logical prerequisite of systematic misrecognition?

The 1949 paper really offers a very striking example of an attempt to give a psychological foundation – including in the full text ethological examples about pigeons and locusts – to an account of a fundamental existential paradox. All human beings, on this view, form their self-concepts on a fundamental misrecognition: they build themselves an imaginary ego and mistake it for the subject that experiences and acts – and, later, speaks. Alienation is built in to self-consciousness. We thus have the support of science for an account of the human condition that sounds very like the myth of the Fall. The biologically very useful tendency to think oneself unified before one is, turns into the eternal philosophical and ethical self-deceit of thinking from a position where one is not.

I don't myself see why one should take a tragic view of this development – *homo sapiens* couldn't survive as a species for a single lifetime if its members didn't routinely develop internal mechanisms, responsive to culture, for controlling the expression of their own instinctual impulses. But both Freud and Lacan do take a tragic view – the classic statement is Freud's *Civilisation and its Discontents*, with its picture of neurosis inevitably increasing as civilised restraint does.

It is worth pausing here to note how firmly Lacan dismisses both the scientific and the perceptual realism which Freud explicitly defends. This position is central to Lacan's work.[11] Freud cannot do without the reality principle: he needs it to explain the way in which, after all, we do learn to deal with a real world outside us and independent of us. But for Lacan it is simply the expression of a scientific prejudice in favour of the view that there **is** a real world outside us, with inherent structures of its own. What Lacan accepts is 'the dialectic of knowledge', with its obvious Hegelian implications. In Hegel's philosophy, the world is actually constructed in the dialectic of knowledge, and exists as part of the self-knowledge of *Geist* (the historically developing human mind or spirit). It is an objective historical idealism. Lacan never goes quite that far; he retains a category of 'the real', though it seems to be almost as unstructured and unknowable as Kant's 'things-in-themselves'.[12] But the whole world in which the speaking subject operates is represented as 'the symbolic' and constructed in language. Language – the symbolic – is thus in philosophical terms pre-ontological: a thing has being only by being signified.[13] This is a structuralism that trembles on the edge of becoming a linguistic idealism.[14]

From the mirror stage to the structure of the psyche

Where does the idea of the mirror stage come from? As Elisabeth Roudinesco points out, Henri Wallon wrote a paper in 1931 on the way the child develops a concept of his own body.[15] His test was the reaction of an animal, or a child, to its own reflection in a mirror. A drake takes the reflection to be his mate; a monkey puts a hand behind the mirror, and becomes agitated when it finds nothing there; a baby before the third month notices nothing at all, but during the next three, will smile at the image as if at a person. At the tenth month the baby sees the image as a detached part of its self; by a year, is beginning to distinguish the self from its image or representation. In the baby's attitude of the tenth month we can see the germ of Lacan's 'imaginary'; in that of the twelfth, of his 'symbolic'.

The mirror stage is a perfectly plausible developmental concept, though it doesn't fit at all well into the standard stages of sexual development that Freud recognised. But there is nothing scientifically absurd about postulating that a human baby has a biological tendency to fantasise itself as a unified whole, modelled on some other person's body or its own seen in a mirror, before motor control is fully established. If one were treating this as a scientific theory, one would want to ask for detailed evidence. It would be nice, for example, if Lacan had provided a discussion of the original experiments of Wallon which are the sole experimental source for his theory, and showed why they had this general cogency; but we don't get that. We do, however, get a number of ethological parallels, to chimpanzees, monkeys, pigeons, locusts, and the fixed action patterns of sticklebacks[16] – which show that Lacan was not wholly hostile to biology and natural science, and even offer parallels to the biological interpretation of Jung that I drew attention to in Chapter 5.[17]

But Lacan's interest in the mirror stage is a philosophical one. The idea of the mirror stage, he says, is an experience that leads us to 'oppose any philosophy directly issuing from the Cogito' – that is, from Descartes' view that I can be certain of my own being on the evidence of my conscious thought. Lacan wishes to use Hegelian ideas: we recognise our own consciousness by recognising another. The child, according to the 1949 paper, is actually 'sunk in motor incapacity and nursling dependence' but identifies with its specular image: this exemplifies the way in which:

(1)   the I is 'precipitated in primordial form' [as an ideal-ego], before
(2)   the dialectic of 'identification with the other' objectifies it, and
(3)   language restores to it its function as subject.[18] (my numbering)

Step 1 is a particular case of the way the image in phantasy (the *imago*) relates the organism to its reality – relating inner and outer worlds. The subject has a succession of phantasies starting with a fragmented body-image and ending with 'the armour of an alienating identity'.

> Thus, to break out of the circle of the **Innenwelt** into the **Umwelt** generates the inexhaustible quadrature of the ego's verifications.[19]

The touch of bombast here prefigures much of Lacan's later style; one of the malign effects of this bombastic language is to hide from us the fact that the central problem of consciousness – how is it that we are aware of the world and ourselves? – is here referred to but not solved. All the same, there is an interesting problem here, and one can dimly see a proposal for the first step of a possible solution: 'how does consciousness develop?' – step one, by developing unifying images of external objects in phantasy and so developing an **imaginary** world. The imaginary world includes a (false) unified image of the self, as ego.

What about the second step – the 'dialectic of identification with the other'? This sounds Hegelian; and sure enough Lacan's teacher Kojève provides us with a precedent, which also has the advantage of telling us something we shall badly need to know later on: the relationship of 'the other' and desire. Consciousness, for Kojève–Hegel, arises not from simple knowledge of some object – that would leave us aware simply of the object and not ourselves – but from a desire *for* the object, which has the effect of separating out a desiring self *from* the object. If food is just there in front of me I am simply aware of it; but if I desire the food, I become aware of my hungry self. What if I eat the food? What is the philosophical significance of that? The action that desire leads to philosophically **negates** the object and the 'I' receives its positive content from the negated non-I. (Hegelian dialectic is never weirder than when a physical action like eating is given a philosophical meaning like negation.) But desire for a body that leads to eating or fucking it would produce a merely animal consciousness; for a human consciousness to be produced you need to desire what is human – that is, to desire the other's desire. From this, presumably, emerges Lacan's lapidary definition 'desire is the desire of the other' – which he constantly repeats, but which seems to make little sense by itself.

It is this metaphysical fairy-tale which Lacan uses to help him rethink Freud's account of the formation of the ego, by successive identification with lost objects. The process becomes a Hegelian dialectic; the ego and its objects are created in this dialectic; both exist in the imaginary. Lacan represents them by a and a' respectively, ('a' stands for l'autre, or 'the other'): can these mere labels be meant to establish them as equivalent to the Hegelian or existential metaphysical category of the other?

We haven't yet sorted out every reference to an 'Other'. The analyst, we are told elsewhere (*Seminar* II, p.246), must aim at the passage of true speech, joining the subject to another subject, on the other side of the wall of language. This is the big Other, not to be confused with the little one above, though it seems eminently confusible. Since we now have no less than three 'a's in our theory of the psyche[20] it is probably time for a diagram.

These four elements of the self are often reified in a square diagram like the one below. (See *Seminar* II, p.242, or *Ecrits*, Chap. 6 for variants. I have added labels in the margins to clarify it a little.)

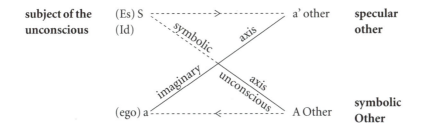

subject of the unconscious	(Es) S (Id)	a' other	**specular other**
	(ego) a	A Other	**symbolic Other**

It will be seen that the subject is identified with the id, not the ego; the ego is an imaginary construction and has an imaginary relation to its objects. The Lacanian unconscious is to be found on an axis we shall learn to call the symbolic, between the subject and the true Other beyond the wall of language. And what marks off the Lacanian unconscious, from what everybody up to Lacan thought was the Freudian one, is its content – not obscure urges and fantasies, but signifiers. The unconscious is the discourse of the Other; it is structured like a language, because it is an effect of language.

To understand this strange concept, we must look at a later stage of the theory (see below).

The third step moves us from the mirror stage to a social stage of development, by way of the Oedipus complex: 'the drama of primordial jealousy' that produces 'the dialectic that will henceforth link the **I** to socially elaborated situations'.[21] This ensures that the whole of human knowledge is mediated 'through the desire of the other' and turns the **I** into an apparatus for which instinctual impulses constitute dangers, even when they are a part of natural maturation, and need to be mediated by culture.

Heresies and expulsions: the Rome Report and the rewriting of psychoanalysis around language

As one might imagine, not all psychoanalysts liked this heavily philosophised version of their discipline. Lacanians, to this day, think of Lacan as a Freudian – the best of the Freudians after Freud himself, and the best precisely because he combines close reading of the master's text with a philosophical sophistication that the master lacked. Substantial differences between Lacan and Freud are in fact usually taken as marks of Lacan's sophistication. But how Freudian is Lacan? Certainly he is a Freudian when compared with Sartre; and I at least find his capsule dismissal of existentialism fairly convincing.[22] But many of the ideas he dismisses – the reality-principle, the ego as centred on the perception-consciousness system – belong to Freud himself. A man who equates the death instinct with existential negativity; who rejects the 'reality-principle' as philosophically crude, and replaces it by the 'dialectic of knowledge'; and who regards the ego as an alienating misrecognition of the I who speaks – such a man is bound to be a Freudian heretic in the eyes of the orthodox. And as we shall see, in due course Lacan was treated as a heretic and suffered excommunication.

Along with a heretical theory went a heretical practice. Psychoanalysis is dominated by the medical model of mental illness. Analysts are confronted with symptoms and look for cures. Many think that to protect patients, it is necessary for analysts to be doctors and follow whatever are the agreed principles of psychoanalytic practice – e.g. as to length of session, frequency of sessions and rules of conduct within the session. All these positions have been opposed. Thomas Szass, for example, rejects the very concept of non-organic mental 'illness';[23] for him there is only deviant behaviour which we choose to stigmatise as illness. Even within psychoanalysis it is very common to oppose the requirement that analysts be doctors. Freud himself was opposed to it.[24]

When the Paris Psychoanalytic Society, in its expansive phase in 1952, was about to set up a training institute, Lacan (though himself qualified) was the leader of the faction in favour of lay analysis. But he stood for more than that: for a cultural, rather than neurobiological conception of psychoanalytic theory, and for a non-medical conception of the very purpose of analysis: to bring the patient to the point at which he could speak his own truth. And for a flexible length of analytic session too; sometimes a few minutes. It is easy to see how this last innovation connects with Lacan's goals – how can the time of the unconscious be measured by a rigid 50-minute rule? But opponents in the Society said that the short sessions, in training analyses, merely enabled him to turn out more trainees, and manufacture, on the production line, lots of little Lacans to take over the world.

Lacan lost that fight and founded a new body: the French Psychoanalytic Society. In 1953 he delivered a 'Report' to a congress of psychoanalysts in Rome, which amounted to a manifesto for the FPS. It was called: 'The Function and Field of Speech and Language in Psychoanalysis'. It began, as one might expect, with an obscure polemic against Lacan's current opponents, and some sharp remarks about American psychoanalysis with its inclination toward the adaptation of the individual to the social environment, and the objectification implied in the notion of 'human relations'. (These remarks had the effect of establishing Lacan's left-wing credentials for many years to come; though anti-Americanism seems to be the **only** way in which Lacan is in the least left-wing. But it was enough during the Vietnam war.)

The main part of the Rome Report, however, is an impassioned, sometimes moving defence of the centrality of speech in the practice of psychoanalysis; in particular of the speech of the analysand as a way of finding his own meaning. The enemy is objectification. The famous 'stages of development of sexuality', for example, are not to be seen as some innate biological programme. They are stages which the analysand has lived through, his own defeats or victories, with a meaning in the past, and another meaning that the analysand can give to them in the present. It is the function of the patient's speech to resume to himself, and give full meaning to, his past. 'The unconscious is that part of the concrete discourse . . . that is not at the disposal of the subject in reestablishing the continuity of his conscious discourse' (Lacan, 1996a, p.49).

These last words are potentially Lacan's most important single claim. They appear to reject the notion of a 'reified' unconscious; an unconscious that is an object, a thing, or a structure, and that serves to **explain** gaps in discourse. They recognise it only as an aspect of the concrete discourse of which the subject **is** unconscious, and which it is the duty of the analyst to make available to him. This is a line of thought which persists throughout

Lacan's work: in 1964 (*Four Concepts of Psychoanalysis*, Chap. 3) he describes 'the gap of the unconscious' as 'pre-ontological' and as 'ethical'. What this means, I think, is that there is no such thing as 'the unconscious' to discover; but the physician has a duty to make available to the patient those aspects of his discourse of which he is unaware.

I am inclined to think that carrying through this line of thought consistently would dissolve the whole body of Freudian thought back from science into philosophy. But there was in Lacan a very strong desire to retain the analytical power – and I think the prestige – of the scientist. Existing scientific models, he felt, were based on a false idealisation of experimental method, and misrepresented the nature of psychoanalysis. But would it not be possible to construct theoretical categories and even modes of formalisation that represent it properly? Might one not even (since psychoanalysis is, after all, the most fundamental way of studying human thinking) find new categories that underlie the hard sciences themselves?

It seems to me obvious that Lacan was partly right to think in this way. There are plenty of examples of successful moves of this kind in the history of science. One of them – very slightly later than Lacan's – occurred in linguistics. Psychologists like Skinner had attempted to account for language use on a behavioristic model;[25] Chomsky provided a much more rigorous model of language, essentially by formalising – making a mathematical model of – the structures of traditional grammar, and incidentally showed Skinner's enterprise to be impossible.[26] Lacan's 'structuralist' move, then, of attempting to import Saussurean linguistic categories into psychoanalysis was in itself a reasonable one; the question is, could he make it work?

But Lacan has a problem that Chomsky does not have. Good formalisations have the essential properties of machines; in fact, they can be made to run as programs on that particular sort of machine we call a digital computer. They are thus eminently testable, since you can use a good formalisation to predict new data and retrodict old. They are also essentially objectifying. Chomsky need have no problem with such an approach; he thinks of himself as an objective scientist anyway; he is only trying to theorise grammar, not human experience in general; and he has never been afraid of data. But Lacan is a passionate opponent of objectification as such. There is thus from the beginning an irresolvable conflict between his 'scientific' presentations and his philosophy; and none of his science actually works.

It is this, in my view, which generated the colossal apparatus of bluff and double-bluff, near-simultaneous assertion and denial, obscure technicality and scalding emotion, paranoid bullying and pathos of the lonely misunderstood excommunicate, that constitutes Lacanian rhetoric, that made life so exciting for his disciples, and makes it so miserable for readers like me, who are not looking for religious leaders, but for bits of psychoanalysis that might fit with the natural sciences and help explain how literature works. It is only fair to Lacan, and Lacanians, to say that they will be profoundly suspicious of the whole procedure I am engaged in – namely, looking for a consistent theory. Lacan speaks of 'the paranoid structure of knowledge', rather as if such consistent theories are always paranoid delusions. Lacanians reject the notion of the analyst as 'a subject supposed to know'. This scepticism about consistent theory is the Lacanian basis of post-structuralism. There is a definite sense in which to try to give a clear and coherent account of Lacanian theory is to work against his intentions.

Nevertheless, in the next few pages I shall build up what might be called a post-1953 Lacanian theory. I can't be sure it is **the** Lacanian theory; the texts are too obscure. It certainly qualifies as a reading of them, though of course an incomplete one. It ignores many important concepts – jouissance, the *objet a*, foreclosure, the four discourses,[27] etc. – as well as almost everything in the later work that seems to be mere paradox or wordplay. Instead, it concentrates on the question of language: on the relationship between Lacan, Lévi-Strauss, Saussure and Jakobson. It is perhaps a piece of **bricolage** built out of Lacanian material: its real value is to show the extreme difficulty of building these materials, with their internal contradictions and misunderstandings, into a comprehensive and connected theory of the psyche.

The general system of Jacques Lacan: a symbolic bricolage of anthropology, psychoanalysis, linguistics, *et al.*

There was a time when Lacan seemed to offer the most astonishing unification of disciplines in recent intellectual history: a foretaste in the 1950s of the glittering promises of French High Structuralism in the early 1960s[28] or indeed – despite the radical philosophical differences involved – of the cognitive sciences now. Anthropology, psychoanalysis and linguistics, Lévi-Strauss, Freud, Saussure and Jakobson, were to be joined in a seamless web, and treated with all the rigour of mathematical formulae. Or, to put it another way, the law of the father and the family would be connected with the symbolism of the phallus and castration, and would explain the workings of language and culture. And the principles involved would be displayed in brief and revealing mathemes. Did this work? Let us consider some key concepts, assuming, perhaps counterfactually, that they belong to a serious philosophical or scientific system and not a literary parody of one.

The symbolic, the imaginary and the real: Lacan

Lacan offers as his basic philosophical categories the famous trio of **the symbolic, the imaginary and the real**. Lacanians attach great philosophical importance to these categories, for epistemology, the theory of knowledge, and ontology, the theory of being. I know of attempts to refound mathematics upon them. Judith Butler, in her book *Gender Troubles*,[29] says that Lacan disputes the primacy of ontology in Western metaphysics; the symbolic is pre-ontological and provides the structure of signification within which a thing takes on the characterisation of 'being'. He subordinates the question 'what is/has being' to the question 'How is "being" instituted and allocated through the signifying practices of the paternal economy?' – which means that there is no access to being without a prior enquiry into the being of the phallus. These are gigantic and very paradoxical philosophical claims, since in its ordinary sense 'being', the fundamental concept of ontology, represents what cannot be allocated or instituted: it just **is**. I don't find any philosophical arguments in Lacan to justify the enormous claim that ontology should be subordinate to linguisterie.

Other commentators find these categories obscure, woolly and variable. (In one standard textbook, which has two authors, one of the authors holds one view and the other author the other.[30]) The most extensive discussion of them was quite late on, in Seminar XXII, RSI, published in four issues of the rare journal *Ornicar?*, 2–5.[31] But Lacan uses here a rhetoric which I find distinctly unhelpful. Thus, the fact that these are interlinked concepts is represented by saying they form a three-link Borromean chain such that if any connection is broken they all fall apart. One feels, at points like these 'If only Lacan would just say what he means and not be so *picturesque!*'[32]

One way of taking them is as fundamental categories of experience; perhaps merely fundamental categories of experience as revealed in the analytic situation. The symbolic is experience structured by the symbolic order of society (human culture); the imaginary is experience structured in phantasy and by images; the real is experience raw and sometimes traumatic. On this view, the real is the impossible because you can't represent it; but you keep on stumbling upon it, particularly in analysis, often represented by gaps and unexplainables in discourse. But neither this nor any other view will cover all appearances of these terms.

Anthropology and the symbolic order: Lévi-Strauss

It was from the anthropologist Claude Lévi-Strauss that Lacan took over the structuralist concept of a pre-existing symbolic order, an order of culture, which comes to constitute the world in which we seem to live. For anthropologists culture covers far more than cultural products like art-works and philosophical systems. It includes all the basic rules that govern the way human beings live in societies. The most important of these for anthropologists govern systems of kinship – they regulate who must marry who. For Lévi-Strauss these are what constitute society as such, and they are determined by incest taboos. The order of culture is therefore marked off from the order of nature by the operation of the incest taboo.

This works in quite a complex way. Since the incest taboo prevents women mating within the family, it forces different men in different families to exchange women. This process of exchanging women between families is what holds society together. Thus the incest taboo, far from being a custom of some particular society, is actually the primal taboo that institutes society as a process of exchange of women. Women are, as it were, the most basic form of social message sent between men. Other cultural forms of message-exchanging are built on this primary one.

> The primordial Law is therefore that which in regulating marriage ties superimposes the kingdom of culture on that of a nature abandoned to the law of mating.
>
> > (*Ecrits*, 1966a, p.66; *Ecrits*, Chap. III, sec. 2. (1953) for general discussion, introducing such concepts as 'the law of the father')

Psychoanalysis and the law of the father: Lacan

How can all this be linked with psychoanalysis? For the psychoanalyst the incest taboo is represented by the Oedipus complex, as it affects the **phallic** phase of sexual development. It is the fear of castration by the father that makes the boy abandon his incestuous desires. Taking this view, it is the castration threat at the phallic phase that inserts the baby, till then just an organism, into the cultural order – the order of law – and makes it a person. Incidentally, the astonishing male chauvinism of these views – which seem to suggest that women are objects rather than persons and have no place in the cultural order – has, by a process of intellectual reaction formation, given rise to a brilliant tradition of Lacanian feminism. It is discussed in the next chapter.

This projected link between the Lévi-Straussian concept of society and the psychoanalytic concept of the self seems theoretically very exciting. It is obvious that sociology and psychology need a link of this kind, if either is to make sense. But will this link work? Lacan seems to be identifying the cognitive unconscious – our unconscious knowledge of the rules of society and language which enable us to function – with the Freudian unconscious.

Is this a major new discovery, as some structuralists thought? Culler, for example, when he claimed that Saussure provided better evidence for the unconscious than Freud did?[33] Or is it a confusion of two different things?

Come to that, it is a standard criticism of Lévi-Strauss that he **confuses** – i.e., identifies without justification – the incest taboo, which is concerned with sex, and marriage regulations, which are concerned with social roles and contracts. Similarly for the connection of the symbolic order with exchange: society is held together by the 'exchange' of women and gifts, and the 'exchange' of verbal messages; is that a reason for confusing women with verbal messages? Lacan too seems to accept such identifications too easily; he seems to think of the symbolic as purely verbal, and yet somehow inaugurated Oedipally.

The attempt to unite Lévi-Straussian anthropology with psychoanalysis is certainly interesting. A sober empiricist would have spent twenty years trying to find evidence for it. For Lacan, however, this theory, which was never completely formulated, was only a way station to a further step of unification, in a theory of language and culture also never completely formulated, but gestured at in all his oratory.

The identification of culture with language: Lacan

Lévi-Strauss modelled his anthropological concept of the order of culture on the Saussurean concept of language, mediated to him in the lectures of Roman Jakobson in 1942.[34] Lacan in the 1950s goes further; he identifies the symbolic order with language; insertion into the symbolic order becomes insertion into language. Such vast identificatory gestures are characteristic of early French structuralism, with its overweening hopes of unifying the human sciences. To a linguist, such an identification is bound to seem highly implausible. Languages are fairly self-contained systems with their own characteristic structure, which is not at all the same as the structure of the culture in which the language is spoken.

We can give a concrete example of this. To read the *Oxford English Dictionary* (the most elaborate and encyclopaedic ever produced) and add to that a Chomskyan generative grammar of English, is not at all the same experience as to read the *Encyclopaedia Britannica*. The reason is that the first describes the language and the second describes general knowledge coded in that language. For Lacan's unification to work, he needs a very complex and inclusive notion of language indeed, for it will have to perform both the functions of the dictionary and those of the encyclopaedia, and some more beside. But in fact, far from adopting a complex and inclusive account of language, he adopts an astonishingly crude and simple one, far cruder than that of Saussure, which is itself inadequate. Human language and human thought alike are reduced to movement from signifier to signifier.

The structuralist model of language: phonemic differences and conceptual oppositions: Saussure

In this section, I will set out the ways in which Lacan's model of language is – from a scientific point of view which many Lacanians will find irrelevant to their interests – distorted and oversimplified until it simply will not work. We might start with the change from the complex Saussurean concept of the **sign** to the crude Lacanian concept of the **signifier**. Saussure defines the **sign** as a **signifier–signified** pair, where a signifier is a sound-image and a signified the concept it represents. In structuralist linguistics, from Saussure to Jakobson,[35] the sound-image is a chain of **phonemes** – the minimal pronounceable units of sound in the language that native speakers recognise as different from each other.

I had better give some examples of this. Here are some words, considered as signifiers or sound-images, each of which consists of a chain of two phonemes only. The sound-images are different in each case by the difference of a single phoneme – which in the first line happens to be the initial consonant, and in the second line the final vowel:

boy, coy, Roy, toy;
boy, bow, bee, by.

These phonemic differences determine how the word is pronounced and perceived as a word, but have no influence on its meaning.

The signified, or meaning, or concept that the word represents, depends on an altogether different set of oppositions. Here are examples of conceptual oppositions:

'boy' is opposed to 'girl' (by sex);
to 'man' (by age-grade);
and to 'kitten' or 'puppy' (by species).

These conceptual oppositions determine the meaning of the word – i.e. its signified – but have no influence on its pronunciation.

Notice that the oppositions of sense are arbitrarily placed in relation to the oppositions of sound and are not reducible to them. There is nothing boyish about the phonemes /b/ and /oi/ separately or in combination; and there is nothing of the sounds /b/ and /oi/ in the concept that combines maleness, immaturity and humanity, and could just as easily be labelled 'puer'. In short, languages are not onomatopoeic (save in occasional words like 'baa' and 'boo').

This independence of sound and sense is the fundamental meaning of Saussure's principle of the arbitrariness of the sign; it is astonishing how many people, including Lacan, have managed to move from this principle to its opposite – namely that it is the signifier that imposes structure on experience. This is completely untrue. It is this common error – or else it is recklessness about the theory he is purporting to borrow – which sometimes leads Lacan to suppress the signified altogether and try to make do with signifiers alone. Taken literally this means that languages are collections of sound-images with no meaning!

Why would anyone want to believe this? One possibility is a form of philosophical materialism, which argues that talk about concepts is mentalistic and empty, and we should replace this by talk about systems of opposition among signifiers. Lacanians often adopt from Saussure the notion that language is a system of oppositions without positive terms; and deduce from this that ideas are differentiated through the differences of the sound-images representing them. This common error, which surfaces again and again in post-structuralist writing, may actually have Lacan as one of its principal sources. It comes from failing to realise, or arrogantly refusing to recognise, that languages have double articulation[36] – that separate systems of opposition exist on the side of the signified and on the side of the signifier. This view is not Saussurean.

What Saussure did say is that thought is cut up into distinct concepts by the signs (not signifiers) making up the language; and it is cut up in different ways in different languages. As a practical warning to philologists and dictionary makers this is an important point: it means, 'don't expect translation ever to run word for word'. But many Lacanians and post-structuralists have made it into something more than that: a radical philosophical interpretation of Saussure, that will be the basis for a theory that culture is based on the conceptual oppositions in the language. As a total theory of meaning, however, it is logically impossible: you cannot construct a semantic system on the basis of pure opposition, or pure difference between signs. There is a full discussion of this, with a demonstration of the logical impossibility of the theory, in Jackson, *The Poverty of Structuralism* (1991). Saussure was strongly criticised for his view by later structuralists like Jakobson (1976), and it is quite inconsistent with his own scientific realism. This view is Saussurean, but false.

Chain and choice: metonymy and metaphor: Saussure and Jakobson

Saussure points out that there are two distinct ways in which linguistic elements can be connected. They can be chained together serially as phonemes are in the sound-image of a word, or as words are in a linguistic expression. He called this the **syntagmatic axis** of language. Or they can be connected by associative links to other words not in the chain. Thus 'education' forms an associative series with 'apprenticeship', 'learning' etc. Later structuralists focused more on the possibility of substituting one item for another in the chain. Thus in the sentence 'the boy kicked the ball' we might replace every sign and produce 'a woman touched a bat'. They called this axis of substitution the **paradigmatic** axis of language. On the paradigmatic axis, one might find a whole set of words like 'girl', 'man', 'woman' etc. that could be substituted for 'boy', or a whole set like 'touched', 'hit', 'thumped' which might be substituted for 'kicked', or one or two, like 'a', 'some' which might be substituted for 'the'.

Roman Jakobson – a bold scholar, immensely fertile in hypotheses, some of which have lasted well[37] – saw far more in the syntagmatic/paradigmatic distinction than anyone before him. In a little book, *Fundamentals of Language* (1956), he connected the two axes of language to two fundamental kinds of operation in the mind, **combination** and **selection**, which could be separated by association tests, and were subject to differential loss in linguistic aphasia (partial loss of language). He thus offered a putative connection between linguistic structure, psycholinguistics and general psychology. In contiguity disorder, you lose combinatory powers; in similarity disorder, you lose selectional powers.

He then connected the mental operations of combination and selection to two figures of rhetoric: **metonymy** and **metaphor**. Metonymy is the figure of speech in which you replace the name of something by the name of an attribute of it or of something closely related to it. There is a closely related figure, synecdoche, in which you give the name of a whole for a part, or a part for a whole. The classic example is the phrase 'thirty sail . . .' meaning 'thirty ships . . .'. Metaphor can be seen as presenting a resemblance as if it were an identity – as when we speak of a man as a dinosaur because we thought men with opinions like his were extinct. It will be seen that the line between these figures is rather difficult to draw. The various figures of speech were named by ancient and mediaeval rhetoricians for practical purposes and on logically rather shaky grounds.

It is not at all clear that these figures are purely linguistic ones; you can use devices very like metonymy and metaphor in film narrative, employing images alone. But Jakobson was a brilliant and imperialistic linguist, always trying to bring fresh territory, like poetics, within the bounds of linguistics. He tried to provide an account of metonymy and metaphor that was purely linguistic, mapping them onto his distinction between combination and selection. Metonymy corresponded to movement along the syntagmatic axis; metaphor to movement along the paradigmatic axis, the axis of substitution. These correspondences don't work too well: both metonymy and metaphor involve substitution of one item for another, and neither necessarily involves any movement along a syntagmatic axis.

Moreover it is absurd to claim that metonymy and metaphor have a different epistemological status. In *The Poverty of Structuralism* I pointed out how the Mafia boss who attends a meeting accompanied by three 'guns' (henchmen with guns – metonymy/synecdoche) is on equal terms with the one who attends accompanied by three 'soldiers' (henchmen with guns – metaphor). My own view is that metonymy and synecdoche are actually particular types of metaphor – all involve representing one thing by another on account of some connection between them, and any connection will do to found a metaphor on. We are dealing with rather arbitrary terminology here, not deep principles of philosophical logic. But Jakobson attached great importance to these distinctions. He related them to stylistics: metonymy goes with realism, and metaphor with romanticism. And he related them to psychoanalysis. Metonymy, based on contiguity, goes with displacement and synecdoche with condensation. Metaphor, based on similarity, relates to identification and symbolism.

Is the unconscious an effect of language? Lacan

Lacan borrowed Jakobson's theory and transformed it. He attempted to map the unconscious processes described by psychoanalysts – repression and the defences, displacement and condensation – onto a list of nine figures of style and four tropes. In this way the unconscious can in a very strong sense be said to be an effect of language.

Lacan claims[38] that linguistics is founded on the basis of an algorithm, which he gives as:

$$\frac{S}{s}$$

read as 'the signifier over the signified'. The scientific linguist is likely to object to this on several grounds. First, linguistics is not actually founded on this formula, which, as Lacan notes, does not actually occur in Saussure. Second, this formula is not an algorithm. (An algorithm is a formula from which you can calculate things, and predict or retrodict data. Generative grammars are algorithms.) This formula, like others appearing in the same chapter, is pictorial. It shows the signifier and signified as being distinct orders separated by a barrier resisting signification. It is said to define the topography of the unconscious in the Freudian sense. That is, Lacan identifies the bar in the formula with the barrier between conscious and unconscious in repression!

Lacan develops a bizarre replacement for the signifier–signified relationship. For Lacan the signified is not a concept but another signifier. The second signifier is to be found beneath the barrier of repression, in the unconscious. Repression has in fact turned into metaphor formation. Signifiers are joined in chains and there are possible connections along the chain – called **metonymic** – and across from one chain to another – called **metaphoric**. Connections between the chains of signifiers that are conscious and the chains that are unconscious don't occur at every signifier. The unconscious set slides about loosely beneath the conscious set and is joined to it at certain key points – like upholstery buttons holding the fabric to what is underneath it. The metonymic and metaphoric connections referred to above are to be identified (quite implausibly) with the processes of **displacement** and **condensation** referred to by Freud. (Note the difference from Jakobson, who thinks condensation is related to synecdoche.)

It is clear in this case that Lacan is no longer talking, as Saussure is, about language as such. He is, I think, talking metaphorically about the use of language in the analytic session. At least, that is the only way of making sense of what he is saying. If he is taken as talking very loosely about chains of associated word representations (not just signifiers, as he says he is) in the conscious and the unconscious mind then there are obviously important insights here; the upholstery button metaphor is a vivid account of the way in which what is said by the analysand in analysis links up, at key points only, with what is in his unconscious. But why is the overall theory described in such an obscure way that one has to resort to conjectures of this kind to make sense of it?

Is there any evidence whatever for an identification of this kind? There is this much: in orthodox Freudian theory we say that repressed material is transformed by processes like displacement and condensation and appears in the end in symptoms, dreams and scripts like those of Schreber the madman,[39] which we treat as having meaning, and interpret, very often, as offering metaphors, metonyms, rebuses and so forth that reveal the unconscious material that must have given rise to them. Lacan wants to collapse the causal processes which orthodox theorists postulate, and identify them with the rhetorical structure of the texts patients produce. The unconscious thus ceases to be a substantive part of the mind, and becomes an effect of language.

Confusing langue *and* parole: *how language speaks people:*
Lacan – misappropriating Saussure

In Lacanian theory, Saussure's distinction between **langue** and **parole**
is usually ignored: this makes phrases like 'the signifying chain' almost
meaningless, since one can't tell whether they refer to a structure or a text,
or simply make a vague gesture in the direction of a process. *Langue* in
Saussure is the systematic structure of language and *parole* the use of it in
speech or writing. A *langue* is a language like English, French, or Japanese,
described in terms of its structure and vocabulary. *Parole* is the discourse
you produce in such a language, by putting together expressions in it, and
speaking or writing them. Linguistics is concerned with languages, not with
the discourses produced in them. The German language is not the same as
the speeches of Hitler or the poems of Goethe, though these are both discourses **in** German. The German language is merely the grammar, vocabulary and idioms of German, which Hitler and Goethe use.

There is indeed a clear relationship between language and subjectivity,
and it is this: language produces (aspects of) subjectivity; a human subject
produces discourse. The *langue* of a community pre-exists the child. It is
reasonable to argue that when it is learnt by the child, it becomes part of his
own subjectivity, providing some of the rules by which he understands the
world and acts in it. The *parole* of the child is produced **in** that *langue*, but
by the child and for his own purposes. Intersubjective relationships are produced when people talk in the same language (produce *parole* in the same
langue) to each other. The existence of intelligent interactive behaviour like
this is our basic evidence for believing in the existence of human subjects
who speak languages and are active agents.

Lacan may well understand the distinction between *langue* and *parole*,
but he almost always ignores it. If you do this, you make a language look like
a vast mass of *parole* waiting to be spoken, rather than what it really is, a
set of principles for making expressions up. And given that Lacan usually
only recognises signifiers, *parole* will have to consist of signifiers: that is,
meaningless sound-images. The speaker, who in all satisfactory theories
is an agent making up new expressions to explain himself to someone else,
becomes a passive subject carried through 'the defiles of the signifier', or
along 'the signifying chain'. Language speaks people rather than people
speaking a language.

Literary theorists have come to love this idiotic paradox, and its consequence that the subject is an effect of language or discourse. But taken
literally it turns the subject into a tape-recorder, and any tape-recorder
becomes a subject. This is as bad as making a desk into a subject.

I am not saying that this is what Lacan intended. On the contrary, no psychoanalyst has been more concerned to reject the view that the subject can be treated as an object. I am saying this is an unintended logical consequence of the theory he has adopted. In this theory, you actually become a subject by speaking (or being spoken). Both subjectivity and the unconscious are now retroactive effects of language, not causes of what you say. The unconscious is structured like a language, because it is an effect of language: it is not, as it was for Freud, something real in itself that may be detected and mapped by its interference with what the patient says, but something constructed out of those interference effects: it is the portion of the patient's discourse not under his control, though God knows what sort of control a human tape-recorder can have.

A misreading of Saussure has thus spawned a new metaphysics of the subject, and of the conscious and unconscious mind; and the whole post-structuralist tradition has followed this metaphysics. I say there is a curious parallelism between this exotic variety of psychoanalysis and the crasser forms of cognitive science. The fundamental thesis of strong artificial intelligence is this: if a computer with sufficient power and appropriate sensori-motor outlets ran the right programs, it would be a subject. We ourselves are no more than damp computers running cultural programs on our wetware. Subjective experience is an effect of data being transferred between programs. But this is an exact parallel to what Lacan himself claims.

In his paper 'The Subversion of the Subject and the Dialectic of Desire in the Freudian Unconscious' (*Ecrits*, Chap. 9), and elsewhere, Lacan offers the crazy formula: 'A subject is what represents a signifier to another signifier'. This is obviously one limiting case of what I have described elsewhere as 'discursive idealism':[40] but it is also the limiting case of cognitive scientific materialism as well. It is the construction of human subjects out of wholly meaningless sound-images.

The phallus as master signifier: Lacan

Sound-images are not the only signifiers Lacan recognises. There are also such entities as 'the gaze'; and there is a master signifier of altogether greater importance: the phallus. The phallus, presumably because of the castration complex, signifies lack; it installs its own lack of being in the signifying chain, and this accounts for signification – though I cannot imagine how. Movement along the signifying chain by metonymy is equated with desire – though it is difficult to see why. These theories are much too vague to be tested empirically; what they gesture at is a fundamental connection between language and sexuality, and in particular between language and male sexuality – the alleged phallo-centrism of human culture, which leaves women no voice. I shall discuss in the next chapter the brilliant feminist response to this claim. What can be said now is that there is actually no empirical evidence whatever that language or language development are linked to sex or sexuality or sexual development. It is a Lévi-Straussian/Lacanian fairy-tale.

There are many theories in the social sciences that appear to offer bread but actually give you a stone. It is perhaps at this point that we realise Lacanian theory is one of them. It has always been a great advantage of Freudian theory that it talks about sex; it discusses the way in which one of the greatest of biological drives, at first utterly non-verbal, is moulded first into fantasy and then into socially acceptable sublimations, some of them verbal. What Lacan offers instead are signifying chains, hanging on a phallus that isn't there, and that represents something Heideggereanly philosophical like lack of being. From the point of view of the literary theorist, of course, this version of the theory seems quite convenient; it only deals with verbal representations, and that is what the literary theorist deals with too. But Freud would have been the first to say – as he always did when somebody suggested leaving sex out – that such a theory was not Freudian.

What is wrong with the linguistic theory of the unconscious?

I have offered the best paraphrase I can of the claims of a quite bewildering theory. From the point of view of a linguist it must, I think, be described as gibberish. In fact, Lacan has simply thrown away Saussure's theory, while keeping some of his terminology. It might be worth asking at this point what motive Lacan had – what evidence, what general argument – for this linguistic rewrite of Freud's theory. It seems to me that he had a single argument, which was enormously potent to him, as versions of it were to all later post-structuralists – and that this argument is entirely unsound. The argument is that psychoanalysis is, exclusively and all the time, a talking cure; nothing happens in the analytic session except talk. The best outcome possible, is that the patient gets control of portions of his discourse formerly outside his control. 'The unconscious' is therefore merely a reification of a gap in discourse; it is an effect of language.

It is an amusing exercise (which remarks of Chomsky suggest) to construct an analogous argument about electricity. We can't directly sense electricity, so we need to measure it with meters. It follows from this (i) that electricity is the result of gaps in our sensory awareness of the world; and (ii) that electricity is an effect of meters. But this is absurd. Electrons are real particles and – quantum uncertainties about position and momentum notwithstanding – their mass movement, which constitutes electrical currents, is also real. We measure currents with meters; but the currents exist whether we measure them or not, and the meters are designed on that assumption.

Freud's theory about the unconscious was invented to explain dreams, symptoms, parapraxes and so on; psychoanalysis is a method justified by this theory, which happens to be verbal throughout; but there is no valid argument back from the verbal character of the method of cure to a purely verbal character of the unconscious. The move to reduce the unconscious to an effect of discourse with gaps in it is far closer in spirit to behaviorism than to Freudian theory. If we put this together with the reduction of discourse to signifying chains without signifieds, we see that Lacan's underlying scientific theory is very close indeed to a crude materialistic behaviorism, decorated in presentation with fantastic flowers of rhetoric. His underlying philosophy, on the other hand, is a kind of linguistic idealism. The paradox is, that the whole world of the symbolic is constructed in language; but language, on this model, is a device too crude and unstructured to construct anything in.

Is there a Lacanian theory?

There was another break-up in 1964, when the French Society, to obtain recognition from the International Psychoanalytic Association, had to agree that Lacan's training should not be recognised. (This was a bizarre requirement, since the society had many members trained by Lacan among its leaders. Were they not properly trained?) As Lacan pointed out (*Four Concepts*, p.3) this amounted to excommunication. Lacan continued to develop his work, in which, often in the very same seminar, he will sometimes wrap his acute but tendentious commentaries on Freud in wild verbal paradoxes, and sometimes, to give himself scientific credibility, express them in pseudo-scientific mathemes – such as algebraic formulae that work according to no known mathematical procedures[41] or topological models of the psyche. (Why do we call them topological models? They are just diagrams!) His personal cult grew till it became international; nobody but a few professionals knew or cared what was happening in official French psychoanalysis; but everybody argued over Lacan. I shall not here discuss the politics of Vincennes, set up in the wake of the 1968 revolutions and leading, as far as Lacanian psychoanalysis was concerned, to another internal war; nor the incidents that led Lacan, in old age in 1980, to dissolve his own School and set up another.

Lacan's general cultural influence dates from this later period: it is since 1968 that there has been Lacanian literary criticism, and Lacanian philosophy, in general circulation, including that quite extraordinary construct, a Lacanian theory of the subject especially for Marxists.[42] One need not perhaps pay too much attention to the various uses of Lacan's optical metaphors in film criticism; criticism is always opportunistic and grabs illuminating parallels from any intellectually fashionable doctrine. Perhaps the most authentic Lacanian criticism is that which simply plays with texts in a Lacanian way, like the master's own reading of 'The Purloined Letter' at the beginning of the French *Ecrits*,[43] and finds brilliant allegories of the master's doctrines.

But the systematic use, by semioticians, of categories like 'the signifier' (carefully divorced, in Lacanian fashion, from any signified) is quite another matter, and a much more important one. It suggests that we have, in semiotics, a regular science of signification, with a grounding in modern psychological theory. Is this true?

It seems to me quite false; and nowhere more false than when semiotics is Lacanian. The fact is that Lacan, so hostile to the objectifications of orthodox psychology, is by the standards of cognitive science guilty of grossly oversimplifying the problem of how human beings can possibly think in language, and what connections there can possibly be between our knowledge of language and the Freudian unconscious.

There is no chance of solving these problems unless you recognise at least the following sub-problems:

(i) the synchronic existence of languages, in the ordinary sense of English, German, French etc., treated by the ordinary methods of linguistics and psycholinguistics, which nowadays include formal logical and mathematical methods (proper mathematics, not Lacanian mathemes);

(ii) the synchronic existence of a symbolic order not identical with language, i.e. what is called in anthropology culture, treated in similarly formal ways, which the cognitive sciences are only just beginning to work out, and which may be beyond formalisation;

(iii) the multifarious and hopelessly ill-defined problems of pragmatics and usage theory, which are concerned with the way expressions from natural languages are used, both in social life, and in private thinking;

(iv) the traditional material of Freudian and Jungian theory alike: spontaneous fantasy, both sexual and otherwise, and the various processes of repression, reaction-formation, projection and so forth that make possible its multifarious cultural transformations.

I am not saying these four problems are the only ones; on the contrary, they subdivide into large numbers of smaller sub-problems, most of which are entirely beyond the beginnings of a solution at the present time. The worst thing one can say about Lacan is that when he was faced with problems like this that he had no real solution for, and no real interest in solving, he hid the fact from himself and his followers by covering it up with philosophical rhetoric. To this day, the rhetoric is still there, and the linguistic theory remains largely vacuous. The obvious reply would be that it is missing the point to see Lacanian theory as science at all; mathemes are not mathematics and linguisterie is not linguistics. They are part of the rhetorical surface of a philosophical teaching that remains loosely in the tradition of Heidegger, and belongs more to the various traditions that make Freud unscientific – phenomenological, existential, humanist, or whatever – than to that which reconciles him with modern science.

Notes and references

Suggestions for further reading are on page 214.

1. **Chomsky**, 1989, Interview in *Radical Philosophy* 53. **Bricmont and Sokal**, 1997, *Impostures Intellectuelles*.
2. In the most famous of the *Ecrits*, on 'The Function and Field of Speech and Language' (p.100), he defends his own analytic technique by analogy with Zen.
3. See **Turkle, Clément**, or **Roudinesco** for the Lacan cult.
4. **Lacan**, 1966a, p.164.
5. **Kojève**, 1947.
6. Though he did distinguish the ego from the ego-ideal and ideal-ego.
7. **Lacan**, *Ecrits*, (1966a) Chap. 4.
8. **Lacan**, 1949: 1966a, p.6.
9. **Lacan**, 1955.
10. **Lacan**, 1949.
11. **Lacan**, 1936, 'Au-delà du "Principe de réalité"' [Beyond the Reality Principle]. See **Benvenuto and Kennedy; Bowie**.
12. **Kant, Immanuel**, *Critique of Pure Reason* (1787) Everyman.
13. **Butler**, 1990, pp.43–4.
14. See **Jackson**, *The Poverty of Structuralism* (1991), and **Jackson**, *The Dematerialisation of Karl Marx* (1994), for a full development of this argument.
15. **Wallon, Henri**, 'Comment se développe chez l'enfant la notion de corps propre', *Journal de psychologie* (Nov–Dec 1931) pp.705–748; quoted in **Roudinesco**, 1990, pp.66–71.
16. *The Seminar*, Vol . I, 1953–4, pp.123, 137.
17. In fact, Lacan consistently treats Jung as someone who is exploring the imaginary.
18. **Lacan**, 1966a, p.2.
19. **Lacan**, 1966a, p.3.

20. Another one, the *objet (petit) a*, inscrutable lost object of desire, arrives in a later development of the theory, which also provides us with a divided subject. See **Lacan**, *The Four Fundamental Concepts of Psychoanalysis* (1977) for this stage of the theory.

21. **Lacan**, 1966a, p.2.

22. 1966a, p.6.

23. **Szass**, 1961.

24. **Freud**, *The Question of Lay Analysis* (1926); in Freud, 1962.

25. **Skinner**, 1957.

26. **Luce, Bush and Galanter**, 1963 Vol. II, 1965 Vol. II.

27. For treatment of these issues, see **Nobus** (ed.) 1998.

28. **Jackson**, 1991.

29. **Butler**, 1990.

30. **Benvenuto and Kennedy**, 1986, p.81.

31. See **Macey**, pp.194–5.

32. See **Thurston**, 1998, in **Nobus** (ed.) for respectful discussion of Lacan's *ten-year* meditation on Borromean rings.

33. **Culler**, 1976, p.76.

34. **Jakobson**, *Lectures on Sound and Meaning* (1976), Preface by Lévi-Strauss; **Lévi-Strauss**, *Structural Anthropology* (1963), Vol. I Chap. IV; **Jackson**, *The Poverty of Structuralism* (1991), Chap. 3, sec. 1.

35. I am simplifying the history here and make no attempt to discuss the emergence of the phoneme concept in the work of Saussure and others at the beginning of the twentieth century, or the Jakobsonian critique of it in the thirties and forties. For a full account see **Jackson**, *The Poverty of Structuralism* (1991).

36. Lacan uses the term 'double articulation' in 'Subversion of the Subject' but in a quite different sense, which has no connection with linguistics.

37. For example, his theory that the different phoneme sets found in different languages can all be distinguished in terms of a small set of universal distinctive features became the basis of all phonological work in generative grammar.

38. **Lacan**, *Ecrits* (1996a), Chap. 5.

39. **Lacan**, 1966a, Chap. 6, for Schreber case.

40. **Jackson**, (1991) Chaps 6 and 7.

41. **Lacan**, 1966a, p.164.

42. **Coward and Ellis**, 1977; **Jackson**, 1994, Chaps 6 and 7; this volume, Chap. 7.

43. Translated in *Yale French Studies*, 48.

Chapter 7

Reading 'otherwise'

SOME VERSIONS OF POST-STRUCTURALIST

PSYCHOANALYTIC CRITICISM

Summary

From the 1970s to the 1990s was the great age of post-structuralism. The idea of looking for a single, if complex, meaning for any text, based on a tacit appeal to the universal human nature of the writer or reader, was replaced by the notions of a fragmented text, producing multiple meanings, and a fragmented subject, reflecting many different identities. And this was made the basis of a radical, though gestural, politics.

The fundamental method was now the analysis of discourses, and psychoanalysis was rarely seen even as a candidate science. It became a set of classic texts, radically reread by Lacan and so available to be read afresh against the whole of literature, but having no scientific authority or explanatory force. But it was still valued for theorising the basic splits and incoherences inherent in human subjectivity. So it was Lacanian theory, joined with Derridan deconstruction, that formed that arcane successor to American New Criticism that Norman Holland indignantly called the New Crypticism. This chapter gives examples of deconstructive psychoanalytic readings and theories by Felman, Spivak, Brooks, and Reinhard and Lupton; brilliant readings, difficult even in my brief summaries, yet not altogether escaping the triviality of the deconstructive grammarian at self-conscious play.

Lacanian theory, joined with Althusserian Marxism, formed a purportedly revolutionary political discourse which helped young French and British critics terrorise old-fashioned humanists, and revolutionised European film criticism; though not, as was hoped, Europe. Reread by feminists like Mitchell and Rose, it made Freud and Lacan pillars of radical feminism, rather than the chauvinist enemies of women they had seemed. Laura Mulvey's classic piece of feminist film criticism illustrates this rereading. Even the discursive theories of Foucault, which might have put an end to Freud, have been combined with Lacanian ideas, both in Europe and the USA, in the most radical micropolitics yet: the epistemological antihomophobia of Sedgwick, Butler and Halperin.

Derrida and deconstruction

The guiding star of American formalist post-structuralism is not Lacan but Derrida.[1] From him, or from some version of him, come the principles of endless dissemination of meaning, endless intertextuality, the self-subversion of the text, productive verbal play. These have exactly replaced the principles of the old New Criticism: the unity of the text, the independence of the text from its contexts, the single all-inclusive meaning for the text that reconciles, or holds in ironic suspension, all contradictions, and gritty analytical seriousness. If we ask: who is the master spirit who presides over modern theoretical criticism in the USA, it is Derrida.

This development is very strange when one considers just how esoteric Derrida's academic interests originally were. Derrida began as a critic of Husserl's phenomenology. This was a sophisticated twentieth century revival of Descartes' seventeenth century attempt to find an absolutely certain basis for knowledge, without engaging in any metaphysical assumptions, and to find it in the immediate presence of ideas and experiences in consciousness. A standard philosophical criticism of any such enterprise (as much Wittgensteinian as Derridan) is that as soon as you put the supposed contents of consciousness in language, as philosophical argument must, they lose their immediate, private and apodictic qualities. It seems that Husserl is, despite his intentions, relying on metaphysical assumptions: specifically (in Derrida's words) on a **metaphysics of presence**, in which immediate presence of meaning to the mind's eye, or in the voice, guarantees truth.

Derrida used deconstructive arguments to question this metaphysics. Deconstruction has had an astonishing showbusiness career; it is nowadays easily the most famous argument form in the world, and a natural choice for a fashion statement or the title of a Woody Allen film. It was at first a way of undermining philosophical arguments by drawing attention to the presuppositions of the text which presents them. It applied to foundational metaphysical assumptions. One shows, from the very text in which such an assumption is presented, that it depends on a suppressed opposite, which must therefore be equally foundational. Thus, as the structuralist model of language shows, meaning is not an immediate property of the symbols present, but depends on their contrast with those not present; this under-mines any metaphysics of presence. Deconstructive arguments in general rely on drawing out of the text under examination presuppositions that undercut the apparent intention of the text.

It is not clear that this technique is valid, save where it can be reduced to a formal *reductio ad absurdum*. Derrida uses it freely, and often with literary texts. In his hands, and even more in those of his followers, it often sounds like fastening on an irrelevant detail, and constructing a far-fetched and im-plausible argument on which one would not hang a dog. It doesn't help that these arguments are often rather ponderously playful.

I made my own inadequate attempt to do justice to Derrida's philo-sophical argument in *The Poverty of Structuralism*,[2] and I won't elaborate it here. What interests me here is that the whole of American literary deconstruction is a metaphorical transfer – effected with Derrida's enthusi-astic support – of the principles of his anti-metaphysical argument in philosophy, into an anti-New-Critical argument in literary criticism. The fundamental New-Critical assumption that you can find the unique single, coherent, complex, balanced meaning for a work of art simply by examin-ing your immediate response to the formal and linguistic properties of that work is analogous to the fundamental assumption of phenomenology that the meaning of an experience is directly revealed by the logical analysis of the experience itself. In fact, in both cases, it is clear that the meaning of an experience is always relative to the context of that experience; and there is no principled way of limiting what contexts might be relevant to it. (An Auden poem about American aircraft carriers that struck my students as pretty and peaceful changed its aspect completely when they learnt that the ships were carrying nuclear weapons; a contextual fact Auden could take for granted for his readers, but I couldn't for my students.)

It is the Derridan context that largely controlled the way Lacan was first interpreted in the USA, with great emphasis on the self-referential and self-undermining qualities of his theory, and the productive qualities of verbal play. These are the features common to the work of Felman, Spivak and the Reinhard Luptons summarised below.

Lacanian verbal games and the abandonment of psychoanalysis as science

*Felman: 'the Hegelian Struggle for Mastery between
Psychoanalysis and Literature'*

Jacques Lacan was imported into the USA by way of the Johns Hopkins Conference[3] 1966, and various numbers of *Yale French Studies*. Of these, the most important for our purposes is perhaps the double issue of *YFS*, 55/6 of 1977, edited by Shoshana Felman, and reprinted as a book in 1982. It was called *Literature and Psychoanalysis, the Question of Reading: Otherwise* which is a post-structuralist pun; it means at once 'reading differently, finding a new reading' – which is what makes it interesting for tenured literary critics, who have to look for publishably new ways of reading old books as a condition of professional advancement – and 'reading according to the Other' which is what makes it Lacanian. I offer a flat-footed explanation of this pun, not because I think it particularly arcane or clever, but to put such puns in question: to ask the reader of this book to judge what value they have. There is a convention in French post-structuralist writing that a pun is more than twice as good as a good argument;[4] it is at this moment in literary history that that convention was entering the American academy and it hasn't gone yet. Its entry is worth noting in passing.

One of the startling things about Felman's approach is that there is a flat contradiction between her basic theoretical claim made and the practice to which it leads. The claim – made explicitly in the introduction to the 1980 book – is to attempt to put the very genius of psychoanalysis in contact with the very genius of the thing called literature, without reducing their basic otherness, or compromising the differences between them. But what it actually does is to reduce the differences between them to nothing, by refusing the status of a theory to psychoanalysis, and treating the relation between literature and psychoanalysis as a relation between texts.

Felman will not accept the normal scientific relationship, in which a theory like psychoanalysis is applied to phenomena, like works of literature, to explain how they work. This, she says, subordinates literature to psychoanalysis. It makes psychoanalysis occupy the place of a **subject**, literature that of an **object**. Alternatively, in Hegel's words, psychoanalysis is the **master** and literature the **slave**. The dynamic encounter between the two is a 'fight for recognition', whose outcome is the recognition of the master; that is, of the truth of psychoanalytical theory. In this case literature's function, like that of the slave, is to **serve** precisely the **desire** of psychoanalytical theory. Psychoanalysis desires **recognition** from literature. It desires to exercise its authority and **power** over the literary field. It desires to hold a discourse of masterly competence. Psychoanalysis, in literature, seems to seek above all its own **satisfaction** (Felman, 1977, pp.5–6).

This is a very odd way to put it. Felman is personifying these discourses, and the personifications are riding away with the argument. If we must apply the master–slave dialectic to philosophy of science, it is actually theories that are the slaves of the facts they try to explain: to the extent that psychoanalysis is trying to explain literature, it is enslaved to literature! But the only conflicts that really involve dynamic encounters, desires for recognition, and searches for satisfaction are conflicts between people. What this conflict is really about is the status of the people who employ these discourses. Jones and even Holland approach their tasks as qualified specialists calling on a knowledge which they are confident the ordinary reader or critic doesn't have available. But it is not literature which is subordinated to psychoanalysis – how could it be? – but the lay theorist who is subordinated to the psychoanalytic one. Rather than accept this, Felman is prepared to abandon the whole idea of scientific explanation!

The abandonment of science

What Felman is refusing to accept is the normal basic relationship between a theory and the world, that connects the two while retaining their specificity: namely that the theory **explains** some features of the world. Yet explanation is the very point – in Felman's word, the very genius – of theory. It is the very genius of psychoanalysis to be a practice based on a set of theories which explain how the mind works. It is the very genius of literature to be a set of fictions and metaphors which people enjoy and are moved by. Putting them in contact without compromising their basic otherness should mean keeping the valuable explanatory qualities of psychoanalysis and the valuable fictional qualities of literature, not mixing them up; and that means using psychoanalysis to explain literature, not the other way round. Anything else loses what is valuable about both literature and psychoanalysis, and loses the specificity of both. And this is precisely what the poststructuralist approach does, not merely here, but generally. It replaces the scientific notion of formulating hypotheses that explain phenomena, with the literary notion of comparing text with text – having texts read each other, as the extravagant metaphor goes; and with the philosophico-political notion of examining texts for their underlying metaphysical assumptions or the interests they allegedly serve.

The claim that psychoanalysis should be treated, not as a science, but as another set of texts has two major disadvantages. The first is that it makes it impossible to criticise any of it as bad science. The kind of criticism I have put forward both in my chapter on Freud and in my chapter on Lacan becomes simply beside the point. Who cares if Lacan gets his linguistics and his algebra and perhaps his topology wrong, delights in wild, paradoxical and unsustainable claims for which evidence is entirely missing, and distorts Freud beyond recognition while claiming to read him better than anybody else – from the point of view of the literary critic it is all part of the rich tapestry of his texts, which calls for comment rather than dismissal.

The consequence of this approach is that you can never find rational grounds for getting rid of any theory at all. Take this approach to chemistry, and you will be stuck with phlogiston theory, or indeed, with the four elements and alchemical transformations. Take this approach to linguistics and if you are lucky you will be stuck with the theories of Saussure and if unlucky with folk-etymology. If you can never find reasons for saying that particular theories are wrong – that they don't make sense or don't fit the facts – then literary theorising as a rational activity collapses, and turns back into untheorised literary criticism. It is my thesis that this is what has happened to a good deal of post-structuralist literary theory. There is a lot to be said against verbal play.

A second disadvantage is that, if you don't make scientific claims for them, there seems to be no particular motive for attending to psycho-analytic texts at all. The critic is making an arbitrary decision to choose to compare a work of literature (say, a great novel) with a paper by Freud or Lacan, because he finds it interesting, just as he might compare one literary work with another because he finds it interesting. No special argument needs to be put forward for doing that: it is what literary critics do all the time. Comparing *Sons and Lovers* with *The Commonest Sources of Degradation in the Erotic Life* is on all fours with comparing *Sons and Lovers* with *Portrait of the Artist as a Young Man*. Both are illuminating; and illuminating in much the same way. And again, literary theory has collapsed as a rational activity, leaving us only with untheorised literary criticism. Theoretical re-flections may be inspired by either comparison; but until we arrange those reflections as a systematic philosophical or scientific theory of literature, which admits counter-arguments or counter-evidence, we are not engaged in rational theory-construction.

In practice, many post-structuralists find themselves unable to behave as their theory suggests they should. It is almost impossible to argue about psychoanalytic theory without treating it as at least a candidate science. Even Lacan has to pretend, again and again, that he is offering a kind of sci-ence, though it always turns out to be pseudo. Peter Brooks, for example, dismisses Lacan as a series of brilliant glosses on Freud rather than a system-atic thinker, and claims that the very survival of psychoanalytic perspectives in literary criticism is evidence that we believe that 'the structure of liter-ature is, in some sense, the structure of the mind'.[5] In arguing this, he is, of course, committing himself to a tacit belief in psychoanalysis, either as a scientific theory of mind, or as a system of metaphysics. I am sure he is right to do this, but such claims should be openly acknowledged and explicitly defended.

Deconstructing the post-structuralists: Brooks

But for Felman and her associates[6] the question of the scientificity of psycho-analysis is dropped; it becomes irrelevant; and in fact it cannot even be posed in the terminology favoured by these American post-structuralists. They would not speak, even to deny its existence, of a science which explained how literature worked. They would speak of a master discourse which acted as a metalanguage for literature; or of claiming a position of mastery for psychoanalytic texts. And they would claim, following Barthes, that there is no metalanguage for literature, and, like Felman, that one can't claim mastery for psychoanalytic texts over literary ones.

This actually sounds open-minded, if you forget the mad person-ifications underlying it, and seems to make a refreshing change from Lacan's assertive pseudo-science and insane dogmatism. But like most forms of post-structuralism, it is very easy to deconstruct. This tentative, uncertain, unstable open-mindedness turns out to rest on the unsupported assertions of some of the most dogmatic writers who have ever written.[7] Peter Brooks, not himself a dogmatist and probably the member of this school I most admire, says in his book, *Psychoanalysis and Story-Telling* (1994) p.24, that if there is one thing that post-structuralist criticism has most usefully 'taught' us, it is 'the suspicion and refusal of this last word in the interpretive process and history, the refusal of any privileged position in analysis.' Brooks is obviously perfectly right; that is what post-structuralist criticism has insistently 'taught' – and by the act of teaching, it has assumed the position of a subject-supposed-to-know, a dogmatic authority. (A valid post-structuralism has to content itself with textual analyses showing dogmatic authority running into logical absurdities or *aporias* – the moment it asserts even a negative dogma, it refutes itself.)

Brooks continues by pointing out that Lacan, with 'the greatest panache and high priestly drama' has 'taught' (that word again) students of liter-ature to understand the basic operations of the 'dream work', condensa-tion and displacement, as the master tropes of rhetoric, metaphor and metonymy, and thus 'to initiate a rereading of Freud attentive to his semio-tic imagination'. It sounds terribly sensitive, but in fact Lacan has no case whatever for identifying condensation and displacement with metaphor and metonymy, and as usual offers no evidence. We have here a case of the arch-dogmatist teaching us something that is almost certainly not true. One is bound to ask: in what possible way can it be more open-minded to replace a putative science of psychoanalysis whose theories are based on evidence and are in principle refutable, with the dogmatic creed of a man who not only behaves as a high priest but is taken as one by a cultish following?

Brooks' article, in Felman, 1977a, was a claim that Freud's paper *Beyond the Pleasure Principle* – which, we will remember, introduced the repetition compulsion and the death instinct – in some sense sets out Freud's master-plot. It is thus a model, not merely for a particular plot that we might find in literature, but for plot in general. ('Narrative always makes the implicit claim to be in a state of repetition, as a going over again of ground already covered . . .': Felman, 1977, edn. 1982, p.285.) In Brooks' best-known work, *Reading for the Plot*, this point is elaborated, and his general position is summarised again in Brooks 1994. It is an interesting scientific claim about the writer's and reader's compulsions.

But Brooks has a very selective attitude to the company he will keep. He is anxious to dissociate himself from the psychodynamics of Norman Holland. He thinks it important that there can be 'a psychoanalytic criticism of the text itself that does not become – as has usually been the case – a study of the psychogenesis of the text (the author's unconscious), the dynamics of literary response (the reader's unconscious), or the occult motivations of the characters (postulating an unconscious for them)' (Felman, 1982, p.299; Brooks, 1984, p.112). Now a psychoanalytic account of the text itself is presumably one that postulates an unconscious for the text itself. To an old-fashioned scientific psychoanalyst, nothing could seem more absurd than to refuse to postulate an unconscious in the three entities logically capable of having one – author, reader, and character – while in some sense postulating one in an entity logically incapable of having one – the text. The post-structuralist defence would be, presumably, that author, reader and character alike are merely effects of the text.

(I would like at this point to break into *this* text and ask a personal question to any teachers of literature who are reading this book. Do you, O sophisticated reader of the year 2000+, ever say to a student: 'If you ever attribute an unconscious mind to Hamlet, or to Shakespeare, or to any-body in the Elizabethan audience, I shall mark you down and think you terribly naïve for treating them as persons, real or imitation. But it is perfectly all right to speak of the unconscious of *Hamlet* (the play not the person), and even better if you refer to it as a political unconscious, or an intertextual unconscious; or to speak of the unconscious of literature in general or of psychoanalysis; or to say that literature and psychoanalysis form the unconscious of each other. In the literary-critical trade I am introducing you to, sophisticated nonsense is much better than unsophist-icated sense.')

I will end this section by considering three examples of post-Lacanian formalist criticism, two from 1977, one from 1993, concerning Henry James, Coleridge and Shakespeare, respectively.

Felman: turning the screw on the critics

Shoshana Felman's own contribution to the book she edited is a striking example of the strengths and weaknesses of the new type of criticism: how it combines utter brilliance with triviality. It is a study of Henry James's *The Turn of the Screw* and seems about the same length as that novella. It is based on an intriguing metacritical insight. Some thirty years after the publication of this ambiguous ghost story, Edmund Wilson came up with a psychoanalytic interpretation that reversed its meaning. The ghosts from which the good governess tried unsuccessfully to rescue the children became projections of her own sexual problems; they existed only in that governess's evil head.

A shooting war ensued, between the old literal critics for whom the ghosts were real and the governess good, and the new Freudian ones for whom the ghosts are projections and the governess sick. Felman takes both sides at once; she recognises that it is the uncertainty of interpretation that produces the whole atmosphere of the work; to decide is to foreclose.

This seems to me a genuine insight and true; but it wouldn't, by itself, produce a novella length criticism. But Felman also examines the imagery of the *critics* as they excoriate each other, bringing out:

> the motif . . . of neurosis and of madness, of hysterical delusion. Robert Heilman . . . accuses Wilson of 'hysterical blindness' which alone would be able to account for the latter's errors in interpretation.

She thus shows how the quarrels between the critics have reflected the effects of the novella itself: Edmund Wilson must be hysterically blind to see the governess as hysterically blind! It would seem one could hardly get more 'meta-' than this; but Felman manages it easily, proposing parallels between critic, text and the technical terminology of Lacan. The governess, and Edmund Wilson, are looking for mastery, trying to stop the meaning and arrest signification (in post-structuralist terms there could be no worse sin than this).

I cannot give a fair summary of the many brilliant ways in which *The Turn of the Screw* is shown to be an allegory of Lacanian psychoanalysis – or, occasionally, of Derridan deconstruction. Nor can I give a fair account of the many arguments used – not, of course, arguments of the sort that would satisfy an analytical philosopher or a natural scientist, but tropes, figures of speech, audacious identifications of apparently distinct ideas, and hectic slides down the signifying chain. The whole thing is a worthy successor of Barthes' *S/Z*.[8]

Spivak's matrioshka: metapsychology around the figure of Coleridge

In the same volume, the translator of Derrida, Gayatri Chakravorti Spivak, presents an almost too exemplary piece of deconstructive psychoanalytic formalism.[9] It is a beautiful example of the way that intense methodological self-consciousness can make critical analysis rather empty. It resembles in structure a *matrioshka*: the doll that splits open to reveal inside a further doll, which splits open . . . In other words, each point Spivak makes is a metalinguistic comment on what she has said just before. By a paradox that characterises post-structuralism, the innermost doll is the largest and most interesting and the outermost dwindles to relative triviality, being a comment on a comment on a comment seven times removed.

The innermost Russian doll of her analysis is Coleridge's theory of the imagination, which he calls 'the living power and prime agent of all human perception', and 'a repetition in the finite mind of the eternal act of creation in the infinite I AM'. This theory is Coleridge's attempt to reconcile object and subject in being and knowledge.[10] An old-fashioned philosopher would want to discuss this important topic.

Spivak, however, focuses on the enclosing doll: Coleridge's textual **presentation** of the theory. Deconstruction is an appropriate technique of analysis here; for notoriously Coleridge's theory is **not** demonstrated in *Biographia Literaria*, two chapters of which half present it, promise to present it, and eventually, by way of a fictional letter from a friend advising Coleridge not to include the proof(!), indefinitely delay it, so that in the end we never get it.

Spivak is going to use psychoanalysis on these dotty chapters. What for? To explain why Coleridge is doing this? No. That would be very unLacanian and even more unDerridan. Her purpose, at the third level of metalanguage, is to 'test' these two chapters by the rules of new psychoanalysis, with its useful vocabulary of the imaginary, the Other, desire, castration. (Thus that fictional letter which cuts off Coleridge's argument is 'castrating' – there's a useful bit of vocabulary!) But Spivak is too sophisticated to perform any such test herself. Her darker purpose – we are now at the fourth level of metalanguage, the fourth Russian doll – is to present a hypothetical example of such a 'test', not by herself but by a hypothetical American common critic.

Or at least, not actually to present it. More to consider (doll five) the likelihood that there will be more such 'tests' in future, as American critics read more of the new psychoanalysis; and that there will be more rude gestures from the sophisticated French who see such 'tests' as opportunistic misunderstanding. And given this likelihood, to do something that only a sophisticated deconstructionist philosopher can do (doll six):

> to make a move toward neutralising at once the appropriating confidence of the former [the Americans] and the comforting hierarchization of the latter [the French]. (Felman, 1982, p.221)

Now that is really worth doing, is it not? And there is a meta-step outward beyond this, to the most pregnant or gaseous philosophical doll, and at last we reach something substantive, even if it is only a question:

> to ask what this sort of use of a psychoanalytic vocabulary in literary criticism might indeed imply. (Felman, 1982, p.221)

And what does it imply? Psychoanalysis might seem to imply that there is a person under analysis – a character, a reader, even an author. It would be an old-fashioned approach that treated Coleridge as a person! Spivak doesn't do this. Does she then believe he is a text? Not at all; unlike some post-structuralists – the common critics she is parodying – she is scrupulously careful to recognise the difference between the two. The answer has been given earlier: what the use of a psychoanalytic vocabulary in literary criticism implies is:

> An ideology of 'applying' in critical practice a 'theory' developed under other auspices, and of discovering an analogy to the task of the literary critic in any interpretative situation inhabiting any 'science of man'. (Felman, 1982, p.209)

So the notion of 'applying' a theory is an ideological one! We have come a long way from Freud and Ernest Jones, and perhaps a longer way from Norman Holland. All they could have done is offer putative scientific accounts of Coleridge's, or the reader's, unconscious. For Spivak, detaching herself from the vulgar ideology of application, the psychoanalytical vocabulary only 'illuminates Coleridge's declaration that the *Biographia* is an autobiography' (Felman, 1982, p.226). Why do I feel that this is rather little for a psychoanalytic vocabulary to do?

Reinhards' rhetoric: Shakespeare as Lacanian trope

There have, since 1977, been many, many brilliant criticisms of the Felman kind. Indeed, the major objection to the whole field of Lacanian post-structuralism is its tendency toward brilliant rhetorical play. One of the most brilliant is called, very cogently, *After Oedipus* (1993). The book seems to be the product of a family collective – Julia Reinhard Lupton and Kenneth Reinhard, with twin sister Ellen Lupton drawing the pictures. These are Lacanian diagrams of the psyche, but in them Lacanian symbols like S or O are replaced with names of characters or plays, or even genres.

Consider the diagram in the previous chapter where four aspects of the self are set out in a square. At the top, we have (to give them names) **the subject of the unconscious** opposite **the specular other**. At the bottom, we have **the ego** opposite **the symbolic Other**. The two diagonal connections are the **symbolic** axis joining the subject to the Symbolic Other, and the **imaginary** axis joining the ego to the specular other. This diagram suggests a kind of ratio: as the subject to the other so the ego to the Other.

By writing in various names in the corners you can indicate literary-historical parallels to this psychic structure: as Hyperion to a satyr so I to Hercules; as ancient tragedy to modern tragedy; so *Hamlet* to *Oedipus Rex*! These may seem whimsical, but the Reinhard Luptons have elaborate arguments for them, developed, no doubt, over some years of work in their Lacanian seminar.

It goes further. In Lupton diagram four, we have a whole universe of discourse at every corner of the diagram: as *Oedipus at Colonus* and the dialectic of ethos and mythos to *King Lear*, opsis and lexis, and the Theatre of Cruelty, so *Hamlet* and the *Trauerspiel* to *Oedipus Rex* and classical tragedy. In this last diagram, *Antigone* sits in the middle at the point where the imaginary and symbolic axes (here labelled *ethos* and *mythos*) cross. Phew!

What this book shows, I think, are the limitations of rhetorical brilliance as a criterion for judging literary criticism. It reads rather like a metaphysical poem 247 pages long, with five or six conceits on every page, in which every conceit is based on Lacanian theory.

And the central claim is itself a literary conceit – in the words of the blurb, which are the shortest I can find, that *Hamlet* and *Lear* are models of 'literary transmission'!

> . . . while *Hamlet* stages melancholia as the tragic scenario of literary inheritance, *King Lear* presents psychosis as a model of the canon and its discontents.

Let us take this slowly. It is not just that *Hamlet* is about melancholia – it is about literary inheritance. It is not just that *Lear* is about madness – it is about the canon.

There is no reason why a literary critic should not adopt this interpretation. It is one of the ordinary procedures of critics to show that some classic is worth attending to because it speaks to our own urgent preoccupations. If you are a teacher of English Literature in an American university, then your urgent preoccupations may well be with literary inheritance and the problem of the canon. It is both natural and comforting if you can provide an argument to show that 'Shakespeare' is handling the very same problem.

It is worth comparing this judgement with the view traditional humanist critics might take. They would probably agree that Shakespeare takes an interest in melancholia and mourning, a keen interest in psychosis, and a mild satirical interest in literary transmission and canon formation. At least that's what one would infer from his plays. (If one wanted a writer who discusses literary transmission and the canon all the time, one would try Milton.) Such a Shakespeare is grossly unsatisfactory to the modern teacher of literature. Fortunately one can call in 'Shakespeare' instead, who is a retroactive construction from the *critics'* text, and has the appropriate academic interests.

The authors see themselves as part of the third generation of psychoanalytic critics. The first generation discussed **applications** of psychoanalytic theory to literature, the second, Felman's, discussed the **interimplications** of psychoanalytic and literary texts. Applications, say the Reinhards, correspond to Lacan's imaginary relationships; interimplications to his symbolic relationships. So the third stage corresponds to Lacan's real. Readers will be pleased to deduce that there can't be any more stages of psychoanalytic criticism to come, as Lacan never introduced any further categories after the real.

But what sort of relationship can you have between literature and psychoanalysis that isn't either application or interimplication? It is 'what Lacan and Jacques-Alain Miller have called *extimité*.' *Extimité* means 'the intimate exteriority of the material letter'. It means 'the mute signifier intransigently lodged through primal repression, incorporation or foreclosure in the significations it sets into motion' (Lupton and Reinhard, p.4). I don't think it would make sense to ask, in the way a cognitive scientist might ask, just how a mute signifier sets the significations in which it is lodged into motion, or where they go.

I confess that I do not believe in *extimité*. I don't think myself that the Reinhards get beyond the interimplications of texts; there is nowhere further to go. What they do seems to me just interimplication taken to the giddy limit. They layer the texts of Lacan on those of Freud, and on those of Shakespeare, and of Walter Benjamin. (Why not?) They follow Felman's practice of personifying inanimates and having them fight for mastery, but take it to new extravagant heights. For them, Shakespeare and psychoanalysis are discourses engaged in 'sibling rivalry and other children's games'. One of these games they name as 'playing doctor' – they mean the application to literature of theories of infantile sexuality originally developed in a medical context. (This neatly sees off Ernest Jones and Norman Holland – and indeed me. Anyone who sees psychoanalysis as a body of scientific theory testable by its ability to help cure mental illness can be spoken of as 'playing doctors'.)

Another children's game is 'the Hegelian struggle for pure prestige'. This they describe as putting the mirror up to philosophy 'in which the structuralist and post-structuralist Shakespeares fruitlessly multiply' (Lupton and Reinhard, p.1). One has to admire these Reinhardian allusions, puns and tropes, which also multiply fruitlessly throughout their book, supplying its main texture, but which I have no time to consider now. They make the scientific approach of Holland, Ernest Jones, or Freud look very plodding and to deploy rational arguments against them would be to aim a cannon-ball against a swarm of gnats. Anyhow, what would one base an argument on? They are not aiming at an underlying truth, only rhetorical comparisons.

The literary theorist's Hegelian struggle for mastery

When we looked at Felman earlier, we saw what was really meant by attributing a Hegelian master–slave struggle to texts: it is a projection onto texts of a struggle between people. In this case, academics: specifically, psychoanalytic literary critics and non-psychoanalytic ones. It is here that you find, literally, a struggle for prestige: a struggle for the academic prestige of the person with the master discourse; a struggle that quite literally cashes out, in material terms, into grants and professorial appointments. And this struggle now has nothing to do with truth. By rejecting the claims of psychoanalysis to be a science (in post-structuralist jargon, a 'master discourse') one neatly excludes scientists of any stripe – psychoanalytic, cognitive, or whatever – from making a contribution: the struggle is now wholly between literary critics.

We can extend this last point, and make it clear that it is a general property of the more textually oriented post-structuralist literary criticism. From Roland Barthes onwards, it has been commonplace to deny the existence of extratextual human subjects, and the relevance of extratextual reference. At the same time, it has been customary to project human attributes onto the text, so that texts are supposed to read each other, engage in Hegelian struggles for prestige, and so forth. To talk in such a way has become a mark of sophistication and shows that one is a member in good standing of a certain critical elite. To claim that it is transparent nonsense, since only people think and texts do not, is sometimes seen as a mark – God save the mark – of philosophical naïvety. What has not been so widely remarked is that this collusive practice of nonsense has a clear economic basis, in entitling a particular occupational group to live off the criticism of literature, while fending off the contributions of all those academic specialisms that describe the world that literature is about.

British quasi-Marxist post-structuralism

Lacan entered the British literary academy under the imprimatur of Louis Althusser. His article 'Freud and Lacan' was published in 1964, and reached *New Left Review* in 1969. This was just in time for the new wave of Althusserian Marxists (who were about to make a critical and anti-humanist revolution) to know that if they were going to be psychoanalytic they had to be Lacanian. As a result, Lacan himself, in his British debut at the age of seventy, became an Althusserian; and young critics sometimes talked as if he really were a minor follower of Althusser, who had filled in a little psychological detail in the Althusserian system. In fact, of course, it was the other way round. Althusser was a follower of Lacan, in all his practice and some of his theory. It was Lacan who showed, from 1953 onwards, that you could dominate French psychoanalysis without any official position, by running a regular seminar offering fantastic rereadings of Freud. It was Althusser who a decade later attempted to dominate French Marxism by running a regular seminar offering fantastic rereadings of Marx. Althusser even practised a 'symptomatic reading' of *Capital*, in which the gaps and absences in the text disclosed a kind of unconscious discourse which turned out to be Marx's – or rather Althusser's – philosophy. And the Althusserian system, as it emerged, can be seen as in part a rational Marxist makeover of the Lacanian one.

Althusser replaces the Lacanian notion of 'the symbolic' with the Marxist notion of 'ideology'. Ideology thus becomes a name for the whole culture in which people live, in which their minds are formed, and within which they have their personal experiences. He conflates the Lacanian notion of the subject (which comes to exist only in and through the symbolic and finds himself in speech) with that of the ego (which is a centre of misrecognitions formed in the imaginary). He comes up with the notion of a subject, formed in ideology by a process of interpellation (being called on to assume a role or reply to a question). Althusser's 'subject' inherits the misrecognitions of Lacan's 'ego'; it has an imaginary relationship to the real conditions of production. (The words 'imaginary' and 'real' here recall Lacan but have quite unLacanian meanings: 'imaginary' means ideological, and 'real' means economic.) The advantage of this position to a Marxist is that it enables him to 'explain' how an awful exploitative system like capitalism appears to retain the consent of its victims, while a good caring one like communism does not. The workers favour things like freedom of employment and political freedom because of the ideology within which they were 'formed as subjects'. This theory really provides a licence to dismiss the actual feelings of the workers.[11]

The advantage of the Althusserian system to the revolutionary young critics of the 1970s was that it allowed them to dismiss the critical judgements and the theories of ideological enemies – 'humanists' or even socialists of a pre-Althusserian variety – since these, however cogently based on immediate experience, could readily be described as ideologically based misrecognitions. Thus we have Eagleton securing an easy triumph over Raymond Williams in *Criticism and Ideology*, 1975. It allowed them to base their own judgements and theories on something much firmer than subjectivity – namely Marxist science, often known as 'theoretical practice' to make it sound more materialist. Thus Catherine Belsey called her book *Critical Practice*. In those days it was possible to believe that the fame of Shakespeare, founded on subjective responses grounded in ideology, might pass away next year when the revolution came; but the science of Marx was a house founded on a rock, and Althusser had built it. Or even, since Althusser had provided the philosophical foundations for some of Marx's least plausible hypotheses, that Althusser **was** the eternal rock on which Marxism was founded.

I have offered an analysis of the last days of British literary Marxism in *The Dematerialisation of Karl Marx*, 1994, and won't repeat it here. There will also be found comments on the great triumphs of *Screen* magazine, when a dullish film journal was taken over by Theoretical Revolutionaries who proposed not merely a new account of film but a new conception of the human subject, as an effect of the text that it is reading, or the film it is watching. This is grand indeed. But the theory of the person that emerges seems to rely entirely on a simple confusion. When we read a book or watch a film, we often identify with an authorial point of view or even with a camera position, and have the illusion of watching the world from a new subjective position. But it is the nature of such 'subject positions' to be ephemeral. They expand the number of ways in which we can look at the world, and to that extent, alter our basic personalities. But however many we adopt, they never add up to the discursive construction of a total, lifelong personality. Yet that is what seemed implicit in the triumphalism of some of the more radical theorists of subject construction or positioning: that we are constructed as subjects by texts, and can be reconstructed as revolutionary subjects by modernist texts.[12]

Feminist film theory and the appropriation of psychoanalysis

Feminism was a second strand of the revolutionary enthusiasm of the seventies, and one that has survived better than Marxism. The surprising thing was the feminist appropriation of Lacanian psychoanalysis. We can see that feminism is vulnerable to a biological argument that women are intrinsically different from men, not merely in their physical bodies but their basic subjectivity: one law for the lion and the ox is oppression. Feminists have always been hostile to Freud because he seems to propose just such a difference in basic subjectivity, but places it at the level of unconscious, rather than conscious desire, so that women cannot even give reliable testimony to their own wants. Women who desire the activities and privileges of the male are driven by penis envy. Granting that desire does not give them the only thing that nature permits them to substitute for a penis: a baby. So justice does not require equal opportunities for women!

Feminists have appropriated psychoanalysis for their own purposes by reading it as an analysis not of the way the unconscious naturally develops, but of the way society installs patriarchal assumptions and attitudes into the unconscious.[13] The Lacanian rereading of Freud has been valuable for this purpose,[14] because it pays at least lip-service to semiotics; and this has enabled feminists to propose a semiotic mechanism for this purpose. The basic assumption is that the world of law, civilisation and language, which Lacan calls **the symbolic**, is the world of the father, which boys enter by identification, through the fear of castration. The phallus is the signifier of that world: that is what we mean by saying that that world is phallocentric. The woman signifies castration. She therefore has no place in the world of the symbolic – of law, logic, reasoning, intelligence, science, culture; she either represents the plenitude of the world of **the imaginary** – of sensuous experience and fantasy – that preceded it, or the threat of castration that precipitated the subject into it.

The catch is that the subject only finds himself as such in the symbolic. (There is no subject in the imaginary, only the ego misrecognised!) So it is not clear that a woman can even *be* a subject: all subjectivity is masculine. And since mature desire is articulated only in the symbolic, where a woman can have no place, woman's desire cannot be articulated. She can speak only with a masculine voice, since language itself is masculine. Women are mute prisoners in a masculine culture. This vision might seem to be despairing; but it had an enormous romantic appeal to feminists of the 1970s. It captured – and majestically exaggerated – the sense of imprisonment in masculine assumptions that they had; and at the same time the revolutionary politics of the period suggested that one might be able to change society, in an utterly radical way, that would change the nature of subjectivity itself in both men and women. An example of such feminist reading is that of Laura Mulvey in 'Visual Pleasure and Narrative Cinema', written in 1973 and published in *Screen* 16, 3, 1975, and collected in Mulvey, 1989, *Visual and Other Pleasures.*

Film, according to Mulvey, offers the twin pleasures of scopophilia and identification. The spectators, in Mulvey's day isolated from each other in the darkness of the cinema, or nowadays, alone watching video, 'watch the hermetically sealed world beyond the screen unfold magically', indifferent to them. Scopophilia – the pleasure of looking at something as an erotic object – is one of the sexual instincts Freud refers to, but doesn't place clearly in his developmental sequence. In 'Instincts and their Vicissitudes',[15] he suggests it can be transformed into exhibitionism – the pleasure of having others look at the self as erotic object. In film, however, the spectator's exhibitionism is repressed and projected onto the performers.

For the pleasures of identification, Mulvey refers to Lacan's 'mirror' stage of development: the child constitutes its own ego in the imaginary by identification with its mirror image, overlaying recognition by misrecognition. This produces an ideal ego, an alienated subject, which, reintrojected as an ego-ideal, prepares the way for identification with others in the future. It appears that in cinema we have a kind of regression to this early phase of identification. (The non-Lacanian, Holland, suggests something similar for literature, particularly the popular kind; he thinks that during reading there is a regression to oral dependency.)

But the position of male and female objects is not the same. Women are passive; they are looked at both by the audience and by the other characters in the film, and displayed exhibitionistically to both. The meaning of woman is sexual difference: she provokes castration anxiety, from which the male unconscious can escape only by two routes: the sadistic story, or the fetishistic spectacle. In the first, we re-enact the trauma of castration: we investigate the woman, demystify her, devalue her, perhaps by finding out her guilt, by punishing her, or by 'saving' her. In the second, we escape by disavowal of castration: we substitute a fetish object for the missing member, or turn the represented figure itself into a fetish 'so that it becomes reassuring rather than dangerous': hence the cult of the film star. Mulvey offers Hitchcock and Sternberg as type-examples of these two approaches, but examples could be multiplied.

By contrast, men are active and attract ego-libido rather than scopophilia: they are identified with as actors rather than looked at as spectacle by the spectator. They themselves become the bearers of the look – those who within the film also look at the heroines. They forward the action, where the fetishised female tends to stop it. We identify with them, participate in their power, and by proxy come to possess the heroine. Hollywood provides a rich array of ego-ideals in its leading men for us to identify with. And in its techniques – as in the camera-work that denies its own materiality so that we seem to be watching the real without mediation, or in the way spectacle stops the audience distancing itself, and hides the castration-fear it provokes. These techniques cater for the needs of the neurotic male unconscious.

This imbalance between women and men Mulvey puts down to the patriarchal unconscious. Films rest on it, manipulate it for their effects, and are partly responsible for installing it in us. Mulvey writes out of a deep love for these films, and loves the voyeuristic-scopophilic pleasures they give; but as a feminist she strongly disapproves of them and thinks we should give them up! Avant-garde film, she thinks, can help in this: the first step is to 'free the look of the camera into its materiality in time and space and the look of the audience into dialectics, passionate detachment'. And she has actually produced some avant-garde films (with Peter Wollen) that try to do this. This seems a belated Brechtian enterprise; but in fact the whole *Screen* project was part of an Anglo-Saxon post-structuralism borrowing from French theory that had an enormous faith in the potential political radicalism of modernist form.[16]

How much credence can we give this theory? The basic datum is certainly correct. Not only in films, but in art in general, there is an imbalance in the representation of men and women. As John Berger put it, in *Ways of Seeing*: 'men act and women appear'.[17] In art, film, pornography and fashion alike, women are looked at and men look. A biologist might conclude that this is probably their natural sexual constitution; but that it doesn't necessarily have any implications for, say, intellectual activities. The Lacanian theory is paranoid, all-embracing, and utterly terrifying. Women represent castration and have no place in the symbolic; they are silenced by the nature of language and culture itself. But the evidence for this is remarkably thin. There is no scientific evidence whatever that language acquisition, language use and the development of logical thinking have anything whatever to do with castration or the phallus, whether absent or present, real or fantasised. It is a Lacanian fairy-tale, that cannot survive the slightest exposure to developmental psycholinguistics. I wonder if there is a single paper in the vast literature of this field (already well developed at the time of Mulvey's paper) which even considers such a connection, or any psycholinguistic researcher who would regard the suggestion as other than silly.

Even if it is a fact that, sexually, women in our society like to be looked at, and men to look, what has that to do with the ability to talk – which little girls are better at than little boys – or to think logically, and do maths and physics – which they can learn equally well? The notion that women's voices are suppressed by the very nature of the last two activities is surely old-fashioned prejudice ('women aren't logical') dressed up as feminist epistemology. Like all grand paranoid epistemological feminisms, this one simply hides the much more detailed systems of sexual prejudice that really have developed historically. I discuss these issues in the next chapter.

The Foucauldian turn and the politics of sexual identity

An entirely non-cognitive path out of Freudian and Lacanian theory has been provided by the same man who gave us all a way out of Marxism: Michel Foucault. Foucault was an analyst of the history of systems of ideas, along with the practices and institutions that embody those ideas. He has had an enormous influence upon modern Anglophone critics, partly because he provided an up-to-date and leftist version of the background history of ideas that all literary scholars once found essential, and showed that it need not involve the conservative identification with the past shown by a Tillyard or a C.S. Lewis.

The post-structuralist elements in his work are the pervasive assumptions (never properly argued or made into explicit philosophical claims) that the discourses, practices, institutions and so forth that we employ construct both the world that we live in and the selves that live in that world. So madness, illness, crime and sexual deviance appear as the constructs of the discourses, practices and institutions of doctors, jurists and moralists, and have no substantive independent reality of their own. Thus in *Discipline and Punish: The Birth of the Prison* we study ways of disciplining bodies which create the kinds of subject needed by particular societies. Such an approach is obviously still indebted to Marxist frameworks.

Foucault's way out of Marxism was provided in his second theoretical period. In the first, quasi-structuralist phase, he spoke of discourses within an 'episteme' – a framework of discourse common to many fields and peculiar to one historical period. In the second, post-structuralist phase, he reworked the old Marxist theory of ideology – particularly the version favoured by his sometime teacher Althusser – as a theory of truth. For Marxists, truth is given by Marxist science; ideology is constructed in relations of power, in order to preserve relations of power; and the world is experienced, and the self is constructed, in ideology. For Foucault in this period, **truth** is created in relations of power.[18] The traditional view that truth is correspondence to an independent reality is abandoned.

This has the advantage for relativistic moderns that they don't have to believe in truth, and can suppose that they are fighting against power every time that they deny the truth of some popular prejudice. And it gets rid of the challenge of Marxism, which claims to expose global and systematic types of economic oppression. Marxism, for Foucault, lived in the nineteenth century like a fish in water; it could survive nowhere else. For me, the world still seems full of just the types of systematic oppression Marxism was created to oppose. The only effect of the experience of the twentieth century is that we now know Marxist solutions only make them worse. But Foucauldian micropower politics can't even diagnose these problems, let alone solve them.

Foucault undermines Freudian theory in his third phase, when he decides that what he has been doing all along is theorising the construction of subjects; and writes a history of sexuality. A key move in that history is to deny the fundamental premise of psychoanalysis: that sex at the end of the nineteenth century is repressed and concealed, and that Freud provided a liberational discourse that lifts that repression. On the contrary, says Foucault, sex is constructed in the discourses that pretend to uncover it, and in the regimes that pretend to regulate it. We live in an intensely confessional age, in which we produce sex in discourse: Freudian theory ranks as one of those discourses which produce sex.

Why did Foucault produce his extraordinary theory? It is in fact part of a fantastically argued, but quite comprehensible trajectory in his work, that begins with *Madness and Civilisation*, and has a personal basis. Foucault was an aggressive homosexual in the fifties, when to be that was to risk being classified as mad, or sick, or criminal, or deviant, or sexually perverted. His whole oeuvre seems to have been an attempt to defend himself against such charges, not by disputing their truth in terms of the conventional classification systems of the day, but by attacking those systems themselves as ungrounded, arbitrary and oppressive, which indeed they were.

Hence he wrote about the way reason constructs madness, doctors construct sickness, systems of order create deviance, penological systems construct crime, and our discourses about sex construct sex.[19] Where nothing is left natural, and everything is constructed, one construct is as good as another. It is part of Foucault's triumph that he hardly had to defend or discuss homosexuality at all; he is rather like a daring general, who protects his home territory by fighting his wars on the enemy's soil. But his approach deeply influences later writers on homosexuality like Halperin, Sedgwick and Dollimore; and it is often used alongside Lacanian and Freudian ideas rather than replacing them.

Like most theories that include discursive construction, Foucault's is highly attractive to literary and cultural critics; it suggests that discourse, their own speciality, is more important than biological instinct in the formation of sexuality – just as Foucault's theory of power suggests that discourse is more important than economics in the distribution of power. It gives literary and cultural critics a central role in sexual politics, like the role his earlier theory gave them in social micropolitics. And there have been brilliant applications of Foucauldian approaches. One of the most impressive is the argument of Halperin's *One Hundred Years of Homosexuality* that homosexuality is not a natural, inborn category; there is no homosexual gene; it is, rather, a cultural construct that has been around for only a hundred years; it is not to be confused with the utterly different social phenomena with which it is sometimes compared, like Greek pederasty, or Arapesh customs. It seems to be a corollary of this that we can't label Leonardo da Vinci or Shakespeare homosexual, since the category didn't exist in their time.

Queer studies are revolutionised by such approaches as this. In the writings of a Halperin, or a Dollimore, or perhaps the most ambitious of all anti-homophobic critics, Eve Kosowsky Sedgwick, the whole concept of gay identity is spread, fragmented and historicised. We separate the question of the gender you identify with from that of what sexual object you want, or that of what relation you have with that object. We ask, do male homosexuals and lesbians form a natural group between the sexes, or rather two opposing groups more masculine and more feminine respectively than heterosexual men and women? We trace the separated fragments of the modern gay identity, though not that identity itself, throughout cultural history. And a key source – sometimes the only possible source – for these fragments is the interpretation of literature. To add my own examples to Sedgwick's: Hector and Patroclus, the Socrates of Plato but also of Xenophon, the Shakespeare of the sonnets (but also of the dialogues of Rosalind and Orlando, of the two Antonios in *The Merchant of Venice* and *Twelfth Night*, of the homosociality of Iago and Othello) join with the cast of *The Importance of Being Earnest* and of *A Passage to India* as the bearers of that love which now shouts its name in a multitude of confused voices.

The interpretations of Sedgwick in particular offer something of the cultural shock that early Freudian ones did, before they faded into commonplaces. The body-language of Marianne Dashwood is read alongside that described in a nineteenth century text diagnosing and condemning masturbation, in a paper on *Sense and Sensibility* called 'Jane Austen and the Masturbating Girl': the very title so alienated the right in America that there were calls to cut research funding. The metaphors of Henry James, in *The Wings of the Dove*, are shown to reveal a deep interest in the practice of 'fisting', and his basic stance is one of homosexual panic. In her major work, *Epistemology of the Closet*, we might say that the Foucauldian tradition of analysis comes defiantly out of the closet and its homosexual nature is revealed. For Sedgwick, 'many of the major modes of thought and knowledge in twentieth-century Western culture as a whole are structured – indeed fractured – by a chronic, now endemic crisis of homo-heterosexual definition, indicatively male, dating from the end of the nineteenth century' (Sedgwick, 1991, p.1). The lifelong crisis of identity that is the deepest experience of twentieth century homosexuals is thus projected outwards as a crisis in the self-knowledge of a homophobic society; and interpretations of Melville, Wilde and James become the evidence.

The weaknesses of post-structuralism and the substantiality of the subject

Post-structuralism has now been around for a quarter of a century, counting from the early classics: Derrida's *Of Grammatology*, Barthes' *S/Z*, or Deleuze and Guattari's *Anti-Oedipus*;[20] or nearly twice that long if one traces it back to Lacan's 'Rome Report' of 1953. It remains an intellectual strategy rather than a philosophical doctrine: a strategy with a serious part and a comic part. The serious part is to challenge intellectual consensus in every field by showing, through close textual examination, the metaphysical assumptions on which that consensus rests, or the interests that it serves. The comic part is to do so by jokes and wordplay, by writing poised on the edge of sense and nonsense, or by the construction of daft systems of extravagant metaphors.

In the strange world of anti-metaphysics, wordplay can be serious argument. For Derrida and his followers the whole of Western thought is imprisoned within the categories of metaphysics; and though it is not actually possible to think outside these, one can make intellectual moves that put them in question, and thus make the whole structure tremble. This is the serious meaning behind the empty wordplay of which I have complained in this chapter. Whether it is useful to extend this wordplay into literary criticism is another matter.

A second strategy for post-structuralist philosophers is to discover the hidden interests behind supposedly objective discourse by attacking the pre-given, rational and universal human subjectivity which philosophers like Kant postulated as the necessary ground for any discourse – scientific, moral, or aesthetic – to be universal and objective. Marxist, feminist and Foucauldian post-structuralists claim that the supposed pre-given universal subject is actually a regulatory fiction rather than a necessary truth or a factual hypothesis about the mind. It is an imaginary construct devised retrospectively to be a ground for the consensus some philosopher favours.

The claim for universality, they say, is a way of repressing alternative subject positions. What is put forward as impersonal and universal reason **is** actually WASHMAG – white, anglo-saxon, heterosexual, masculine, and governing class – and rests on the suppression of black, gay, feminine, and working-class or colonised positions. The post-structuralist therefore proceeds by taking the texts that are supposed to issue from this pre-given WASHMAG subject (which might mean almost any text – literature as much as philosophy) and looking at them for what is excluded in order to make them function – looking at anomalies, gaps, uncertainties, aporias. In this way one can recover the ignored and suppressed, the subjected, subject positions.

There is in principle no limit to this process. A feminist subject, for example, is as much a regulatory fiction as a humanist one; and a post-structuralist analysis like that of Butler's *Gender Troubles* has no difficulty in dissolving it. Not that we needed post-structuralist arguments to tell us gender is a performative category rather than one that expresses an inner truth. The old sociological category was role. Joan Riviere's psychoanalytic category was masquerade. These older approaches reinforce the post-structuralist attack on the notion of a fixed inner identity,[21] whether feminist or otherwise.

Post-structuralist argument once had a devastating effect, cutting from under our feet any ground we thought we had, and suggesting to some that a political revolution would soon follow the intellectual one. But now it is a ruling orthodoxy: the ideology of a wholly predictable, and indeed almost compulsory, intellectual dissidence. Post-structuralists read Otherwise: and you can predict exactly how they will read. They will be anti-racist, anti-sexist, anti-homophobic, anti-colonialist and discreetly anti-capitalist. But aren't we all? And they will read literature in those senses, with stunning ingenuity. And they will be as anti-authoritarian as is compatible with treating Foucault or Derrida or Lacan as Gospel.

The weakness of post-structuralism is the same as its strength. This intellectual strategy has an irresistible drive toward relativism and anti-realism: to a point where, as Derrida nearly put it, there is nothing outside the text. Early post-structuralists take from Lacan the view that the subject is an effect of the text; later ones, like Butler, make even the body a textual construct. There can be no prediscursive body; only a body constructed in some discourse (like biology) as prediscursive![22] In the limit, the whole universe is a textual construction, and we have returned to full-blown philosophical idealism. This line of argument bothers me more than Butler's conclusions, some of which – such as that masculinity and femininity are performative categories or regulatory fictions – seem fair enough.

But the concept of 'the subject', so much used in post-structuralist theory, is a multiply ambiguous one. If it is a regulatory fiction then it is constructed in discourse and is eminently deconstructible. But if it is what cognitive science would make it, a system of cognitive organisation in the brain, with a biological basis and a cultural overlay developed over a lifetime, which is causally responsible for the nature and quality of subjective experience, then it is something we may form theories about in discourse, but it is not a retroactive effect of discourse, and is not itself constructed in discourse.

We need to remind ourselves that the whole notion of 'construction in discourse' is a metaphor; it would be truer to say that nothing (literally nothing) is constructed in discourse than that everything is. All you can literally construct in discourse are descriptions and, by implication, concepts. You can specify a wooden chair, a body, a human subject, or a star in words but to construct the chair you need wood, and tools; to construct the body you need genes and genitalia; to construct a human subject you need a lifetime living in society; and you cannot construct the star at all; it is just there, and would be there, produced by the elementary physical processes the discourse of astronomers probably describes, even if no human beings and no such discourse had ever existed. Post-structuralism can read discourses against themselves and undermine metaphysical assumptions. But it is powerless against objects. What exists can sometimes be destroyed but can never be deconstructed.[23]

Notes and references

Suggestions for further reading are on page 215.

1. **Derrida**, 1962, 1967. See **Jackson**, 1991 for discussion.

2. **Jackson**, 1991, Chap. V.

3. **Macksey and Donato**, 1970.

4. For discussion of the role of facetiousness in post-structuralism, see **M. Pêcheux**, '*Les Verités de la Palice*' (1975) (trans. **Harbans Nagpal**, *Language, Semantics, and Ideology: stating the obvious* (1982)).

5. **Peter Brooks**, *Psychoanalysis and Story-Telling* (1994), on Lacan, p.110, on structure of the mind, pp.24ff.

6. **Felman**, 1977a: Shoshona Felman, Daniel Sibony, Gayatri Spivak, Roger Dragonetti, Charles Méla, Peter Brooks, Jean-Michel Rey, Phillipe Sollers, Fredric Jameson, John Brenkman, Barbara Johnson. A useful later list is given by **Brooks**, 1994 (p.23): Shoshana Felman, Neil Hertz, Leo Bersani, Sarah Kofman, Malcolm Bowie, Jane Gallop, Jacqueline Rose, Toril Moi. We are dealing here with a substantial school who share the almost automatic assumption that one can use Lacanian and late Freudian theory freely for critical purposes, but have no interest in the theory as science. See **Ellman**, 1994 for a recent book on these lines.

7. Not only Lacan and most Lacanians, but Althusser and most Althusserians. Derrida is not a dogmatist; his fault is to misrepresent texts – see **Jackson**, 1991 for a discussion of his misrepresentation of Saussure.

8. For discussion of *S/Z* see **Jackson**, 1991, Chap. IV.

9. **Spivak, G.C.**, 'The letter as cutting Edge' (1977), Felman, 1982, pp.208–226.

10. **Coleridge, Samuel Taylor**, *Biographia Literaria*, Chaps 12 and 13.

11. **Althusser**, 1984.

12. *Screen*, Reader 2 (1981) (The Society for Education in Film and Television); **Easthope**, 1988; **Lapsley and Westlake**.

13. **Mitchell**, 1974.

14. **Mitchell and Rose**, 1982.

15. S.E. XIV; Penguin Freud, XI.

16. **Coward and Ellis**, 1977; **Easthope**, 1988; **Jackson**, 1994.

17. **Berger**, 1972, p.47.

18. See **Jackson**, *The Dematerialisation of Karl Marx* (1994), Chap. 8, sec. 2.

19. **Foucault**, 1961, 1963, 1966, 1975, 1976–85.

20. See **Jackson**, 1991 for discussion and references.

21. See, for example, Chap. 2, sec. 2, 'Lacan, Riviere and the Strategies of Masquerade' in *Gender Trouble: Feminism and the Subversion of Identity*, **Butler**, 1990.

22. **Butler**, *Bodies that Matter: the Discursive Limits of Sex* (1993). For a more moderate view, see **Thomas Laqueur**, *Making Sex: Body and Gender from the Greeks to Freud* (1990).

23. Detailed defences of a realist metaphysical position will be found in **Jackson**, 1991, 1994.

Chapter 8

The structure of unconscious sexual fantasy

SEXUAL DIFFERENCE, BEHAVIORAL GENETICS AND

SYMBOLIC MEANING

Summary

What is really shocking about modern biology is its reductiveness: it decentres the human subject in a much more thoroughgoing way than any version of Freudian theory can. For post-structuralists, mind is an effect of discourse; changes in discourse can produce a different 'human nature'. For behavioral geneticists, mind and cultural discourses alike are side effects of a competition between genes or spermatozoa. We are cognitively programmed and physically adapted to speak languages, build societies, have complex thoughts, exhibit gender differences, marry, commit adultery, masturbate (while denying we do so) and rape, because over geological ages these have been effective reproductive strategies. Social control of this behaviour thus seems more difficult than we thought, and discourse a weak instrument to use.

Nevertheless, human consciousness, fantasy and discourses like literature do exist and themselves need to be explained. I argue that the extension of radical biological reductionist theories still leaves a logical space for systems of dynamic psychology along Freudian or Jungian lines. We can recognise many levels of unconscious thought which can neither be reduced to instinctive behaviour nor attributed to a retroactive effect of language. They include a primary-process, imaginary, or archetypal level at which instincts are shaped into images; a level of repressed thought created by the internalisation of social taboos; and a set of historically constructed metaphors, sexual and otherwise, which produce a cultural unconscious where we can find such internalised ideologies as patriarchy. These processes of unconscious construction are what underlie morality, culture and politics alike. The elaborate cultural structures through which we understand and act in the world are built on them and discourses ranging from high literature to fashion and pornography can be drawn on to illuminate them.

The biological accounts of sexual difference and sexuality[1]

Sexual differences: the biological view

Sexual differences are deeply built into human biology; yet the most important finding of modern biology about sexual difference is a negative one, which is so taken for granted that it is never put in print. It is that while the human race shows physical dimorphism – men are about a third heavier than women and have twice the fighting strength – there are no significant differences in intellectual ability. There are no definable intellectual tasks which one sex can handle and the other cannot. All that objective investigation shows is a slight statistical bias in the kinds of skill the sexes have. Girls and women are significantly better at language skills; boys and men at spatial skills, mathematics and science. But the mental differences between men and women are far smaller than the physical ones.

Biologists thus give no support to the oldest and most damaging stereotype about women: that they are inherently limited intellectually, compared with men. Curiously enough, the only significant support for this position has come in recent times from certain traditions within feminism. Some people have argued for a 'feminist epistemology' – that is, a special theory of knowledge, truth and justification, for women, that is different from that used by men.[2] They have argued that logic and science are essentially male ways of viewing the world.[3] This is an upside-down version of the old saloon-bar prejudice that women can't be logical or scientific! Some in the Lacanian tradition have argued that language is essentially male, since it depends on the phallus, and thus women, trapped in male language, can have no voice of their own.[4] In so far as a claim like this is meant to have any connection with the real world at all, it seems to be false in every possible way. Language does not depend in any way on the phallus. Women's language skills are superior to men's. They are especially good at finding a voice for their own feelings, which is something men don't do at all well.

Claims of this sort are obviously false – even lunatic – and damaging to women. The interesting question is why anyone should make them. In the last section of this chapter I am going to suggest that they belong – along with claims that the differences between the sexes are **metaphysical** – to a realm of cultural metaphorics – of fantastic but culturally pervasive metaphors in which a changing sexual politics is fought out in the cultural unconscious of society. It is precisely because these battles are fought out in fantasy and metaphor that those who fight them – the MacKinnons, the Irigarays and the old saloon-bar chauvinists alike – find it necessary to talk such extravagant nonsense. They find in it a certain mythical sense.

There is another set of differences, however, recognised in the familiar masculine and feminine stereotypes, for which modern biology gives clear and objective justification. These are differences of temperament, including levels of aggression and sexual urgency. As in most species of animal, most male humans are far more competitive, aggressive and promiscuous than most females, and far more prone to murder and rape. Cultural theorists often talk as if this difference must be caused by social conditioning: letting male children play with warlike toys, or letting men read pornography. They see masculinity and femininity as culturally constructed genders with only the loosest fit to biological sex, yet make them causally responsible for major differences in male and female behaviour.

In fact, each biological sex has its own characteristic complex hormonal systems which produce characteristic effects on development, physique, behaviour and mood. Thus testosterone levels have a complex feedback relationship with aggressive behaviour, in both sexes.[5] But they are consistently far greater in the male. The testicles of the male begin to operate about six weeks into the foetal stage, and produce testosterone, which modifies the organisation of the brain to make typically aggressive male behaviour likely in childhood, more or less whatever mothers do. There is a further surge of testosterone at puberty, which renders most adolescent boys far rougher, and in due course more promiscuous, than most adolescent girls.

It looks as if gender categories are constructed in societies because there already exist in nature, as a result of purely biological processes, systems of brain organisation that produce characteristically male and female behaviour. The social constructs of gender are, as one would expect, a human social adaptation to the brute facts of biological sex, in which humans are similar to many other animals. Humans, of course, go beyond this simple adaptation to produce elaborate unconscious patriarchal fantasies, of the kind discussed below.

Cultural commentators have not yet come to terms with biology; many of them still deny its relevance. Presumably this is because most cultural commentators retain from the sixties (when the biology was not known in such detail) Utopian hopes of changing the facts. I believe one cannot hope to change the social and cultural facts, or the unconscious fantasies, without understanding their biological basis.

The evolution of human sexual behaviour

Evolutionary biology has always recognised that what is selected for is, in the first instance, successful reproductive behaviour; bodily form is important only so far as it supports this. It follows that fundamental behaviour patterns are inherited and are under genetic control: and this must be as true for human beings as for any other animals. Indeed, examples of this are obvious: if you are born a human being you will develop a large brain and speak a language; if you are born a chimpanzee, with a very slightly different genome, you will develop a small brain and not speak a language. Biologists claim that the same thing is true for sexual as for cognitive behaviour.

Why do we inherit certain physical characteristics and behaviour patterns? Because they have contributed to reproductive success or at least have not been eliminated by causing reproductive failure. It is easy to see the reproductive advantages of some forms of behaviour: going on two legs, to free the hands for toolmaking; communicating in language; socially cooperating over complex courses of action; even developing monogamous pairings, so that there are two parents to bring up the children. But how does one explain unproductive practices like masturbation or lethal ones like infanticide?

There seems to have been enormous progress in the biological theory of sexuality in the last twenty years. A classic work like Symons (1979) is still debating such questions as whether female orgasm is a functionless by-product of functional male orgasm. Baker and Bellis (1995) seem not merely to have settled this question, but to give a plausible account of several different functions of orgasm in males and females in routine heterosexual sex, masturbation, and infidelity.[6] In a speculative fictional extension of the theory, Baker (1996) describes the subconscious decision-making that has to take place during episodes of routine sex, adultery, etc.; he thus gives an implicit biological theory of the unconscious which can be usefully contrasted with that of Freud.

In this section I shall give a brief account of Baker and Bellis's biological theory, which I broadly accept; it is still controversial, but it explains far more of human sexual behaviour than anything else I have seen. In doing so, it reveals something about human nature: namely, that there are complex systems of alternative sexual behaviours (not simply a single system of behaviour) slightly different for men and for women, built into the human genome, existing prior to any historically known social system or system of cultural conditioning, and forming the necessary basis of these.

The first striking point is that many features of human sexual behaviour are inherited from a very distant pre-human past. Life began on earth around 4,000 million years ago, and sexual reproduction – reproduction by the amalgamation of cells with sharing of genetic material – about 1,000 million. Around 900 million years ago the gametes began to differentiate in size: small ones (sperm) containing only genetic material and produced in very large numbers combined with large ones (ova) containing both genetic material and nutrients for the developing organism, and produced in much smaller numbers. The many sperm produced compete with each other to fertilise the ova.

Organisms producing sperm – males – have a much smaller energy investment in each sperm than those producing ova – females. Males need to fertilise as many ova as possible; females, to produce ova which are fertilised by the genetically best males. What Baker and Bellis call male urgency and female coyness thus appear in the evolutionary series 800 million years ago, before life on dry land, and of course are still present in most species including the human. One of the peculiar things about cultural theorists is that they sometimes try to explain, on the basis of cultural conditioning, features of behaviour like the promiscuity of men and the selectivity of women, which are shared with most other species and have a clear biological functional basis. Why does one need a cultural explanation? Very little cultural conditioning was available for brainless organisms in the pre-Cambrian seas!

As soon as organisms became complex enough for the male to have organs for sperm storage, two possible reproductive strategies emerged for the male. One is to outproduce other males with sperm. The other is to guard the female and prevent the sperm of other males from reaching her. A basic female strategy of accepting economic resources for sexual services also emerges at this point. Baker and Bellis call it 'prostitution' – rather a tendentious word, considering that they apply it equally to human females, fish and sepsid flies: 'partial economic dependence' would be better.

Internal fertilisation began about 300 million years ago, and it cleared the way for animal life on dry land. It also cleared the way for a number of physical changes that made possible much more complex forms of behaviour. To understand this we must recognise that there are conflicting interests in reproduction. The male interest in fertilising as many females as they can – all the females in the world, if they can manage it – favours reproductive strategies including promiscuity and rape. In species ancestral to human beings, rape (copulation forced by the male on an unwilling female) begins at the reptile level. Some would say that a human rapist remains at that level; but the Baker and Bellis point is that rape is a regular reproductive strategy found in many animals including some far from the human lineage, such as the scorpion fly.

Females need to secure fertilisation from the one male with the best genes and in some species (including human beings and most birds) they need economic support from one or more males, but not necessarily from the one which fertilised them. In some monogamous birds the female chooses a partner as much for the economic resources he controls as for his genetic merit; such birds will often mate with another partner, deceiving their regular one, who helps bring up chicks not his own. The parallel with human adultery is obvious; for Baker and Bellis it is, in a sense, not a parallel but an identity; both species are pursuing the same reproductive strategy for the same reasons.

The war between males and females is sometimes fought out within the body of the female. The vagina and uterus of the female become a kind of obstacle course for sperm, giving her a great deal of control over conception, including, even at the reptile stage of evolution, the possibility of ejecting sperm, killing them internally, or killing the fertilised egg. Baker and Bellis refer to this as 'contraception', which would be absurd if it implied conscious intention; but their point is that the conscious contraception human beings employ is the lineal descendant of these capacities and not a wholly new reproductive strategy.

A war between males and other males is also fought out within the body of the female. The sperm of two or more males may be present, like competing armies, in the genital tract of the female at the same time; according to Baker and Bellis, sperm competition is one of the driving forces of evolution, affecting both male and female bodies and behaviour. The ejaculates of mammals have become complex, including sperm specialised simply to kill or block the path of other males' sperm: this differentiation of sperm is particularly marked for human beings, which is evidence for a long evolutionary history of rape, promiscuity and adultery. (To an outsider, one of the most interesting features of the new biology is the way one can write an evolutionary history of behaviour, including human behaviour, from studies of the physiology of the cervical mucus, or the male ejaculate. It is as spectacular in its way as the demonstration from DNA that we came out of Africa.)

In higher animals, reproductive strategies become more complex; thus both mate guarding and sperm warfare may occur within the same species. Among primates the gorilla is mainly a mate guarder, the chimpanzee a sperm warrior. Male gorillas are much larger than female, but have very small genitals. They produce little sperm, but the silverback male intimidates all competitors. Male and female chimpanzees are much of a size, but the male has enormous genitals. Mating is fairly promiscuous, so sperm from different males compete inside the genital tract of the female.

Human beings fall between gorillas and chimpanzees, in terms of size difference between the sexes and size of male genitals, and also in favoured reproductive strategies: humans are basically monogamous and most males guard their mates, if necessary with violence; but there is some promiscuity and adultery, and some sperm competition occurs. Unlike other primate females, humans are never on heat; so the male never has any way of knowing when to inseminate her; this 'sexual crypsis' is the basis of most human sexual strategy for both sexes. It keeps him attentive and makes it easy for her to deceive him when she is unfaithful.

Perhaps the most interesting finding of Baker and Bellis is the subtle interaction between copulation, masturbation and infidelity in human beings. Mammals can reach orgasm by copulation or masturbation; the function of masturbatory climax in a man is to get rid of older sperm and leave fresher ones for the next hoped-for copulation. Men try to keep their regular partners topped up with an appropriate level of sperm, and to prepare a fresh and potent set for an irregular partner.

Women are different. Masturbatory climax leaves the mucal channels in the cervix blocked, and prevents sperm swimming up them at the next copulation. Copulatory climax has the opposite effect: while not actually necessary for fertilisation, it opens the channels for the sperm being ejaculated, and improves the chances of fertilisation. A woman who masturbates to climax over a fantasy of her lover, copulates with her husband with no climax or a fake one, and climaxes again during copulation with a lover, has assisted the lover's sperm to fertilise, rather than the husband's. This appears to be a fairly regular reproductive strategy, though it is not, of course, a conscious one.

The interesting thing about this theory scientifically speaking is the number of familiar sexual behaviour patterns it shows to be biologically functional, which other discourses have treated as merely irrational and immoral. It even explains why some of these practices are condemned – why, for example, though almost all men, and at least a third of women masturbate, the practice is universally condemned and a word like 'wanker' is a mortal insult. (It is because it is to each person's reproductive advantage that they alone should masturbate and nobody else should, and that nobody should know when they do it.)

The theory is still fairly new and controversial; one would not be surprised if some of the detailed explanations were changed. But it suggests fairly strongly what a full-scale biological theory of inherited human behaviour patterns might look like. Such a theory would designate the pre-social and pre-discursive biological reality on which social construction and discursive elaboration build. On this view a category like 'adultery' would not be merely a social construction; it would, rather, be the way in which a particular reproductive strategy, found not only in human populations but many animal ones, was practically constructed and conceptually elaborated in a particular human society. The same would go for other categories like rape, promiscuity, marriage, etc.

Baker's extension: a new theory of the unconscious

In his books, *Sperm Wars* and (with Elizabeth Oram) *Baby Wars*, written at a popular level and illustrated with fictional case studies, Baker tries to extend the theory above to account not merely for the inheritance of certain behavioral patterns, but for the individual human actions taken in accordance with those patterns. The woman masturbates when she does, knowing nothing of its connection with fertility, because her body, or her unconscious mind, has decided that she wants her lover's baby rather than her husband's.

This would imply that the real reason an Emma Bovary takes an aristocratic lover is that her body regards him as a better genetic bet than her dull husband; and her romantic reveries, far from being the cause of her actions, would be a side effect of her body's techniques for ensuring that her lover will father her child. It is a point Flaubert missed! But it is not implausible. Can one plausibly extend it into the view that she is unconsciously motivated by the desire to have the greatest possible number of great-grandchildren?

Baker is here, I think, misled by his own theory. What I am given by biology is not an internal representation of an unconscious desire for ultimate descendants whom I may never know, along with the intellectual problem of planning unconsciously how to get them. It is rather the several desires for food, for sex with some partners and not others, for sleep, for action to impose my will upon the world, and so forth. These desires occur in patterns which cause me to act in ways which may eventually lead to descendants; that is why these desires, in those patterns, will be part of the genetic inheritance of my descendants.

The interesting question for cultural theory is of course how are the several desires and practices which arise from our biology integrated and transformed into the vast cultural structures which actually determine our experience of the world? The essential step, I think, is the spontaneous generation of fantasies directly from the instincts, which are projected upon the world of the higher animal and become the basis of its consciousness. In human beings, of course, elaborate cultural systems are built on these fantasies, and the illusions of an Emma Bovary are in turn built on these – being thus at two removes from fundamental biology.

The domain of sexual fantasy

Fantasy, planning and decision-making

A fantasy is a narrative or fragment of a narrative – perhaps as little as a single image – generated spontaneously by the mind in response to some instinctual impulse. As we saw in Chapter 2, the capacity to form fantasies is a necessary part of the functioning of the mind of any intelligent animal. The reason is that intelligent animals do not simply respond to stimuli, nor simply act at random. They spontaneously form plans for future action.[7] These are sometimes fragmentary, and consist of little more than a vision of a desired goal, sometimes quite detailed, and with human beings may be worked out in verbal form. Higher animals live in a world of future possibilities, not merely of present experiences.

At the moment of action, choices are made among alternative plans; one is put into action but the others are not completely forgotten; a future action might involve following a plan that was not followed this time. Actions thus have a mental penumbra; we steer ourselves through a landscape with alternative paths, rather than run on railway lines through a dark tunnel. Human beings can take conscious decisions. In these the mind explores a number of alternative scenarios for the future (usually in quite fragmentary form) and selects one.

We are not dealing with wholly conscious or wholly rational processes here. The plans we select are rarely worked out; the intellectual process that has produced them is rarely conscious. The criteria we apply when we choose between them are also rarely conscious. Fantasies seem to be generated and elaborated as much by processes of projection and identification of the kind long studied by Freudians, Jungians and other dynamic psychologists as by linear reasoning. Criteria for judgement seem to involve the same unconscious processes. Only in the most unimportant cases can we clearly set out the criteria by which we make decisions; and these are the only decisions that could be made by a computer.

Far the most important content of fantasy is sex, both in the waking state and in REM sleep. This is exactly what one would expect, given the importance to natural selection of reproductive strategies. Fantasy is much closer to the genes than social reality is – indeed, social reality can be viewed, as Freud viewed it, as an elaborate construction designed to channel, repress, and guide the operations of instinct. For human beings, in some societies, the repressive nature of culture is such that it is possible for them honestly to deny that they think much about sex. Freudian theorists have traditionally taken it as their task to show that virtually every aspect of culture is a transformation of thinking about sex; and this is a view that modern biologists should find wholly congenial.

Fantasy and social learning: infantile and archetypal fantasies

Fantasy is also indispensable for the social learning of complex concepts and skills. Complex social learning involves forming hypotheses about the world, and hypotheses, like plans, start as fantasies.

Fantasy plays a necessary role in learning when a higher animal finds itself genetically programmed to perform a single act, or a whole strategy, that it does not yet know how to perform. For human beings, the sexual act itself is a good example. We do not initially know the procedures for this; and unless we get them from social learning of some kind, will never know them. What we are given by nature is merely spontaneous desire for a certain type of sexual object. We also have the capacity to project that desire on real objects in the world, and see desirable qualities in them. Desire then motivates continual repetitive fantasy about sexual action – fantasy which may be wildly different from real possibilities, and is only quite slowly brought into harmony with the facts of adult sexual behaviour in a particular society.

The most elaborate accounts of childhood sexual fantasy ever produced are those of the Freudians and Kleinians. The reliability of these is quite uncertain. An adverse critic might say that what Freud did was to take the sexology of his day, with its account of standard sexual perversions – polymorphous sexuality, oral sex, anal sex and incestuous sex – and assign the corresponding fantasies, in the order given, to the development of normal children. To these were added hypothetical traumas in childhood – the primal scene, for example – and childhood sexual theories. It is the peculiar mark of Freudian theory that everything of psychological interest seems to happen in childhood. For Freudians adult life and literature are perpetually haunted by unconscious infantile fantasies drawn from the developmental processes just summarised. To fall in love, or to experience transference in the analytic situation, is to project an infantile love onto the adult other.

The orthodox stance of the classical Freudian critic is that which is made systematic by Norman Holland (Chapter 4 above). We can read off the core fantasies at the heart of every work of art in the world from a dictionary of infantile fantasy, often fantasy about body parts. The hero of a thriller – Erroll Flynn, Arnold Schwarzenegger – is a phallus facing oral engulfment in some fearful place. *Hamlet* evokes Oedipal fantasy; *Macbeth* and *Dover Beach* the primal scene of the parents coupling. The core of each reading experience is an infantile fantasy; the basic experience of reading itself is paralleled with one of the most infantile fantasies of all, that of sucking at the breast and passively receiving nourishment. The artistic elaboration of the art work, which takes it beyond crude fantasy, involves complex processes of projection and identification, and evokes in the reader all sorts of ego-defences.

Freud's analyses find the infantile beneath the adult. Jung's find the archetypal beneath the everyday. To fall in love, for a Jungian, is to be captured by an archetype. In Jung's theory we deny the primacy of the infantile and claim that the unconscious is working out the problems of the present and the future, rather than repeating those of the infantile past, and doing so largely by manipulating archetypal images. In Jungian therapy, those images are taken as images of an inner reality of impulse and emotion, and the patient is essentially learning to come to terms with inner reality.

Jung's position is not a wholly biological one; his 'archetypal images' are drawn from culture, not biology; but it is in some ways an easier position to align with biological realities than Freud's. One identifies the instinct – in the sense of an intellectual/emotional process which the organism is genetically preprogrammed to engage in – with the archetype; and the object that sets off that instinctual process can be identified with the archetypal image. Thus the archetypal image for a heterosexual man's sexuality would be the image of a woman, rather than, say, the phallus; the archetypal image for maternal feeling would be a smiling or crying baby; these are the objects to which the human subject is preprogrammed to respond.

Unfortunately, as we have seen, Jungians have a tendency toward a baroque multiplication of archetypes, until every passing tendency in modern life is dignified with an archetypal label of a suitably mythic character. This turns the archetype into a social-historical stereotype, and Jungian theory comes close to being a historical study of cultural metaphors, of the kind that I have attempted in the last section of this chapter. The treatment of art is much the same. Every thematic element in a work of art becomes a version of an archetype; every powerful image an archetypal image, particularly if it is archaic. But this loses the central biological insight of Jungian theory: that the archetypes are the subjective side of human instincts, and the archetypal images are a natural iconography of human instincts. What we would really expect is that the elementary archetypes would be combined to form the complex unconscious fantasies that underlie both daily life and literature.

The archetypal fantasy structures of sex and violence: six bodies in the marriage bed

Here is a speculative account of how aggressive and erotic archetypes may be combined in both lovemaking and literature. The epic and romance traditions, which are continuous with modern thriller fiction, action films, space opera etc., familiarise us with certain cultural versions of archetypal images: the beautiful woman as object of quest – sexual object, victim to be saved, temptress; the hero pursuing the quest, fighting with villains or monsters, etc. We might note here the sexual imbalance of the imagery; as Berger said about European art, and Mulvey agreed about Hollywood film, men act and women appear. A similar content is found outside the realm of professed fiction. The beautiful woman as object of female fantasy turns up in the fashion magazines, and as object of male fantasy, in pornography; the man of action in the lifestyle magazines and, as an implied subject, in magazines about cars or photography.

One might argue that this is a superficial response to a sexist society; if things were different we could envision an alternative fantasy world of beautiful willowy male sex objects and harsh-faced action heroines just as easily. But it is much more probable that this difference at the level of fantasy is a direct reflection of the unequal structure of heterosexuality itself, whether that is thought of as an imposed social pattern[8] or, as I suppose, an instinctual pattern. Within this fantasy structure sexuality is envisaged as a female on show; aggression as a male in action. Mythologically, Venus and Mars; practically, a Victorian woman tight-lacing for her subaltern, or a 1940s woman putting on her lipstick for her flight-lieutenant. So much is commonplace; what is not commonly recognised is how deeply this fundamental imbalance in archetypal imagery can penetrate into heterosexual experience.

Archetypal projection is probably at its strongest for both sexes during lovemaking. When men make love they try to project their archetypal image of sexuality onto the body of the real woman, so as to respond sexually to her. They are not doing anything wrong in this; they are not even doing anything avoidable. You cannot respond sexually to a real body; it is just meat. You can respond only to a projected body; or, to put it more exactly, what makes your response a sexual one is your projection of the archetypal image of sexuality onto the body you are having intercourse with. In one sense this is obvious: it is a man's desire that makes the body of the woman erotic for him. But to speak of the projection of an archetypal image of sexuality goes beyond that commonplace, and indicates the psychic mechanism involved.

Insofar as the archetypal image of sexuality, whether for man or woman, is female, a woman who is sexually aroused is one projecting her image of sexuality upon her own body. Meanwhile the man is also projecting his image upon her body. There are, metaphorically, four bodies in the bed, two real ones, male and female, and two imaginary ones, both female, and both projected on the woman's real body. The woman is behaving according to her image of sexuality, and the man is acting on the assumption that she is behaving according to his image.

They are not necessarily at odds. There are, after all, two real bodies there, which communicate with each other; their real actions and their real physical responses affect the projections that each makes. It is possible for two people to remake their projections so that they coincide. Perhaps this is the real meaning of the phrase 'making love'. Two human beings are between them making an archetype – Venus – come into existence in their shared world. This is an epiphany. More often, no doubt, they are at cross-purposes. Venus is not born from the foam; though some physical satisfaction may be felt, by one or other party, or even both.

I am not sure whether it is a defect of human nature or its normal functioning that usually brings two more bodies into this crowded bed. In the first version of psychoanalysis Freud refused to recognise aggression as a primary instinct; it arose from frustrated sexuality. There is likely to be plenty of that in our bed, if the two projections never coincide, and the behaviour of one party continually frustrates the sexual satisfaction of the other. But the later Freud thought aggression – in the form of a Death Instinct – was independent, and primary; and there is some confirmation here, for most animals, from ethology, and the beginnings of an understanding of its hormonal basis in neurophysiology.[9]

Let us suppose that aggression is indeed an independent instinct. Then it will have its own archetype, and complexes that surround it, and its own system of projections. What will its archetypal image be? I don't think there is any reasonable doubt about this. It is the image of the hero, or to be more precise, the hero/villain: Milton's Satan. And this image is usually male. There are, it is true, aggressive women and warrior-queens in fiction and mythology, and also in life. But they are much rarer, and intuitively they seem to belong to a more sophisticated layer of the mind, just as male gods of love do. Athene and Cupid belong to the study and the court: it is Ares and Aphrodite – Mars and Venus – whom we find in bed together. In the archetypal structure of heterosexuality, the man projects his own aggression, as an image of manliness, and on his own body; and the woman projects hers in the same form, and also on his body. In the full heterosexual experience, the man has the joy of the successful hero, attacking the woman's real body. The woman has the fear of a real person, being attacked by a frightening imaginary hero.[10]

We now have six bodies in the bed, two real and four imaginary, but I doubt if we have reached the full complexity of the situation. The doubtful assumption is that our hero is attacking something real. No doubt his real body is; and perhaps he is hurting her real body; but in the imaginary realm, heroes need monsters. The hero projects upon the woman's body an imaginary monster, and his attack is justified, and he is triumphant. And what does the woman do? I think she projects the image of a garden, a paradise, a retreat, which is broken into, violated, and she is devastated. But I don't think that is all, because it would not give psychic satisfaction. I think she also identifies with the hero in his triumph over the monster.[11]

What happens if both parties collaborate on that image is something which cannot be described as making love. It is more like making hate, making degradation, or even making war – providing we understand this last phrase to mean not making war with each other, but collaborating to produce a psychic image of aggression and destruction. Such an image has pleasures of its own; both sexes are born able to fight and enjoy fighting – even if men have better equipment, hormonal and muscular, to feel and be aggressive. Of course, the pleasure of enjoying an aggressive assault on oneself is not quite the same as the pleasure of making an assault on someone else; but it can still be a real pleasure – in fantasy.

It is not, however, in itself a sexual pleasure. The next turn of the screw comes when aggression is eroticised. When this happens in a man, the image projected on the woman combines both sexuality and monstrousness. Behaviour towards such an image must therefore be both concupiscent and destructive. It is clearly in this realm that the fantasies of the very rare violent type of pornography belong. These naturally do not appeal very much to women. It is certainly possible for a woman to see herself as a monster. But, in general, she is more likely to see herself as a victim. She projects upon her own body the archetype of the victim. And sometimes she splits the aggressor into two archetypes, hero and villain; and in her fantasies of violence and sex, the hero rescues the victim from the violence of the villain. This is the archetypal structure of the romance, whose primary appeal is to women; though masculine/feminine role identifications are mobile enough in fantasy for it to appeal to men as well.

This is a highly speculative account of the interlocked archetypal fantasies that probably underlie both heterosexual lovemaking and a great deal of literature. But it is at least as plausible as Freudian primal scene and castration scenarios, whether in their original or Lacanian form. My thesis is that fantasies of this kind are the basic instinctual building blocks of both complex human actions and complex art works: they account for the emotional meaning of both. The proper development of a theory of such fantasies, on the lines on which Holland developed his Freudian dictionary of fantasy, could throw light on a great many cultural forms, including both popular and serious literature. It would also be satisfyingly reductive, as a cultural theory ought to be. One is saying that every time one reads *Pamela* or *Pride and Prejudice* one is running through courtship and aggressive fantasies, projecting the image of sexuality on the heroine, and that of aggression on the hero. Whether one should think of them as occurring at a primary-process or archetypal or imaginary level depends on whether one is Freudian, Jungian, or Lacanian. I am not satisfied with any of these; but do not presume to offer an alternative.

In these three sections I have stressed the biological and universal. But most of our thinking, conscious or unconscious, is cultural, historical and constructed. I close the book by illustrating this. We can see how what we take as myth is actually intensely contemporary politics; and literature shows us this.

Societies, taboos and the unconscious

Human actions are free in a special sense; they are choices from the set of possibilities for action available in a particular society at a particular time, made by a human subject who has been formed in that society. It is this fact which has led sociologically inclined thinkers – which in our context must include the 'theoretical anti-humanists' who followed Althusser – to make of the human subject no more than a locus, a point in sociological space in which the social influences brought to bear on the subject in the past meet the social restrictions on the subject in the present, and generate a decision. In this context it is mere sentimentality to speak of persons, and the concept of human nature is meaningless. Essentially the same position can be formulated in terms of discourse and ideology; the subject is formed in ideology and lives in ideology, which consists of a set of discourses. The subject is an effect of these discourses – actually it is an illusion which comes from our supposing that a discourse must have an author.

These approaches forget that a subject is always an aspect of the functioning of the brain of an animal, with an animal's genetically pre-programmed strategies to carry out, generating spontaneous pre-cultural fantasies of how to effect them. It is that animal's brain which has been affected by social influences or elaborate discourses in the past, and which is evaluating social and discursive possibilities now. And that brain is of more than sufficient complexity to make decisions which are essentially unpredictable, even by another brain. Biological materialism thus comes, quite unsentimentally, to the aid of human nature. A person is a socialised human animal who can understand discourses well enough to use the information they give to make decisions that will secure whatever personal goals he has managed to generate from his (or of course her) own animal needs.

From a genetic point of view, a human society is something human beings are programmed to construct and belong to, in order to appropriate natural resources and to control and modify instinctive reproductive strategies, in the interests of overall reproductive success. Societies thus have both economic and moral functions: it is to society, not nature, that one must look to suppress both starvation and rape. But controlling human instincts like aggression and sexuality is a fearsomely difficult matter. Theoretical anti-humanism makes society's tasks seem too easy.

The fundamental method by which societies control human instincts is by applying a taboo to the object of those instincts. Lévi-Strauss suggested that the incest taboo was what marked off the realm of culture from the realm of nature. Marriage regulations – which for anthropologists form the basic grammar of human societies – derive from this; and so, presumably, in due order, does the whole raft of institutional regulation of behaviour that gives us roles like husband, father, son, wife, mother, child, and so forth, and eventually constitutes the total framework of a society in which we live. Lacan took this up and, equating the incest taboo with the Oedipal experience, made it the foundation of the unconscious as well. I have discussed this theory, rather sceptically, in Chapter 6; but one doesn't have to be a Lacanian to see taboo as central to society and the unconscious.

Taboos attempt to outlaw not merely an action, but the very thought of that action; not merely the following out of an instinctual pattern, but the image that arouses that instinctual pattern. They thus simultaneously limit the set of social possibilities, and construct a limited human subject to live within these possibilities. But the human subject is only limited by being socially forbidden to think about certain actions; the subject's instincts may still generate fantasies about them, which the subject is forbidden to recognise. Taboo therefore creates a Freudian unconscious full of forbidden fantasies. Taboos are not confined to sex; they cover religious matters, creating realms of the sacred and the blasphemous; and codes of diet and hygiene, creating categories of cleanliness and pollution. In early societies these categories are not separate; as *Oedipus Rex* and *The Oresteia* show, you may incur pollution that no god can cleanse either by marrying your mother or killing her.

Taboos can apply to what is allowed to be seen as well as what is allowed to be done. Most cultures taboo the genitals; some a woman's breasts; there are some religions which require a woman's whole body to be hidden. Theologically, women are here seen as occasions of sin rather than sinners; the target is to suppress the impure thoughts of men by suppressing the image that arouses those thoughts. The visual taboo is usually extended to visual representations as well as realities. These taboos enter in a very complex way into our relationship with social practices and discourses. Two useful examples come from the fashion industry and pornography.

In all societies, there are significant differences between male and female clothing; and sometimes, as in the case of Victorian tight-lacing, clothing is designed around a sexual fetish. In those cultures where clothing varies with fashion, the key to the fashion is a continual variation in the degree of concealment of the sexual organs, breasts, etc.; hemlines move from the floor up to the thigh and down again; bosoms are covered and uncovered, jut out and flatten. In cases like this, it is clear that clothing is not merely a covering and practical impediment; it has a social meaning, and that meaning is a sexual one. In effect, women are constructing body images for themselves which at once invite and control potential sexual overtures: men, body images which make sexual overtures.

When this process goes wrong, it can have tragic consequences. Anorexia is a serious mental disease leading to self-starvation and often death; its victims – nearly always women – look as if they had been in Auschwitz. It appears to be purely psychogenic and based on a false body image: the fashion press is often blamed for this, for using thin models whose physique normal women cannot emulate. But presumably an internalised taboo on sex drives the victim to make the body pre-pubescent, sexually unattractive and anovulatory. (Baker and Bellis classify this as a female contraceptive technique.)

Pornography is theoretically interesting since it is a form of discourse read almost exclusively by men, and throws special light on male sexual fantasy. Most of the interesting studies come from within the feminist tradition. It has a complex relationship with taboo which does not seem to be properly discussed in any of the studies I have read. Pornography varies enormously, but I will take one popular form only. A typical pornographic image of a kind available in Britain over the last fifty years will be a picture of a young woman smiling and making a gesture of crude sexual invitation. Fifty years ago this would have been a display of breasts; nowadays it would be a display of genitals. If we imagine taboo away, such pictures would be mildly attractive to heterosexual men, and leave heterosexual women indifferent. But taboo enters into the very constitution of the self and the unconscious, and can produce wildly different readings of these pictures, similar only in their intensity and irrationality. The very same picture can make a strong man, or woman, physically sick, or produce intense erotic excitement, or both at once.

How does this happen? Puritans, ancient or modern, constitute part of their egos around a taboo on imagery arousing sexual desire, which makes such images sacred in the context of marriage or serious love, and rejects them otherwise as no part of the self – that is, in unconscious fantasy, as excrement. For such a mind, male or female, to be confronted with the erotic image may mean any of the following: (i) to be forced to break an internal taboo that limits the possibilities of experience – hence to be liberated. This is the experience of many male teenagers, and was the experience of many left-wingers at the time of the 'sexual revolution' of the sixties. (ii) To be forced to incorporate the sexuality of another into the self against one's will – hence, symbolically, to be raped. This, according to commentators like Dworkin, was the experience of some of the left-wingers' female consorts! (iii) To be forced, symbolically, to ingest excrement. Hence to be disgusted and nauseated. This is an experience many women, and a surprising number of men have, and is why pornography is called 'filth'. (iv) By projecting the taboo into the mind of the model, the observer can read her nakedness and gestures as something forced on her – hence rape – and can respond either by disgust or by a symbolic rapist's feeling of triumph over her.

Most of the public discussion of pornography has been a dialogue of the deaf between people who have had entirely different conscious experiences of it, due to the different unconscious internal taboos they have brought to it. These experiences are so compelling that they may render it impossible to see the actual text for what it is. For anti-pornographers like Dworkin and MacKinnon, who seem to equate symbolic representation with reality, and masturbation over a picture with rape of a woman, pornography just **is** violence against women, even if no physical violence has occurred or been depicted.[12] Other feminists have protested against this crude identification, and even suggested that what is needed socially is more pornography for and by women.[13] Those who have not internalised the sexual taboos in any strong form are likely to find the whole controversy puzzling: in terms of violence, the material seems so tame compared with Hollywood teen thrillers, *The Perils of Pauline*, or children's cartoons; and they will conclude that the imagined violence of pornography is largely a projection of the violent feelings that it provokes. It is a nice example of the social importance of unconscious internalised taboos, and the way they can impair rational debate about culture.

The metaphorics of feminism and the cultural history of patriarchy

Metaphysical fairy-tales of post-structuralism

French feminists, who sucked in philosophy with their father's milk, often present sexual difference as a matter of **metaphysics**. What is meant by that

– or at least what should be meant by that – is that the opposition between masculine and feminine is one of the fundamental categories, like the opposition between form and substance, in terms of which we analyse the universe as a whole. Indeed from one point of view these are the same metaphysical opposition: it is quite traditional to see form as masculine and substance as feminine. If the oppositions constructing sexual identity are metaphysical, we can use deconstructive techniques, which were designed for the purpose of detecting and attacking metaphysical assumptions, to analyse and undermine them; and a busy universe of discourse opens up for us. We can, for example, argue that one of a pair of categories is privileged over the other – e.g. that masculine is privileged over feminine – and yet is only definable in relation to the other; sexual identity is set up by privileging masculine over feminine. Antihomophobic writers like Butler or Sedgwick do the same for the categories of heterosexual and homosexual.

These are exciting metaphysical fairy-tales in which the realities of political oppression are worked out allegorically. If we take them literally, we fall into the central delusion of post-structuralism, which is that of the omnipotence of discourse. Butler, for example, argues that there can be no pre-discursive human nature; we construct human nature in discourse and then use discourse to project it as pre-discursive![14] But this is to confuse things with the concepts of things. All we can construct in discourse is concepts. A zoologist like Baker or a doctor like Bellis is not using verbal magic to construct a dinosaur or a human being, but using technical terminology to construct a reasonably accurate description of both. They are not using further verbal magic to banish their construct into the realm of the unconstructed. They are describing animals that existed long before the modern discourses of zoology and medicine attempted to describe them, though their descriptions may still be correct. The universe is both historically and logically prior to any scientific account of the universe.

To someone who thinks of the universe as a physical thing, and life as a phenomenon within it, to see sexual identity as a metaphysical category is idiotic: galaxies, mathematical abstractions and physical forces don't have sexes. To someone who thinks of the universe as a universe of possible experience, it is less implausible; for everything we know of, that has experiences of any kind, is sexed. When it comes to offering an account of what these basic categories are, French philosophers often resort to picturesque metaphor: my favourite, I think, is that of Luce Irigaray, when she suggests that you can describe men, using the science of mechanics, but for women you need the science of fluid mechanics – and actually advises her readers to go away and read a book on fluid mechanics![15]

Metaphysics of this kind should really be renamed metaphorics.[16] These are archetypal metaphors – or at least, attempts to provide new metaphors for an old archetype. The opposition that these metaphors are representing exists, not in the material world, but in the world of unconscious fantasy, or, in Irigaray's case, of feminist political fantasy. But archetypal metaphorics may indeed play a central role in the feeling of sexual identity.

Epistemology is the theory of knowledge, truth, evidence, etc.; we have seen that some feminists argue for a different epistemology for men and women. It is suggested that logic, mathematics and science represent an essentially male way of viewing the world; thus Catharine MacKinnon, the anti-pornographer, explicitly compares them to voyeurism, seeing the scientist as a pornographic photographer of nature, and offers consciousness-raising as an alternative epistemological model.[17] Taken literally, the theory has absurd consequences. It would imply that one might have a different chemistry for men and women: the oxygen theory of combustion could be true for men, and the phlogiston theory for women. And men and women would pursue knowledge differently: the men by observation in the laboratory; the women by consciousness-raising in the kitchen. A view like this could be immensely damaging to women's career prospects in chemistry! It at once inverts and confirms what is, despite its august metaphysical antecedents, the standard saloon-bar prejudice that women can't think rationally. Theories like this become no better when dressed in Lacanian clothing, though they are more difficult to spot.

What seems silly to a scientific realist is not necessarily silly within phenomenology. By 'phenomenology' I mean in general the logical analysis of experience, and in particular that branch of philosophy practised by Husserl and others which attempts to achieve apodictic certainty about the essential nature of our world, without making any metaphysical assumptions, by the direct logical analysis of immediately intuited experience.[18] It is logically possible that experience comes in different kinds; possible, even likely, that the experience of a bat is qualitatively different from the experience of a human being. It is also possible to found a certain type of essentialist feminism on the claim that the experience of a woman is as qualitatively different from that of a man as a bat's is: but there is not much evidence that this is so. Again I think we are in the realm not of sober truth but of unconscious fantasy about sexual difference.

Patriarchal ideology and the history of unconscious sexual metaphors

I would argue that the distinction between masculine and feminine is neither metaphysical nor epistemological; and it is certainly not biological.

It belongs to the world of cultural stereotypes; but they are very deep ones, constructed for political purposes over historical time on a biological basis; and they map onto most of the fundamental metaphors with which we order our experience of the world. Helen Haste, in *The Sexual Metaphor*, argues that we map this distinction onto the oppositions **light–dark, public–private, science–arts, rational–intuitive, rationality–chaos, sun–moon, active–passive, hard–soft, thinking–feeling**.[19] I would agree with these, and suggest more: **mind–body, conscious–unconscious**, and **human–animal**. For feminists there is another opposition more important than any of these: **oppressor–oppressed**.

Modern feminism has changed our reading of the whole of cultural history, and turned the literature and mythology of the world into a series of metaphors for the political oppression of women. In my reading the process begins at the beginning of historical time. We read the earliest Sumerian myth, and find that the development of Sumerian civilisation by taming the swamplands of the Tigris–Euphrates delta is translated into the triumph of a male city god – the particular one varies – over a female earth-monster, Tiamat. It is a myth like this that lies historically behind the creation story in Genesis and the philosophical theologies that have been founded on it; and it is a myth like this that lies obscurely behind the 'metaphysical' categories of masculine 'form' and feminine 'substance' or 'content', and carries obscure notions of conquest and control.

Later on we can read, translated into drama, the history of the way that the greatest cultural flowering of the Greeks was built on the political suppression of Greek women. The fears of Greek men are embodied in the powerful women who stalk through their drama: Clytemnestra, Medea, the Bacchae, whose leader, under the influence of Dionysus, tore off the head of her own son; and good women like Alcestis, far stronger than her worthless husband. The story of that political suppression is told in powerful metaphors in the first great dramatic trilogy we have: *The Oresteia* of Aeschylus. Every fear of women in power and 'manoeuvring like men' is embodied in the figure of Clytemnestra, who runs her city like a military camp and murders her husband when he returns from the Trojan war. His death must be avenged by his son: so says the God of Greek enlightenment, Apollo, who (we are told at the start of the third play) long ago took over control of the ancient shrine of the Earth-Goddess at Delphi.

But Apollo's power over goddesses is a very limited one. When Orestes has killed his mother, Apollo cannot protect him against the ancient, pre-Olympian goddesses who stand for the mother, and hunt him down. We can note here an identification of the feminine with the archaic, while Apollo is modern. If we take the story as an allegory of the powerlessness of conscious enlightenment to deal with the unconscious forces within us, we shall not be altogether distant from Greek thought; a similar point is made thirty to forty years later in *The Bacchae* of Euripides, though here it is Dionysus, the new male god, who releases the underlying passions of women.

The Oresteia displays the progressive politics of its era: it favours the advance of democracy among men, and Athenian imperialism, and the suppression of women. So it is only in Athens (Imperial Athens, which was busy trying to centralise all trials in its own courts) that Orestes can be tried and acquitted: by a male jury under the presidency of a Goddess. Athene is the only woman in public life in all Athens; but she is everywhere. She can be trusted, because she was reborn from Zeus's head, and speaks only what the Father commands. She is the goddess of wisdom, and wisdom comes from the father. This is the primal myth of patriarchal epistemology: it lies at the beginning of Western culture, and conditions everything that is to come.

In due course, mind itself will be seen as masculine, and body as feminine; the word will be seen as masculine, and the world that it orders as feminine. These identifications, it must be stressed, make no logical or philosophical sense; but they are deeply embedded in general culture, and affect the way we all think. They even affect, by a long historical develop-ment, the Christian doctrine of the immaculate conception, the creaturely status of Mary, mother of the Lord, the all-male Trinity, and the place of the Word in Christian theology. The Word towers above the world with masculine authority. Can one wonder if, at the other end of Western time, the post-structuralists talk of phallogocentrism, and the feminists want a revolution of knowledge and a feminist epistemology? Outside myth, this desire makes no sense. But myth matters.

Susan Griffin (1981) argues that our society – she seems to be thinking of almost every society in the modern world and of most historically known societies too, particularly those that descend from the Judaeo-Christian tradition and share its anti-sexual attitudes – embodies what she calls a 'pornographic' or 'chauvinist' mind; pornography is the mythology of that mind; a 'poetry of oppression'.[20] The chauvinist mind is a split between culture and nature, mind and body, in which culture or mind is taken as dominant, and nature or the body degraded or rejected. It finds in the image of the rejected race, negro or Jew, and the rejected sex, woman, a rep-resentation of the rejected body, or nature; and projects on that image everything it hates.

To take this view is to go beyond the claim that the various oppositions onto which masculinity and femininity are mapped belong to a kind of semantic unconscious of language, which affects the way we think and feel.

It is to claim, rather, that the 'feminine' side of each opposition is dynamically repressed, and often unconscious in the clinical sense. It is not altogether at odds with Freud's thought to suggest that civilisation itself is built on the repression of the feminine, where the feminine is identified with the bodily. J.C. Smith has recently drawn on feminist thought to argue that the foundations of the social order itself are neurotic[21] in the clinical sense.

In what might be called the normal cultural stereotype the father is the source of knowledge: the mother is the source of life. Some versions of patriarchal ideology deny the second proposition! What does Apollo say in the trial scene of the *Oresteia*? 'The woman you call the mother is not the parent, but merely the nurse of the man's seed, which is the real source of life: witness Athena, who shows how the father Zeus can bear a child without a woman'.[22] Such a claim as this is a transparent legal fiction, designed to protect male inheritance rights; yet it becomes a standard part of Greek science. It represents the basic denial of maternity on which masculine initiation ceremonies world-wide and much of patriarchal culture seem to be based. The parallel Hebrew myth is the birth of Eve from Adam's rib. These are among the many ideological concepts which have been used to project the real political oppression of women by men into a natural or God-given difference between them. Every age, on this view, has defended an oppressive politics with an appeal to natural differences which are often outrageous denials of natural facts.

Those 'natural' sexual differences which the Greeks and the moderns see as biological are for seventeenth century Christians, and some contemporary Muslims, the law of God. Men and women are alike in being God's creatures, created in God's image, and capable of showing truth, wisdom and even holiness. But they are, as Milton tells us in the most impressive account of patriarchal ideology in English literature:

> Not equal, as thir sex not equal seemd;
> For contemplation hee, and valour formd,
> For softness shee and sweet attractive grace,
> Hee for God onely, shee for God in him.[23]

They do not have equal access to God, so it is natural that women can't be priests (or mullahs, or rabbis). According to Christian, Islamic, Jewish, Hindu, and general post-neolithic religious ideology, as well as to popular biology and basic saloon-bar chauvinism, it is men who are designed as thinkers, leaders, hunters and fighters. They understand logic, mathematics, science and machinery and are natural heads of society and of the family:

> His fair large Front and Eye sublime declar'd
> Absolute rule[24]

Adam's 'higher intellectual' and even his physical prowess were feared by Satan; and even his hair was not too long: it came down only to his shoulders, while Eve's reached her waist. Women are designed as wives and mothers, and though they have a right and a duty to rule their young children, are by nature subordinate to their husbands; and this enters into the very nature of the erotic bond between them: even when Eve is unfallen and naturally good, her hair curls in 'wanton ringlets'

>   which impli'd
> Subjection, but required with gentle sway,
> And by her yeilded, by him best receivd,
> Yeilded with coy submission, modest pride,
> And sweet reluctant amorous delay.[25]

C.S. Lewis, a great Milton scholar, used his fiction rather than his criticism to put the Miltonic point with absolute and brutal clarity: obedience (by women to men) is an erotic necessity (for women).[26] The feminist, Catharine MacKinnon, put it much more crudely by saying that women get off on their own subordination.[27] But she thought this pathological; Lewis, the Taliban Islamic warriors of Afghanistan, the saloon-bar chauvinists and the sociobiologists think it natural.

What is the relationship of a mythological and literary tradition like the one we are examining to the unconscious assumptions of society at large? The modern tendency to overemphasise discourse effects would lead us to say that these images of men and women are constructed in the poems we have looked at, and these constructed images have fundamental effects on society. I strongly doubt this: it seems to me as unlikely as the long-exploded idea that the poets fix and develop the language. Attitudes to men and women in society are generated by powerful unconscious processes of identification in fantasy, and transmitted from one generation to another by innumerable informal contacts that leave no written trace.

A work of literature is diagnostic rather than causal: it performs a kind of cultural psychoanalysis by showing us what stereotypes and metaphors form the basic topography of the cognitive unconscious, in its time, and enables us to illustrate and examine them, as I have just done. It does not create them. But there is no better clinical evidence that they exist. Even someone like me, who broadly accepts the biological account given earlier of the real innate differences between men and women, can be led by the evidence of literature to accept also the existence of a powerful ideology of patriarchy, developing over millennia, but present in the cognitive unconscious to this day.

Notes and references

Suggestions for further reading are on page 215.

1. For an authoritative account of the basic research in this field, up to 1979, see **Donald Symons**, 1979, *The Evolution of Human Sexuality*. **Robin R. Baker** and **Mark A. Bellis**, 1995, *Human Sperm Competition: Copulation, Masturbation, and Infidelity* takes the story to 1995. I follow these save where stated. For popular mainstream summaries of currently orthodox positions, see **Pinker**, 1997, **Ridley**, **Dawkins**, 1976, 1982, **Diamond**. For sexual differences, **Moir and Jessel**, *Brainsex*, provides an excellent summary of results and a fine bibliography up to 1989; **Moir and Moir**, 1998 *Why Men Don't Iron* is a Channel 4 television tie-in, written in popular style, but has good notes.

2. **Stanley and Wise**.

3. **MacKinnon**, 1983, pp.111–113.

4. See **Laura Mulvey**, 1989 for a fine critic who has adopted this strange theory – discussed in previous chapter.

5. See **Kemper**, 1990, *Social Structure and Testosterone: Explorations of the Socio-Bio-Social Chain* for a detailed study. Also **Damasio**, 1994 for emotion and the brain.

6. The crucial finding that women who have an orgasm during copulation retain sperm better has been independently confirmed, e.g. by a team at Cardiff University: report from the British Association 1998, in *The Times*, September 1998.

7. The centrality of plans to intelligent behaviour was one of the earliest insights of the cognitive revolution; cf. **Miller, Galanter and Pribram**, 1960. It is discussed in Chapter 2 above.

8. **MacKinnon**, 1983, **Wittig**, 1992.

9. The death instinct is not exactly equivalent to aggression, in the sense Lorenz gives it; it is more like aggression directed at the self. For social structure and testosterone see, e.g. **Kemper**, 1990.

10. Cf. **Dworkin**, 1987, *Intercourse*.

11. Garden-bowers connect in fantasy to the pudenda. Students of epic will recall the use of the garden/bower image as a representation of sexuality in Ariosto, Tasso, Spenser and Milton. A rather elaborate analysis of this tradition underlies this section, but can't be given here.

12. **Dworkin**, 1979; **MacKinnon**, 1982, 1983, 1994.

13. **Segal and MacIntosh**; **Vance**, 1984; **Williams**.

14. **Butler**, 1993.

15. **Irigaray**, 1977. For exasperated comment on such misuse of science, see **Sokal and Bricmont**.

16. I hold these to be different; on attempts to reduce one to the other, see 'White Mythology', **Derrida**, 1972, Chap. 8.

17. **MacKinnon**, 1983.

18. **Edmund Husserl**, *Cartesian Meditations: an Introduction to Phenomenology* (1950).

19. **Helen Haste**, *The Sexual Metaphor* (1993) p.3. I have inverted the opposition arts–science, which is an obvious error.

20. **Judy Grahn**, quoted in **Griffin**, 1981, pp.1–2.
21. **J.C. Smith**, *The Neurotic Foundations of Social Order: Psychoanalytic Roots of Patriarchy* (1990).
22. *Eumenides*, trans. Fagles, 665–678.
23. **John Milton**, 1667–9, 1694, *Paradise Lost* IV, 296–299.
24. *P.L.*, IV, 300–1.
25. *P.L.*, IV, 307–11.
26. **C.S. Lewis**, *That Hideous Strength* (1945) (London: The Bodley Head) pp.178–9.
27. **Catharine MacKinnon**, 'Desire and Power: a Feminist Perspective' (1988) in **Nelson and Grossberg**, 1988.

Suggestions for further reading

Chapter 2: The new cognitive psychology

Introductions

Pinker, Stephen. *How the Mind Works* (1997).

Johnson-Laird, Philip. *The Computer and the Mind: an Introduction to Cognitive Science* (1988).

Sagan, Carl. *The Dragons of Eden: Speculations on the Evolution of Human Intelligence* (1977).

Lorenz, Konrad. *Behind the Mirror: a Search for a Natural History of Human Knowledge* (1973).

Jackson, Leonard. *The Poverty of Structuralism* (1991) (Contains discussion of the cognitive significance of language and the vacuity of structuralist and post-structuralist approaches for which I have no space in this chapter).

Further reading

Language: Chomsky, Noam (general) 1979, 1980, 1982, 1986, 1989; (technical) 1956, 1957, 1965 and articles in Luce, Bush and Galanter 1963, 1965; Botha; Fodor and Katz 1964; Jackendoff; Jackson 1991; Lakoff 1980, 1987; Lenneburg; Lieberman 1975, 1984; Skinner 1957; Winograd.

Philosophy: Boden 1990; Churchland; Dennett 1978, 1979, 1984a, 1984b, 1991; Dreyfus and Dreyfus; Hodgson; Hofstadter and Dennett; Lockwood; Midgley; Penrose 1989, 1994; Ryle; Searle 1984, 1987; Young.

Cognitive science: Blakemore; Blakemore and Greenfield; Boden 1987, 1991; Calvin; Damasio; Edelman 1987, 1989; Fodor 1975, 1983, 1987, 1990; Gardner 1977, 1985; Neisser; Prigogine and Stenders; Pylyshin; Rose 1993; Schank 1972, 1977, 1990; Sternberg.

More technical: Aleksander and Morton; Bobrow and Collins; de Gelder; Ellis and Young; Fodor and Pylyshin; Johnson-Laird 1977, 1983; Kirsh; McLelland, Rumelhart, *et al*; Minsky 1975, 1979; Pollock; Rumelhart; Shallice; Shapiro; Shinghal; Thayer; Walsh; Wegman; Wilensky.

Behavioral ecology: Darwin; Diamond; Lorenz 1952, 1963, 1973; Ridley; Tinbergen 1951, 1953, 1968; Wilson 1975, 1978.

Chaos theory: Gleick, Stewart.

Computers, meaning and literary theory: Colomb and Turner in Cohen; discussed in Jackson 1991, pp.217–18.

This is a formidable, though selected, booklist for the non-scientist but I can vouch for the interest of everything here, at popular or serious level. My own idiosyncratic view is that serious students of cognitive science should (i) take a good course in formal logic; (ii) read the articles by Chomsky and Chomsky and Miller in Luce, Bush and Galanter 1963, 1965: these demonstrate how one can formalise a body of unconscious human knowledge and establish a basic level of mathematical competence; (iii) read and follow up the references in Shapiro (1992 or later edition) *Encyclopedia of Artificial Intelligence*. There are many ways into cognitive science, but language is surely the key.

Chapter 3: The sceptical Freudian

Texts and critique

Freud, Sigmund. *Two Short Accounts of Psychoanalysis* (1962) (The early and late systems).

Freud, Sigmund. *Introductory Lectures on Psychoanalysis* (1915–17).

Freud, Sigmund. *New Introductory Lectures on Psychoanalysis* (1933).

Freud, S. and Breuer, J. *Studies on Hysteria* (1895).

Freud, Sigmund. *The Interpretation of Dreams* (1900).

Freud, Sigmund. *The Psychopathology of Everyday Life* (1904).

Freud, Sigmund. *Jokes and their Relation to the Unconscious* (1905).

Freud, Sigmund. *On Sexuality: Three Essays on the Theory of Sexuality and Other Works* (1905–31).

Freud, Brunswick and Gardiner, M. (ed.) *The Wolf-Man and Sigmund Freud* (1973).

Freud, Sigmund. *Case Histories I: 'Dora' and 'Little Hans'* (1977).

Freud, Anna. *The Ego and the Mechanisms of Defence* (1936).

Klein, Melanie, Heimann, Paula and Money-Kirle R.E. *New Directions in Psycho-analysis* (1955).

Fisher and Greenberg. *Freud Scientifically Reappraised: Testing the Theories and Therapy* (1996).

Further reading

Studies: Chasseguet-Smirgel and Grunberger; Ellenberger; Frosh; Gay 1985, 1990; Gray, Bowers and Fenz; Limentati; Marcus; Mitchell 1974; Obholzer; Orne; Riviere; Sandler; Segal 1973; Wegman; Wollheim.

Critiques: Aldridge-Morris; Crews 1995; Eysenck 1957, 1965, 1985; Eysenck and Wilson; Fromm; Grünbaum; Healy; Kline; Malcolm 1982, 1984; Masson 1984, 1989, 1990; Ofshe; Ricoeur; Timpanaro; Vološinov; Wakefield *et al*; Webster; Wells; Wepman; Wollheim.

Freudians: Abraham 1927, 1955; Boss; Bowlby; Freud (Anna); Greenson; Guntrip; Horney; Jones 1923; Klein 1932, 1921–45, 1946–63; Mitchell; Rank 1909, 1929; Reich 1932, 1942, 1949, 1967; Reik; Riviere; Segal 1978; Winnicott 1964, 1988.
Others: Adler; Caudwell; Chodorow; Cooper; Davidson; Groddeck; Prince; Sacks.
Biographies: Jones 1953–7; Sulloway; Gay 1988; Appignanesi and Forrester (Freud's Women); Clancier and Kalmanovich (Winnicott); Grosskurth (Klein); Kerr (Freud, Jung, Spielrein); Roazen (Deutsch); Rubins (Horney); Sayers 1991 (Deutsch, Horney, A. Freud, Klein); Segal 1973 (Klein); Young-Bruehl (A. Freud).

Chapter 4: Art as fantasy and defence

Texts

Freud, Sigmund. *Art and Literature* (1985). Pelican Freud Vol. 14 containing: *Delusions and Dreams in Jensen's 'Gradiva', The Relation of the Poet to DayDreaming, Leonardo, The Theme of the Three Caskets.*

Kuttner, A.B. '*Sons and Lovers*: A Freudian Interpretation' (1916), *P. Anal. Review.*
Jones, Ernest. *Hamlet and Oedipus* (1923–54).

Holland, Norman N. *The Dynamics of Literary Response* (1968).
Holland, Norman N. *The Critical I* (1992).

Further reading

Aristotle; Bloom 1973, 1975; Crews 1975; Edel; Fiedler; Gay 1985, 1990; Hoffman; Holland 1975; Jackson 1994b; Jacobus; Lesser; Manheim and Manheim; Marcus; Skura; Tallack; Trilling; Wilson 1952.

Chapter 5: Instinct, archetype and symbol

Texts and introductions

Jung, C.G. *Symbols of Transformation: an Analysis of the Prelude to a Case of Schizophrenia* (1952) C.W. 5.
Jung, Emma. *Animus, and Anima: Two Essays by Emma Jung* (1934–55).

Stevens, Anthony. *Archetype: a Natural History of the Self* (1982).
Stevens, Anthony. *On Jung* (1990).
Samuels, Andrew. *Jung and the Post-Jungians* (1985).

Bodkin, Maud. *Archetypal Patterns in Poetry* (1934).

Further reading

Jung: 1913, 1919, 1920, 1933–59, 1952, 1960.
Studies: Bennett 1961, 1967; Fordham; Hopcke; Jacobi; Papadopoulos and Saayman; Rolfe; Schwarz-Salant and Stein; Staude; Stevens 1995; Stevens and Price; Wehr.

Jungians: Castillejo; Cowan; Franz; Hillman 1983, 1990; Johnson 1991; Moore and Gillette; Rowan; Ulanov and Ulanov.
Others: Bowlby; O'Brien (case).
Mythographers: Frazer; Graves 1955, 1961; Harrison 1903, 1912, 1913; Murray; Raglan 1936, 1940; Rank 1909, 1929.
Literary Critics: Donington; Fiedler; Frye; Lewis 1936; Propp.

Chapter 6: The first post-structuralist

Introductions

Benvenuto, Bice and Kennedy, Roger. *The Works of Jacques Lacan* (1986).

Roudinesco, Elisabeth. *Jacques Lacan & Co.: A History of Psychoanalysis in France 1925–1985* (1990).

Further reading

A fair selection from Lacan's work is now available in English, of which far the best and clearest are the *Seminar*, Vol. I 1953–4, Vol. II 1954–5, Vol. III 1955–6. Otherwise there are *Ecrits*, 1966a, and a paper delivered in Baltimore, 1966b 'Of Structure as an Inmixing of an Otherness Prerequisite to any Subject Whatever' in Macksey and Donato, 1970; *The Four Fundamental Concepts of Psychoanalysis*, 1977; articles from the Ecole Freudienne in the Mitchell and Rose reader, *Feminine Sexuality*, 1982; and one-off translations of articles on Edgar Allen Poe and on Hamlet in *Yale French Studies 48* and 55–6, (or Felman, 1977a) respectively. Lacan's best known manifesto, the 'Rome Report' of 1953, has been translated twice, by Anthony Wilden 1968 (2nd edn 1986) with notes and commentary; and by Alan Sheridan in 1977, as chapter three of *Ecrits* (Fr. date 1966). There is a transcript of Lacan interviewing an obviously paranoid schizophrenic patient in Schneiderman (ed.) 1980. The patient had read *Ecrits* a short time before and politely obliged with a Lacanian psychosis. There is a complete Lacan bibliography in Roudinesco 1993 (not yet translated).

Commentaries: There are also useful commentaries, by Lemaire 1970, Muller and Richardson 1982, Smith and Kerrigan 1983, Ragland-Sullivan 1986, Benvenuto and Kennedy 1986, Macey 1988, Forrester 1990, Bowie 1991, Nobus 1998.

Politics: The politics are described by Sherry Turkle 1979, Catherine Clément 1981, Stuart Schneidermann 1983 and magisterially, Elisabeth Roudinesco 1990. They are very exciting if you are excited by that sort of thing; they are not the concern of this book, but I am afraid they will keep intruding.

Post-structuralist response: Deleuze and Guattari; Derrida 1980; Easthope 1980.
Philosophers in the background: Descartes; Hegel (Kojève); Heidegger 1926, 1959; Husserl; Sartre 1943, 1945.
Anthropologist in background: Lévi-Strauss 1949, 1958, 1976.
Linguists in background: Saussure, Jakobson 1956, 1976.
Chomsky's dismissal of Lacan: Chomsky 1989.

Chapter 7: Reading 'otherwise'

Texts and introductions

Felman, Shoshana (ed.). *Literature and Psychoanalysis: a Question of Reading: Otherwise* (1977, 1982).
Brooks, Peter. *Reading for the Plot* (1984).
Lupton, J.R. and Reinhard K. *After Oedipus: Shakespeare in Psychoanalysis* (1993).

Ellman, Maud. *Psychoanalytic Literary Criticism* (1994).
Lechte, John. *Writing and Psychoanalysis: a Reader* (1996).

Althusser, Louis. 'Freud and Lacan' (1964) in *Essays on Ideology* (1984).
Berger, John. *Ways of Seeing* (1972).
Mulvey, Laura. *Visual and Other Pleasures* (1989).

Butler, Judith. *Gender Trouble: Feminism and the Subversion of Identity* (1990).
Sedgwick, Eve Kosowsky. *Epistemology of the Closet* (1991).

Further reading

Structuralism: Clarke; Culler 1975, 1976; Jackson 1991; Shalvey.
Althusserianism: Althusser; Althusser and Balibar; Belsey; Coward and Ellis; Elliot; Rée (critique of Coward and Ellis).
Foucauldianism: Barrett; Cousins and Athar; Dollimore; Foucault 1961, 1963, 1966, 1969, 1975, 1976–85, 1980, 1984; Gane; Halperin; Hoy; Macey 1993; Sedgwick 1991, 1995; Sheridan.
Post-Structuralism and Psychoanalysis: Barthes; Betterton; Brenkman; Brooks 1977, 1994; Butler 1990, 1993; Burgin; Derrida 1962, 1967c, 1980; Donald; Easthope 1980, 1988; Finucci and Schwarz eds. (includes extensive bibliography for psychoanalytic studies covering the renaissance period); Forrester 1990, 1991; Irigaray; Jameson; Johnson 1977; MacCabe; Muller and Richardson 1988; Squires.

Chapter 8: The structure of unconscious sexual fantasy

Texts and introductions

Baker, R.R. and Bellis, M.A. *Human Sperm Competition: Copulation, Masturbation, and Infidelity* (1995).
Baker, R.R. *Sperm Wars: Infidelity, Sexual Conflict, and Other Bedroom Battles* (1996).
Symons, D. *The Evolution of Human Sexuality* (1979).

Lakoff, G. and Johnson, M. *Metaphors We Live By* (1980).
Haste, Helen. *The Sexual Metaphor* (1993).
Laqueur, Thomas. *Making Sex: Body and Gender from the Greeks to Freud* (1990).
Butler, Judith. *Bodies that Matter: on the Discursive Limits of Sex* (1993).

Further reading

Deep Metaphor: Lakoff; Jackson 1991.

Sex, Gender and Sexual Difference: Archer and Lloyd; Baker; Baker and Oram; Brownmiller; Cook; Delacoste and Alexander; Ehrenreich; Friday; Kaplan; Kemper; Moir and Jessel; Moir and Moir; Symons; Symons and Ellis; Weitz.

Feminism and its Other: Abel and Abel; Belsey and Moore; Butler 1990, 1993; Castillejo; Conley; Feldstein and Roof; Goldberg; Gray; Lewis 1942, 1945; McNay; Miller, J.B.; Miles; Millett; Mitchell; Mitchell and Rose; Mitscherlich; Morgan; Rhodes and McNeill; Richards; Rose 1986; Sayers 1986; Sedgwick 1991, 1994; Segal 1994; Smith, J.C.; Stanley and Wise; Warhol and Herndl; Warnock; Whitford; Wittig; Wolf; Wright 1991, 1992.

Pornography: Christensen; Dworkin 1979, 1987, 1990; Griffin; Lederer; Lovelace; MacKinnon 1982, 1983, 1994; Segal and McIntosh; Vance; Williams.

Select bibliography

Abel, Elizabeth and Abel, Emily K., eds. *The Signs Reader: Women, Gender and Scholarship*. Chicago and London: University of Chicago, 1983.

Abraham, Karl. *Selected Papers on Psychoanalysis*. London: Hogarth, 1927.

—. *Clinical Papers and Essays on Psychoanalysis*. London: Hogarth, 1955.

Aldridge-Morris, Ray. *Multiple Personality: an Exercise in Deception*. Hove: Erlbaum, 1989.

Aleksander, Igor and Morton, Helen. *Neurons and Symbols: the Stuff that Mind is Made of*. London: Chapman and Hall, 1993.

Althusser, Louis. *Essays on Ideology*. London: Verso, 1984.

Althusser, Louis and Balibar, Etienne. *Reading Capital*. London: Verso, 1968.

Appignanesi, Lisa, ed. *Postmodernism: ICA Documents*. London: Free Association Books, 1989.

Appignanesi, Lisa and Forrester, John. *Freud's Women*. London: Weidenfeld and Nicolson, 1992.

Archer, John and Lloyd, Barbara. *Sex and Gender*. London: Penguin, 1982.

Aristotle. *Poetics* 4th century BC a. Translation and commentary, Halliwell; 1987. London: Duckworth.

—. *Metaphysics* 4th century BC b. Edited and translated Warrington; London: J.M. Dent, 1956.

Baker, R. Robin and Bellis, Mark A. *Human Sperm Competition*. London: Chapman and Hall, 1995.

Baker, R. Robin. *Sperm Wars*. London: Fourth Estate, 1996.

Baker, R. Robin and Oram, Elizabeth. *Baby Wars*. London: Fourth Estate, 1998.

Barrett, Michele. *The Politics of Truth: from Marx to Foucault*. Cambridge: Polity, 1991.

Barthes, Roland. *S/Z*. Paris: Editions du Seuil, 1970.

Belsey, Catherine. *Critical Practice*. New Accents. London: Methuen, 1980.

Belsey, Catherine and Moore, Jane. *The Feminist Reader*. London: Macmillan, 1989.

Bennett, E.A. *C.G. Jung*. London: Barrie and Rockliff, 1961.

—. *What Jung Really Said*. NY: Schocken Books, 1967.

Benvenuto, Bice and Kennedy, Roger. *The Works of Jacques Lacan*. London: Free Association Books, 1986.

Berger, John. *Ways of Seeing.* London: BBC and Penguin, 1972.

Betterton, Rosemary, ed. *Looking On: Images of Women in the Visual Arts and Media.* London: Pandora, 1987.

Blakemore, Colin and Greenfield, Susan. *Mindwaves: Thoughts on Intelligence, Identity and Consciousness.* Oxford: Basil Blackwell, 1987.

Blakemore, Colin. *The Mind Machine: the Book of the TV Series.* London: BBC Books, 1988.

Bloom, Harold. *The Anxiety of Influence: a Theory of Poetry.* Oxford: OUP, 1973.

Bobrow, D.G. and Collins, A.M., eds. *Representation and Understanding.* NY: Academic Press, 1975.

Boden, Margaret A. *Artificial Intelligence and Natural Man.* London: MIT, 1987.

—. *The Philosophy of Artificial Intelligence.* Oxford: OUP, 1990.

—. *Artificial Intelligence in Psychology: Interdisciplinary Essays.* London and Cambridge, Mass.: MIT, 1991.

Bodkin, Maud. *Archetypal Patterns in Poetry.* Oxford: OUP, 1937.

Boss, Medard. *Psychoanalysis and Daseinanalysis.* NY: Basic Books, 1963.

Botha, Rudolf P. *Challenging Chomsky: the Generative Garden Game.* Oxford: Blackwell, 1989.

Bowie, Malcolm. *Lacan.* London: Fontana, 1991.

Bowlby, John. *Attachment and Loss. Vol. I: Attachment. Vol. II: Separation. Vol. III: Loss.* London: Hogarth/Penguin Books, 1969.

Brenkman, John. 'The Other and the One: Psychoanalysis, Reading, the Symposium' (1977) in Felman, 1977a, 1982.

Brooks, Peter. 'Freud's Masterplot' (1977) in Felman, 1977a, 1982.

—. *Reading for the Plot: Design and Intention in Narrative.* NY: Knopf (and Vintage Books), 1984.

—. *Psychoanalysis and Storytelling.* Oxford: Blackwell, 1994.

Brownmiller, Susan. *Against Our Will: Men, Women and Rape.* London: Secker and Warburg, 1975.

Burgin, Victor; Donald, James; and Kaplan, Cora, eds. *Formations of Fantasy.* London: Methuen, 1986.

Burr, Chandler. *A Separate Creation: How Biology Makes us Gay.* London: Bantam, 1996.

Butler, Judith. *Gender Trouble: Feminism and the Subversion of Identity.* NY: Routledge, 1990.

—. *Bodies that Matter: on the Discursive Limits of Sex.* NY: Routledge, 1993.

Calvin, W. *How Brains Think: Evolving Intelligence Then and Now.* London: Orion/Phoenix, 1996.

Castillejo, Irene Claremont de. *Knowing Woman: a Feminine Psychology.* Boston and Shaftesbury: Shambhala, 1990.

Caudwell, Christopher. *The Concept of Freedom* (includes part of *The Crisis in Physics*). London: Lawrence and Wishart, 1938, 1948, 1949.

Chasseguet-Smirgel, Janine and Grunberger, Bela. *Freud or Reich: Psychoanalysis and Illusion* (1976). London: Free Association Books, translated by Claire Pajaczkowska, 1986.

Chodorow, Nancy. *The Reproduction of Mothering: Psychoanalysis and the Sociology of Gender.* Berkeley, London: University of California, 1978.

Chomsky, Noam. 'Three Models for the Description of Language' (1956) in Luce, Bush and Galanter, 1965.

—. *Syntactic Structures.* The Hague: Mouton, 1957.

—. 'On Certain Formal Properties of Grammars' (1959) in Luce, Bush and Galanter, 1965.

—. 'Introduction to the Formal Analysis of Natural Languages' (1963) in Luce, Bush and Galanter, 1963.

—. *Aspects of the Theory of Syntax.* Cambridge, Mass.: MIT, 1965.

—. *Language and Responsibility.* Sussex: Harvester, 1979.

—. *Rules and Representations.* Oxford: Blackwell, 1980.

—. *The Generative Enterprise.* Dordrecht: Foris, 1982.

—. *Knowledge of Language: Its Nature, Origin and Use.* NY: Praeger, 1986.

—. 'Noam Chomsky: An Interview' *Radical Philosophy 53.* London: Radical Philosophy Group, 1989.

Chomsky, Noam and Miller, George. 'Finite State languages' (1958) in Luce, Bush and Galanter, 1965.

Christensen, F.M. *Pornography: the Other Side.* NY: Praeger, 1990.

Churchland, Patricia Smith. *Neurophilosophy: Towards a Unified Model of the Mind-Brain.* Cambridge, Mass. and London: MIT, 1986.

Clancier, Anne and Kalmanovich, Jeannine. *The Paradox of Winnicott* (1984). London: Tavistock, translated by Prince Masud Khan, 1987.

Clarke, Simon. *The Foundations of Structuralism.* Sussex: Harvester, 1981.

Clément, Catherine. *The Lives and Legends of Jacques Lacan.* NY: Columbia UP, 1983, Fr. 1981.

Cohen, Ralph, ed. *The Future of Literary Theory.* London: Routledge, 1989.

Colomb, Gregory and Turner, Mark. 'Computers, Literary Theory and Theory of Meaning' (1989) in Cohen, 1989.

Conley, Verena Andermatt. *Hélène Cixous.* Sussex: Harvester Wheatsheaf, 1992.

Cook, Mark. *The Bases of Human Sexual Attraction.* London, NY, etc: Academic Press, 1981.

Cooper, David. *Psychiatry and AntiPsychiatry.* London: Tavistock, 1967.

Cousins, Mark and Hussain, Athar. *Michel Foucault.* London: Macmillan, 1984.

Cowan, Lyn. *Masochism: A Jungian View.* Dallas, Texas: Spring, 1982.

Coward, Rosalind and Ellis, John. *Language and Materialism.* London: Routledge, 1977.

Crews, Frederick. *Out of My System: Psychoanalysis, Ideology and Critical Method.* NY: OUP, 1975.

—. *The Memory Wars: Freud's Legacy in Dispute.* London: Granta Books, 1995.

Culler, Jonathan. *Structuralist Poetics.* London: Routledge, 1975.

—. *Saussure.* London: Fontana, 1976.

Damasio, Antonio R. *Descartes' Error: Emotion, Reason and the Human Brain.* London: Macmillan, 1994.

Darwin, Charles. *The Expression of the Emotions in Man and Animals.* London: John Murray, 1872.

Dawkins, Richard. *The Selfish Gene.* Oxford: OUP, 1976.

—. *The Extended Phenotype: the Long Reach of the Gene.* Oxford: OUP, 1982.

De Gelder, Beatrice, ed. *Knowledge and Representation.* London: Routledge, 1982.

Delacoste, Frédérique and Alexander, Priscilla, eds. *Sex Work: Writings by Women in the Sex Industry*. Pennsylvania and San Francisco: Cleis/London: Virago, 1987.

Deleuze, Gilles and Guattari, Felix. *Anti-Oedipus: Capitalism and Schizophrenia*. London: Athlone, 1983, Fr. 1972.

Dennett, Daniel. *Brainstorms*. Montgomery Vt: Bradford Books, 1978.

—. Review of Popper and Eccles (1977) in *Journal of Philosophy* 76, 1979.

—. *Elbow Room: The Varieties of Free Will Worth Wanting*. Cambridge, Mass: MIT, 1984a.

—. 'Carving the Mind at Its Joints', review of Fodor (1983) in *Contemporary Psychology*, 29, 1984b.

—. *Consciousness Explained*. London: Allen Lane Penguin, 1991.

Derrida, Jacques. *Husserl's Origin of Geometry: An Introduction*. Sussex: Harvester, 1962.

—. *Of Grammatology*. Baltimore: Johns Hopkins, 1967.

—. *Margins of Philosophy*. Sussex: Harvester, 1972.

—. *The Post Card: from Socrates to Freud and Beyond*. Chicago: Chicago UP, 1980.

Descartes, René. *Descartes: Philosophical Writings*. London: Thomas Nelson, 1954.

Diamond, Jared. *The Rise and Fall of the Third Chimpanzee: How Our Animal Heritage Affects the Way We Live*. London: Random House, 1991.

Dollimore, Jonathan. *Sexual Dissidence: Augustine to Wilde: Freud to Foucault*. Oxford: OUP, 1991.

Donald, James, ed. *Psychoanalysis and Cultural Theory: Thresholds*. London: Macmillan, 1991.

Donington, Robert. *Wagner's Ring and its Symbols*. London: Faber, 1961.

Dreyfus, Hubert L. and Dreyfus, Stuart E. *Mind over Machine: The Power of Human Intuition and Expertise in the Era of the Computer*. Oxford: Blackwell, 1986.

Dworkin, Andrea. *Pornography: Men Possessing Women*. USA: Perigree Books/London: The Women's Press, 1979.

—. *Intercourse*. London: Secker and Warburg, 1987.

—. *Mercy*. London: Secker and Warburg, 1990.

Easthope, Anthony. 'Reply to Rée'. *Radical Philosophy 25*. London: Radical Philosophy Group, 1980.

—. *British Post-Structuralism since 1968*. London: Routledge, 1988.

Edel, Leon. *Stuff of Sleep and Dreams: Experiments in Literary Psychology*. London: Chatto and Windus, 1982.

Edelman, G. *Neural Darwinism*. NY: Basic Books, 1987.

—. *The Remembered Present: A Biological Theory of Consciousness*. NY: Basic Books, 1989.

Ehrenreich, Barbara; Hess, Elizabeth; and Jacobs, Gloria. *Re-Making Love: the Feminization of Sex*. NY: Doubleday Anchor, 1986.

Ellenberger, Henri F. *The Discovery of the Unconscious: the History and Evolution of Dynamic Psychiatry*. London: Allen Lane Penguin, 1970.

Elliott, Gregory. *Althusser: the Detour of Theory*. London: Verso, 1987.

Ellis, Andrew W. and Young, Andrew W. *Human Cognitive Neuropsychology*. Hove and London: Erlbaum, 1988.

Ellman, Maud. *Psychoanalytic Literary Criticism*. London: Longman, 1994.

Eysenck, Hans. *Sense and Nonsense in Psychology*. London: Pelican, 1950.

—. *Fact and Fiction in Psychology*. London: Pelican, 1965.

—. *Decline and Fall of the Freudian Empire*. London: Penguin Viking, 1985.

Eysenck, Hans and Wilson, Glenn. *The Experimental Study of Freudian Theories*. London: Methuen, 1973.

Featherstone, Mike, ed. *Theory, Culture and Society Vol. 5 No. 2–3: special issue on Postmodernism*. London: Sage, 1988.

Feldstein, Richard and Roof, Judith. *Feminism and Psychoanalysis*. Ithaca and London: Cornell UP, 1989.

Felman, Shoshana, special editor. *Literature and Psychoanalysis: the Question of Reading: Otherwise*. Yale French Studies (55–6), 1977a.

—. 'To Open the Question' (Introduction to Felman 1977a). Yale French Studies (55–6), 1977b.

—. *Literature and Psychoanalysis: the Question of Reading: Otherwise*. Baltimore: Johns Hopkins, 1982.

Ferguson, John, ed. *Socrates*. London: Macmillan, 1970.

Fiedler, Leslie A. *Love, Sex and Death in the American Novel*. London: Penguin, 1960.

Finucci, Valerie and Schwarz, Regina, eds. *Desire in the Renaissance*. Princeton: Princeton UP, 1997.

Fisher, Seymour and Greenberg, Roger P. *Freud Scientifically Reappraised: Testing the Theories and Therapy*. NY: John Wiley, 1996.

Flugel, J.C. *A Hundred Years of Psychology*. London: Duckworth, 1933.

Fodor, Jerry A. and Katz, Jerrold J. *The Structure of Language: Readings in the Philosophy of Language*. NJ: Prentice-Hall, 1964.

Fodor, Jerry and Pylyshin, Z. 'Connectionism and Cognitive Architecture: a Critical Analysis'. *Cognition*, 28, 1988.

Fodor, Jerry A. *The Language of Thought*. Scranton, PA: Crowell, 1975.

—. *The Modularity of Mind*. Cambridge, Mass: MIT, 1983.

—. *Psychosemantics*. Cambridge, Mass: MIT, 1987.

—. *A Theory of Content and Other Essays*. Cambridge, Mass: MIT, 1990.

Fordham, Frieda. *An Introduction to Jung's Psychology*. London: Penguin, 1953.

Forrester, John. *The Seductions of Psychoanalysis: Freud, Lacan, Derrida*. Cambridge: CUP, 1990.

—. 'Psychoanalysis: Telepathy, Gossip, and/or Science' (1990) in Donald, ed. (1991).

Foucault, Michel. *Madness and Civilisation*. London: Tavistock, 1961.

—. *The Birth of the Clinic*. London: Tavistock, 1963.

—. *The Order of Things*. (*Les Mots et les Choses*). London: Tavistock, 1966.

—. *The Archaeology of Knowledge*. London: Tavistock/NY: Pantheon, 1969.

—. *Discipline and Punish*. London: Penguin, 1975.

—. *The History of Sexuality*: Vols I–III. NY and London: Penguin, 1976–85.

—, ed. Colin Gordon. *Power/Knowledge – interviews, etc. 1972–77*. Sussex: Harvester, 1980.

—. selection ed. Paul Rabinow. *The Foucault Reader*. London: Penguin, 1984.

Franz, Marie-Louise von. *Puer Aeternus*. Los Angeles: Sigo, 1981.

Frazer, J.G. *The Golden Bough*. London: Macmillan, 1890–1915.

Freud, Anna. *The Ego and the Mechanisms of Defence*. London: Hogarth, 1936.

Freud, Sigmund. *The Standard Edition of the Complete Psychological Works of Sigmund Freud*; ed. James Strachey. London: Hogarth and the Institute of Psychoanalysis. 24 Volumes (Abbreviated S.E. Vol. Num.), 1953–74.

—. I. *Pre-Psychoanalytic Publications and Unfinished Drafts*, 1886–1899.

—. II . . . and Breuer, J. *Studies on Hysteria*, 1895.

—. III *Early Psychoanalytic Publications*, 1893–9.

—. IV, V *The Interpretation of Dreams, On Dreams*, 1900–1.

—. VI *The Psychopathology of Everyday Life*, 1901.

—. VII *A Case of Hysteria, Three Essays on the Theory of Sexuality, and Other Works*, 1901–5.

—. VIII *Jokes and their Relation to the Unconscious*, 1905.

—. IX *Jensen's 'Gradiva' and Other Works*, 1906–8.

—. X *The Cases of 'Little Hans' and the 'Rat Man'*, 1909.

—. XI *Five Lectures on Psychoanalysis, Leonardo, and Other Works*, 1910.

—. XII *Case History of Schreber, Papers on Technique, and Other Works*, 1911–13.

—. XIII *Totem and Taboo, and Other Works*, 1913–14.

—. XIV *On the History of the Psychoanalytic Movement, Papers on Metapsychology, and Other Works*, 1914–16.

—. XV, XVI *Introductory Lectures on Psychoanalysis*, 1915–17.

—. XVII *An Infantile Neurosis, and Other Works*, 1917–19.

—. XVIII *Beyond the Pleasure Principle, Group Psychology, and Other Works*, 1920–22.

—. XIX *The Ego and the Id, and Other Works*, 1923–5.

—. XX *An Autobiographical Study, Inhibitions, Symptoms and Anxiety, Lay Analysis, and Other Works*, 1925–6.

—. XXI *The Future of an Illusion, Civilisation and Its Discontents, and Other Works*, 1927–31.

—. XXII *New Introductory Lectures on Psychoanalysis, and Other Works*, 1932–6.

—. XXIII *Moses and Monotheism, An Outline of Psychoanalysis, and Other Works*, 1937–9.

—. XXIV Indexes and Bibliographies.

The standard edition is one of the greatest translations of any scholar in any language. However, I have found the following Penguin books convenient:

—. *Two Short Accounts of Psychoanalysis*. Penguin, 1962.

—. *The Penguin Freud Library*, ed. Angela Richards and Albert Dickson, 15 volumes 1973–86 (Abbreviated P.F. Vol. Num.).

1. *Introductory Lectures*; 2. *New Introductory Lectures*; 3. *Studies on Hysteria*; 7. *On Sexuality*; 11. *On Metapsychology – The Theory of Psychoanalysis*; 14. *On Art and Literature* (Contains 'Jensen's Gradiva', 'Leonardo', and other works.).

Freud, Sigmund. *The Origins of Psychoanalysis: Letters to Wilhelm Fliess*. London: Imago, 1887–1902.

Freud, Sigmund and Brunswick, R. Mack, ed. Gardner, M. *The Wolf-Man and Sigmund Freud*. London: Penguin, 1973 (1971).

Friday, Nancy. *My Secret Garden: Women's Sexual Fantasies*. London: Virago, 1975.

Fromm, Erich. *The Crisis of Psychoanalysis*. London: Penguin, 1970.

Frosh, Stephen. *The Politics of Psychoanalysis: an Introduction to Freudian and Post-Freudian Theory*. New Haven and London: Yale UP, 1987.

Frye, Northrop. *Anatomy of Criticism*. Princeton: Princeton University, 1957.

Gallop, Jane. *Reading Lacan*. Ithaca: Cornell UP, 1985.

Gane, Mike, ed. *Towards a Critique of Foucault*. London: Routledge, 1986.

Gardner, Howard. *The Shattered Mind: the Person After Brain Damage*. London: Routledge, 1977.

—. *The Mind's New Science: A History of the Cognitive Revolution*. NY: Basic Books, 1985.

Gay, Peter. *Freud for Historians*. Oxford: OUP, 1985.

—. *Freud: A Life for Our Time*. London: Dent, 1988.

—. *Reading Freud: Explorations and Entertainments*. New Haven and London: Yale UP, 1990.

Gleick, James. *Chaos*. London: Cardinal (Sphere), 1987.

Goldberg, Stephen. *Male Dominance: the Inevitability of Patriarchy*. London: Sphere Books, 1979.

Graves, Robert. *The Greek Myths*. London: Penguin, 1955.

—. *The White Goddess: a Historical Grammar of Poetic Myth*. London: Faber, 1961.

Gray A.L., Bowers K.S. and Fenz W.D. 'Heart Rate in anticipation of and during a negative visual hallucination' (1970) in *International Journal of Clinical and Experimental Hypnosis*.

Gray, Elizabeth Dodson. *Patriarchy as a Conceptual Trap*. Wellesley, Mass: Roundtable, 1982.

Greenson, Ralph R. *The Technique and Practice of Psychoanalysis, Volume 1*. London: Hogarth, 1973.

Griffin, Susan. *Pornography and Silence: Culture's Revenge Against Nature*. NY: Harper and Row/London: The Women's Press Ltd, 1981.

Groddeck, George. *The Book of the It* (1923). London: C.W. Daniel, 1935.

Grosskurth, Phyllis. *Melanie Klein*. London: Maresfield, 1986.

Grünbaum, Adolf. *The Foundations of Psychoanalysis: a Philosophical Critique*. Berkeley and London: University of California, 1984.

Guntrip, Harry. *Personality Structure and Human Interaction*. London: Hogarth, 1968.

Halperin, David M. *One Hundred Years of Homosexuality: and Other Essays on Greek Love*. Routledge, 1990.

Harrison, Jane. *Prolegomena to the Study of Greek Religion*. Cambridge: CUP, 1903.

—. *Themis: A Study of the Social Origins of Greek Religion*. Cleveland and NY: Meridian, 1912.

—. *Ancient Art and Ritual*. Bradford: Moonraker, 1913.

Haste, Helen. *The Sexual Metaphor*. London: Harvester Wheatsheaf, 1993.

Healy, David. *Images of Trauma: From Hysteria to Post-Traumatic Stress Disorder*. London: Faber, 1993.

Hegel, G.W.F., *The Phenomenology of Mind*, 1807. London: Allen and Unwin, translated by Baillie, 1931.

Heidegger, Martin, *Being and Time* (1926). Oxford: Blackwell, translated by Macquarrie and Robinson, 1962.

—. *On the Way to Language* (1959). NY: Harper and Row, translated by Peter D. Hertz and Joan Stambaugh, 1972.

Hillman, James. *Archetypal Psychology: A Brief Account*. Dallas: Spring, 1983.

—. *The Essential James Hillman: A Blue Fire*. London: Routledge, 1990.

Hodgson, David. *The Mind Matters: Consciousness and Choice in a Quantum World*. Oxford: OUP, 1991.

Hoffman, F.J. *Freudianism and the Literary Mind*. Louisiana: State UP, 1957.

Hofstadter, D.R. and Dennett, D.C. *The Mind's I: Fantasies and Reflections on Self and Soul*. NY: Basic Books, 1981.

Holland, Norman N. *The Dynamics of Literary Response*. Oxford: OUP, 1968.

—. *5 Readers Reading*. London: Yale UP, 1975.

—. *The Critical I*. NY: Columbia UP, 1992.

Honderich, Ted. *A Theory of Determinism*. Oxford: OUP, 1988.

Hopcke, Robert H. *A Guided Tour to the Collected Works of C.G. Jung*. Boston and Shaftesbury: Shambhala, 1989.

Horney, Karen. 'The Flight from Womanhood: the Masculinity Complex in Women, as Viewed by Men and Women' (1926), *International Journal of Psycho-Analysis 7*.

Hoy, David, ed. *Foucault: A Critical Reader*. Oxford: Blackwell, 1986.

Husserl, Edmund, posthumous, ms 1929; French translation 1933; new English translation 1960. *Cartesian Meditations: an Introduction to Phenomenology*. The Hague, London: Martinus Nijhoff, 1960.

Irigaray, Luce. *This Sex Which is Not One*. Ithaca, NY: Cornell UP, 1977.

Jackendoff, Ray. *Patterns in the Mind: Language and Human Nature*. London: Harvester Wheatsheaf, 1993.

Jackson, Leonard (review). The Highest Consciousness. *HER* Autumn, 1969.

—. *The Poverty of Structuralism*. London: Longman, 1991.

—. *The Dematerialisation of Karl Marx*. London: Longman, 1994a.

—. 'Drop the Dead Linguist!' London: *The Times Higher Education Review*, August, 1994b.

Jacobi, Jolande. *The Psychology of C.G. Jung*. London: Routledge, 1942.

Jacobus, Mary. *Reading Woman: Essays in Feminist Criticism*. London: Methuen, 1968.

Jacoby, Mario. *Individuation and Narcissism: the psychology of self in Jung and Kohut*. London: Routledge, 1994.

Jakobson, Roman and Halle, Morris. *Fundamentals of Language*. The Hague: Mouton, 1956.

Jakobson, Roman. *Sound and Meaning (Six Lectures on: 1976)*. Sussex: Harvester, 1978.

—. *Verbal Art, Verbal Sign, Verbal Time*, ed. K. Pomorska and S. Rudy Oxford: Blackwell, 1985.

Jameson, Fredric. 'Imaginary and Symbolic in Lacan', 1977 in Felman, 1977a.

Johnson, Barbara. 'The Frame of Reference: Poe, Lacan, Derrida', 1977 in Felman, 1977a.

Johnson, Robert A. *Transformation: Understanding the Three Levels of Masculine Consciousness*. San Francisco: HarperCollins, 1991.

Johnson-Laird, Philip. *Thinking: Readings in Cognitive Science*. Cambridge: CUP, 1977.

—. *Mental Models: Towards a Cognitive Science of Language, Inference and Consciousness*. Cambridge: CUP, 1983.

—. *The Computer and the Mind: an Introduction to Cognitive Science*. London: Fontana, 1988.

Jones, Ernest. *Essays in Applied PsychoAnalysis*. London: Hogarth, 1923.

—. *Hamlet and Oedipus*. London: W.W. Norton and Co, 1923–54.

—. *Sigmund Freud: Life and Work*. London: Hogarth, 1953–7.

Jung, C.G. *Collected Works*. Princeton: Princeton University/London: Routledge (includes all listed below), 1972–83.

—. *Psychology of the Unconscious*, 1913.

—. *On the Relation of the Unconscious to Poetic Art*, 1919.

—. *Psychological Types*, 1920.

—. *The Archetypes and the Collective Unconscious*, 1933–59.

—. *Symbols of Transformation: an Analysis of the Prelude to a Case of Schizophrenia*, 1952.

—. *The Structures and Dynamics of the Psyche*, 1960.

Jung, Emma. *Animus, and Anima: Two Essays by Emma Jung*. Dallas, Texas: Spring, 1934–55.

Kaplan, Louise J. *Female Perversions: the Temptations of Madame Bovary*. London: Penguin, 1991.

Kemper, Theodore D. *Social Structure and Testosterone: Explorations of the Socio-Bio-Social Chain*. London: Rutgers University, 1990.

Kerr, John. *A Most Dangerous Method: the story of Jung, Freud, and Sabina Spielrein*. London: Sinclair-Stevenson, 1994.

Kirsh, David, ed. *Foundations of Artificial Intelligence*. Cambridge, Mass: MIT, 1992.

Klein, Melanie. *Love, Guilt, and Reparation, and other works, 1921–45; Envy and Gratitude, and other works, 1946–63*. London: Hogarth, 1975.

Klein, Melanie, Heimann, Paula and Money-Kirle, R.E. *New Directions in Psychoanalysis*. London: Tavistock, 1955.

Kline, Paul. *Fact and Fantasy in Freudian Theory*. London: Methuen, 1972, 1981.

Kojève, Alexandre. *Introduction to the Reading of Hegel: Lectures on the Phenomenology of Spirit assembled by Raymond Queneau*. NY: Basic Books, 1947.

Kuttner, A.B. 'Sons and Lovers: A Freudian Interpretation' (1916) *P. Anal. Review*.

Lacan, Jacques. *Speech and Language in Psychoanalysis*, 1953 (aka 'The Rome Report') Baltimore: Johns Hopkins UP (as *The Language of the Self*, 1968), translation, notes and commentary by Anthony Wilden, 1981.

—. *The Seminar of Jacques Lacan, Book I: Freud's papers on Technique* (1953–4). Cambridge: CUP, 1988.

—. *The Seminar of Jacques Lacan, Book II: The Ego in Freud's Theory and in the Technique of Psychoanalysis* (1954–5). Cambridge: CUP, 1988.

—. *The Psychoses: the Seminar of Jacques Lacan 1955–6*. London: Routledge 1982, 1993.

—. 'Desire and the Interpretation of Desire in Hamlet' (1959). Translated in Felman 1977a.

—. *Ecrits – A Selection*. London: Tavistock, 1966a, 1977.

—. 'Of Structure as an Inmixing of an Otherness Prerequisite to Any Subject Whatever' in Macksey and Donato, 1966b.

—. *The Four Fundamental Concepts of Psychoanalysis*. (*The Seminar – XI* – given 1964) London: Penguin, 1977.

—. *The Seminar XX* (1972–3) Chapters 6, 7. In Mitchell and Rose.

—. Seminar of 21 June 1975 (1975). In Mitchell and Rose.

Lakoff, George and Johnson, Mark. *Metaphors we Live by*. Chicago: University of Chicago, 1980.

Lakoff, George. *Women, Fire and Dangerous Things: what categories reveal about the mind*. Chicago: University of Chicago, 1987.

Lapsley, Robert and Westlake, Michael. *Film Theory: an Introduction*. Manchester: Manchester UP, 1988.

Laqueur, Thomas. *Making Sex: Body and Gender from the Greeks to Freud*. Harvard: Harvard UP, 1990.

Lechte, John. *Writing and Psychoanalysis: a Reader*. London: Arnold, 1996.

Lederer, Laura, ed. *Take Back the Night: Women on Pornography*. NY: William Morrow/ Bantam, 1980.

Lemaire, Anika. *Jacques Lacan*. London: Routledge, 1970.

Lenneburg, Eric H. *Biological Foundations of Language*. NY: Wiley, 1967.

Lesser, Simon O. *Fiction and the Unconscious*. Chicago and London: University of Chicago, 1957.

Lévi-Strauss, Claude. *The Elementary Structures of Kinship* (1949; 2nd edn, 1967). London: Eyre and Spottiswoode, translated by R. Needham, 1969.

—. *Structural Anthropology Vol. 1* (1958). London: Penguin, 1968.

—. *Structural Anthropology Vol. 2* (1973). London: Penguin, 1976.

Lewis, C.S. *The Allegory of Love: a Study in Mediaeval Tradition*. Oxford: OUP, 1936.

—. *A Preface to Paradise Lost*. Oxford: OUP, 1942.

—. *That Hideous Strength*. London: The Bodley Head, 1945.

Lieberman, Philip. *On the Origins of Language*. NY and London, 1975.

—. *The Biology and Evolution of Language*. London: Harvard UP, 1984.

Limentati, Adam. *Between Freud and Klein: the Psychoanalytic Quest for Knowledge and Truth*. London: Free Association Books, 1989.

Lockwood, Michael. *Mind, Brain, and the Quantum*. Oxford: Blackwell, 1989.

Lorenz, Konrad. *King Solomon's Ring*. London: Methuen, 1952.

—. *On Aggression*. NY: Harcourt Brace/London: Methuen, 1963.

—. *Behind the Mirror: a Search for a Natural History of Human Knowledge*. London: Methuen, 1973.

Lovelace, Linda (Linda Marchiano) with McGrady, Mike. *Ordeal*. London: Citadel, 1980.

Luce, R.D., Bush, R.R. and Galanter, E. *Handbook of Mathematical Psychology vol. II*. NY: Wiley, 1963.

—. *Readings in Mathematical Psychology vol. II*. NY: Wiley, 1965.

Lupton, Julia Reinhard and Reinhard, Kenneth. *After Oedipus: Shakespeare in Psychoanalysis*. Ithaca and London: Cornell UP, 1993.

Lyotard, Jean-François. *The Postmodern Condition*. Manchester: Manchester UP, 1984.

MacCabe, Colin, ed. *The Talking Cure: Essays in Psychoanalysis and Language*. London: Macmillan, 1981.

Macey, David. *Lacan in Contexts*. London: Verso, 1988.

—. *The Lives of Michel Foucault*. London: Hutchinson, 1993.

MacKinnon, Catharine. 'Feminism, Marxism, Method, and the State: an Agenda for Theory' (1982) in Abel and Abel, 1983.

—. 'Desire and Power: a Feminist Perspective' (1983) in Nelson and Grossberg, 1983.

—. *Only Words*. London: HarperCollins, 1994.

Macksey, Richard and Donato, Eugenio. *The Languages of Criticism and the Sciences of Man: the Structuralist Controversy*. Baltimore and London: Johns Hopkins, 1970.

Malcolm, Janet. *Psychoanalysis: the Impossible Profession*. London: Pan, 1982.

—. *In the Freud Archives*. London: Cape, 1984.

Manheim, L. and Manheim, E. *Hidden Patterns – Studies in Psychoanalytic Literary Criticism*. London: Macmillan, 1966.

Mannoni, Octave. *Fictions Freudiennes*. Paris: Editions du Seuil, 1978.

Marcus, Steven. *Freud and the Culture of Psychoanalysis*. NY and London: Norton, 1984.

Masson, Jeffrey. *Freud: The Assault on Truth*. London: Faber/NY: Farrar, Straus and Giroux, 1984.

—. *Against Therapy*. London: Fontana/Collins, 1989.

—. *Final Analysis: the Making and Unmaking of a Psychoanalyst*. London: Harper Collins, 1990.

McAllister, Pam, ed. *Reweaving the Web of Life: Feminism and Nonviolence*. Philadephia: New Society Publishers, 1982.

McClelland, James L., Rumelhart, David E., and the PDP Research Group. *Parallel Distributed Processing: Explorations in the Microstructure of Cognition Vol. 2: Psychological and Biological Models*. Cambridge, Mass. and London: MIT, 1986.

McClintock, Anne. *Imperial Leather: Race, Gender, and Sexuality in the Colonial Context*. London: Routledge, 1995.

McNay, Lois. *Foucault and Feminism*. Cambridge: Polity, 1992.

Mead, George Herbert. *George Herbert Mead on Social Psychology: selected papers*. Chicago: University of Chicago, 1956.

Midgley, Mary. *Beast and Man: the Roots of Human Nature*. Sussex: Harvester, 1978.

Miles, Rosalind. *The Rites of Man: Love, Sex, and Death in the Making of the Male*. London: HarperCollins, 1991.

Miller, George A. and Chomsky, Noam. 'Finitary Models of Language Users' (1963) in Luce, Bush and Galanter, 1963.

Miller, J.B., ed. *Psychoanalysis and Women*. London: Penguin, 1973.

Miller, Jonathan, ed. *States of Mind*. London: BBC, 1983.

Miller, G.A., Galanter, E., and Pribram, K. *Plans and the Structure of Behaviour*. NY: Holt, 1960.

Millett, Kate. *Sexual Politics*, London: Virago, 1969, 1977.

Minsky, Marvin. 'A Framework for Representing Knowledge' (1975) in P.H. Winston, ed. *The Psychology of Computer Vision*. NY: McGraw Hill, 1975.

—. 'The Society Theory' in Winston, P.H. and Brown, R.H., eds. *Artificial Intelligence: an MIT Perspective* Vol. 1. NY: McGraw Hill, 1979.

Mitchell, Juliet. *Psychoanalysis and Feminism*. London: Allen Lane Penguin, 1974.

Mitchell, Juliet and Rose, Jacqueline, eds. *Feminine Sexuality: Jacques Lacan and the Ecole Freudienne*. London: Macmillan, 1982.

Mitscherlich, Margaret. *The Peaceable Sex: On Aggression in Women and Men*. NY: Fromm, 1985.

Moir, Anne and Jessel, David. *BrainSex: The Real Difference between Men and Women*. London: Michael Joseph, 1989.

Moir, Anne and Moir, Bill. *Why Men Don't Iron*, 1998.

Moore, Robert and Gillette, Douglas. *King, Warrior, Magician, Lover: Rediscovering the Archetypes of the Mature Masculine*. San Francisco: Harper, 1990.

Morgan, Robin. *The Demon Lover: On the Sexuality of Terrorism*. NY and London: Norton, 1989.

Muller, John P. and Richardson, William J. *Lacan and Language – A Reader's Guide to Ecrits*. NY: International Universities, 1982.

—. *The Purloined Poe: Lacan, Derrida and Psychoanalytic Reading*. Baltimore: Johns Hopkins, 1988.

Mulvey, Laura. *Visual and Other Pleasures*. London: Macmillan, 1989.

Murray, Gilbert. *Five Stages of Greek Religion*. London: Watts & Co, 1935.

Neisser, Ulric. *Cognition and Reality*. San Francisco: Freeman & Co, 1976.

Nelson, Cary and Grossberg, Lawrence. *Marxism and the Interpretation of Culture*. London: Macmillan, 1988.

Nobus, Dany. *Key Concepts of Lacanian Psychoanalysis*. London: Rebus, 1998.

O'Brien, Barbara. *Operators and Things: Revelations of a Schizophrenic*. London: Elek, 1958.

Obholzer, Karin. *The Wolf-Man: Sixty Years Later*. London: Routledge, 1982.

Ofshe, Richard and Watters, Ethan. *Making Monsters: False Memories, Psychotherapy, Sexual Hysteria*. London: André Deutsch, 1995.

Orne, M.T. 'Hypnosis: Artefact and Essence' (1959) in *Journal of Abnormal Psychology*, 58.

Papadopoulos, R.K. and Saayman, Graham S. *Jung in Modern Perspective*. Wildwood, 1984.

Penrose, Roger. *The Emperor's New Mind*. Oxford: OUP, 1989.

—. *Shadows of the Mind: a Search for the Missing Science of Consciousness*. Oxford: OUP, 1994.

Pinker, Stephen. *How the Mind Works*. London: Allen Lane, 1997.

Plato. *Five Dialogues of Plato bearing on Poetic Inspiration* 4th c BC a. London: Dent, 1929.

—. *The Republic* 4th c BC b. London: Penguin translated by H. D. Lee, 1955.

Pollock, John. *How to Build a Person: a Prolegomenon*. Cambridge, Mass: MIT, 1989.

Popper, Karl. *The Logic of Scientific Discovery*. London: Hutchinson & Co, 1959.

—. *Conjectures and Refutations: the Growth of Scientific Knowledge*. London: Routledge, 1963.

—. *Objective Knowledge: An Evolutionary Approach*. Oxford: OUP, 1972.

—. *Unended Quest*. London: Fontana, 1974.

Popper, Karl R. and Eccles, John C. *The Self and its Brain: an Argument for Interactionism*. London: Springer International, 1977.

Prigogine, Ilya and Stenders, Isabelle. *Order out of Chaos: Man's New Dialogue with Nature*. London: Heinemann, 1984.

Prince, Morton. *The Dissociation of a Personality* (1905). NY: Meridian, 1957.

Propp, Vladimir. *Morphology of the Folk-Tale*. Austin and London: University of Texas, 1928.

Pylyshin, Zenon W. *Computation and Cognition: Toward a Foundation for Cognitive Science*. Cambridge, Mass: MIT, 1984.

Raglan, Lord. *The Hero*. London: Watts/Thinkers Library, 1936.

—. *Jocasta's Crime*. London: Watts/Thinker's Library, 1940.

Ragland-Sullivan, Ellie. *Jacques Lacan and the Philosophy of Psychoanalysis*. London: Croom Helm, 1986.

Rank, Otto. *The Myth of the Birth of the Hero*. London: Kegan Paul, 1909.

—. *The Trauma of Birth*. London: Kegan Paul, 1929.

Rée, Jonathan. 'Marxist Modes' (1979) *Radical Philosophy,* 23. London: Radical Philosophy Group.

Reich, Wilhelm. *The Invasion of Compulsory Sex Morality*. London: Souvenir, 1932.

—. *The Function of the Orgasm*. London: Penguin, 1942.

—. *Character Analysis*. NY: Noonday (Farrar, Straus and Giroux), 1949.

—. *Reich Speaks of Freud*. London: Penguin, 1967.

Reik, Theodor. *Myth and Guilt – The Crime and Punishment of Mankind*. NY: George Braziller, 1957.

Rhodes, D. and McNeill, S. eds. *Women against Violence against Women*. London: OnlyWomen, 1985.

Richards, Janet Radcliffe. *The Sceptical Feminist: a Philosophical Enquiry*. London: Routledge, 1980.

Ricoeur, Paul. *Freud and Philosophy*. New Haven and London: Yale UP, 1970.

Ridley, Matt. *The Red Queen: Sex and the Evolution of Human Nature*. London: Penguin, 1993.

Riviere, Joan, ed. *Developments in Psychoanalysis*. London: Hogarth, 1952.

Roazen, Paul. *Helene Deutsch: A Psychoanalyst's Life*. NY: Doubleday, 1985.

Rolfe, Eugene. *Encounter with Jung*. Boston: Sigo, 1989.

Rose, Jacqueline. *Sexuality in the Field of Vision*. London: Verso, 1986.

Rose, Stephen. *The Making of Memory: from Molecules to Mind*. London: Bantam, 1993.

Roudinesco, Elisabeth. *Jacques Lacan & Co.: A History of Psychoanalysis in France 1925–1985*. London: Free Association Books, 1990.

—. *Jacques Lacan: Esquisse d'une vie, histoire d'un système de pensée*. Paris: Fayard, 1993.

Rowan, John. *The Horned God: Feminism and Men as Wounding and Healing*. London: Routledge, 1987.

Rubins, Jack L. *Karen Horney: Gentle Rebel of Psychoanalysis*. London: Weidenfeld and Nicolson, 1979.

Rumelhart, D.E. 'Notes on a Schema for Stories' in Bobrow and Collins, 1975.

Rumelhart, David E., McLelland, James L., and the PDP Research Group. *Parallel Distributed Processing: Explorations in the Microstructure of Cognition: Vol. I, Foundations*. Cambridge, Mass. and London: MIT, 1986.

Ryle, G. *The Concept of Mind*. London: Penguin, 1949.

Sacks, Oliver. *Awakenings*. London: Duckworth, 1973.

Sagan, Carl. *The Dragons of Eden: Speculations on the Evolution of Human Intelligence*. London: Hodder and Stoughton, 1977.

Samuels, Andrew. *Jung and the Post-Jungians*. London: Routledge, 1985.

Sandler, Joseph, ed. *Projection, Identification, Projective Identification*. London: Karnac Books, 1988.

Sartre, Jean-Paul. *Being and Nothingness: an essay on Phenomenological Ontology*. NY: Philosophical Library, 1943.

—. *Existentialism and Humanism*. London: Methuen, 1945.

Saussure, Ferdinand de. *Course in General Linguistics* (1916). London: Fontana/NY: McGraw-Hill, 1959.

Sayers, Janet. *Sexual Contradictions: Psychology, Psychoanalysis, and Feminism*. London: Tavistock, 1986.

—. *Mothering Psychoanalysis: Helene Deutsch, Karen Horney, Anna Freud, Melanie Klein*. London: Hamish Hamilton, 1991.

Schank, R.C. 'Conceptual Dependency – a Theory of Natural Language Understanding' (1972) *Cognitive Psychology* 3, 552–631.

—. *Tell Me a Story: a New Look at Real and Artificial Memory*. NY: Charles Scribner's Sons, 1990.

Schank, R.C. and Abelson, R. *Scripts, Plans, and Understanding.* Hillsdale, NJ: Lawrence Erlbaum, 1977.

Schneiderman, Stuart. *Returning to Freud: Clinical Psychoanalysis in the School of Lacan.* New Haven and London: Yale UP, 1980.

—. *Jacques Lacan: Death of an Intellectual Hero.* Harvard: Harvard UP, 1983.

Schwartz-Salant, Nathan and Stein, Murray. *The Body in Analysis.* Wilmette, Illinois: Chiron Publications, 1986.

Searle, John. 'Minds, Brains, and Programs' (1980) in Boden, 1990.

—. *Minds, Brains, and Science.* London: BBC (Reith Lectures, 1984), 1984.

—. 'Minds and Brains without Programs' (1987) in Blakemore and Greenfield, 1987.

Sedgwick, Eve Kosofsky. *Epistemology of the Closet.* NY: Harvester, 1991.

—. *Tendencies.* London: Routledge, 1994.

Segal, Hannah. *Introduction to the Work of Melanie Klein.* London: The Institute of Psychoanalysis; Karnac Books, 1973.

—. *The Work of Hannah Segal: A Kleinian Approach to Clinical Practice.* London: Free Association Books/ with Maresfield Library, 1978.

Segal, Lynn. *Straight Sex: the Politics of Pleasure.* London: Virago, 1994.

Segal, Lynn and McIntosh, Mary, eds. *Sex Exposed: Sexuality and the Pornography Debate.* London: Virago, 1992.

Shallice, Tim. *From Neuropsychology to Mental Structure.* Cambridge: CUP, 1988.

Shalvey, Thomas. *Claude Lévi-Strauss: Social Psychotherapy and the Collective Unconscious.* Sussex: Harvester, 1975.

Shapiro, Stuart C., editor in chief. *Encyclopedia of Artificial Intelligence Vols I and II.* NY: Wiley, 1992.

Sheridan, Alan. *Foucault: the will to truth.* London: Tavistock, 1980.

Shinghal, Rajjan. *Formal Concepts in Artificial Intelligence: Fundamentals.* London: Chapman and Hall, 1992.

Skinner, B.F. *The Behavior of Organisms.* NY: Appleton Century Crofts, 1938.

—. *Science and Human Behavior.* NY: Macmillan, 1953.

—. *Verbal Behavior.* NY: Appleton Century Crofts, 1957.

—. *Cumulative Record.* NY: Appleton Century Crofts, 1959.

—. *Beyond Freedom and Dignity.* NY: Knopf, 1972.

Skura, Meredith Anne. *The Literary Use of the Psychoanalytic Process.* New Haven and London: Yale UP, 1981.

Smith, Joseph H. and Kerrigan, William, eds. *Interpreting Lacan.* New Haven and London: Yale UP, 1983.

Smith, J.C. *The Neurotic Foundations of Social Order: Psychoanalytic Roots of Patriarchy.* NY and London: NY University, 1990.

Sokal, Alan and Bricmont, Jean. *Intellectual Impostures.* London: Profile Books, 1998.

Spivak, Gayatri. *In Other Worlds: Essays in Cultural Politics.* NY: Routledge, 1988.

Squires, Judith, ed. *New Formations: A Journal of Culture/Theory/Politics: Perversity.* London: Lawrence and Wishart, 1993.

Stanley, Liz and Wise, Sue. *Breaking Out Again.* London: Routledge, 1993.

Staude, John-Raphael. *The Adult Development of C.G. Jung.* London: Routledge, 1981.

Sternberg, R.J. *In Search of the Human Mind.* London: Harcourt Brace, 1995.

Stevens, Anthony. *Archetype: a Natural History of the Self.* London: Routledge, 1982.

—. *On Jung*. London: Routledge, 1990.

—. *Private Myths: Dreams and Dreaming*. London: Hamish Hamilton/Penguin, 1995.

Stevens, Anthony and Price, John. *Evolutionary Psychiatry: a New Beginning*. London: Routledge, 1996.

Stewart, Ian. *Does God Play Dice? The New Mathematics of Chaos*. London: Penguin, 1989.

Sulloway, Frank J. *Freud, Biologist of the Mind: Beyond the Psychoanalytic Legend*. London: André Deutsch, 1979.

Symons, D. *The Evolution of Human Sexuality*. Oxford: OUP, 1979.

Symons, D. and Ellis, B. 'Human Male–Female Differences in Sexual Desire' in Rasa, A.E., Vogel, C. and Voland, E., eds. *The Sociobiology of Sexual and Reproductive Strategies*. London: Chapman and Hall, 1989.

Szass, Thomas. *The Myth of Mental Illness*. NY: Harper and Row, 1961.

Tallack, Douglas, ed. *Literary Theory at Work: Three Texts*. London: Batsford, 1987.

Thayer, Robert E. *The Biopsychology of Mood and Arousal*. Oxford: OUP, 1989.

Timpanaro, Sebastian. *The Freudian Slip*. London: New Left Books, 1974.

Tinbergen, Niko. *The Study of Instinct*. Oxford: OUP, 1951.

—. *Social Behaviour in Animals*. London: Methuen, 1953.

—. *Curious Naturalists* (1968). London: Penguin, 1974.

Trilling, Lionel. *The Liberal Imagination*. London: Secker and Warburg, 1950.

Turkle, Sherry. *Psychoanalytic Politics: Jacques Lacan and Freud's French Revolution*. London: André Deutsch, 1979.

Ulanov, Ann and Ulanov, Barry. *Two Archetypes of Human Sexuality*. Wilmette, Illinois: Chiron Publications, 1989.

Vance, Carole S., ed. *Pleasure and Danger: Exploring Female Sexuality*. London: Routledge, 1984.

Vološinov, V.N. *Freudianism: A Critical Sketch* (1927; formerly: *A Marxist Critique*). Indiana: Indiana University, 1976.

Wakefield, Hollida and Underwager, Ralph. *Return of the Furies: an Investigation into Recovered Memory Therapy*. Chicago and La Salle, Illinois: Open Court, 1994.

Walsh, Kevin W. *Understanding Brain Damage: A Primer of Neuropsychological Evaluation*. Edinburgh and London: Churchill Livingstone, 1984.

Warhol, Robyn R. and Herndl, Diane Price. *Feminisms: an Anthology of Literary Theory and Criticism*. New Brunswick, New Jersey: Rutgers University, 1991.

Warnock, Donna. 'Patriarchy is a killer: what people concerned about peace and justice should know' (1982) in McAllister, ed., 1982.

Webster, Richard. *Why Freud Was Wrong: Sin, Science, and Psychoanalysis*. London: Collins/Fontana, 1995.

Wegman, Cornelis. *Psychoanalysis and Cognitive Psychology: A Formalisation of Freud's Earliest Theory*. London: Academic Press, 1985.

Wehr, Demaris S. *Jung and Feminism: Liberating Archetypes*. London: Routledge, 1988.

Weitz, Shirley. *Sex Roles: Biological, Psychological, and Social Foundations*. Oxford: OUP, 1977.

Wells, Harry K. *The Failure of Psychoanalysis: from Freud to Fromm*. NY: International Publishers, 1963.

Wepman, J.M. and Heine, R.W. *Concepts of Personality*. London: Methuen, 1964.

Whitford, Margaret. *Luce Irigaray: Philosophy in the Feminine*. London: Routledge, 1991.

Wilden, Anthony. *Speech and Language in Psychoanalysis*. Baltimore: Johns Hopkins, 1986 – see Lacan, 1953.

Wilensky, R. *Planning and Understanding: a Computational Approach to Human Reasoning*. Reading, Mass: Addison-Wesley, 1983.

Williams, Linda. *Hard Core: Power, Pleasure, and the 'Frenzy of the Visible'*. London: Pandora, 1990.

Wilson, Edward O. *Sociobiology: the New Synthesis*. Cambridge Mass: Harvard UP, 1975.

—. *On Human Nature*. London: Harvard UP, 1978.

Wilson, Edmund. *The Triple Thinkers*. London: Penguin, 1952.

Winnicott, D.W. *The Child, The Family and the Outside World*. London: Penguin, 1964.

—. *Human Nature*. London: Free Association Books, 1988.

Winograd, Terry. *Language as a Cognitive Process*. London: Addison-Wesley, 1983.

Wittig, Monique. *The Straight Mind and Other Essays*. Hemel Hempstead: Harvester Wheatsheaf, 1992.

Wolf, Naomi. *The Beauty Myth: How Images of Beauty are Used against Women*. Toronto: Random House, 1990.

Wollheim, Richard. *Freud*. London: Fontana, 1973.

Wright, Elizabeth, ed. *Feminism and Psychoanalysis: a Critical Dictionary*. Oxford: Blackwell, 1992.

—. 'The Reader in Analysis' (1991), article in Donald, 1991.

Young, J.Z. *Philosophy and the Brain*. Oxford: OUP, 1987.

Young-Bruehl, Elisabeth. *Anna Freud: a Biography*. London: Macmillan, 1988.

Zohar, Danah. *The Quantum Self*. London: Bloomsbury Publishing, 1990.

Index of topics

Index of names, works and characters